EX AUDITU

An International Journal for the Theological Interpretation of Scripture

VOL. 31 **2015**

Ex Auditu is published annually by Pickwick Publications, an imprint of
Wipf and Stock Publishers, 199 West 8th Avenue, Suite 3, Eugene, Oregon 97401, USA

SUBSCRIPTIONS

Individuals:
U.S.A. and all other countries (in U.S. funds): $20.00
Students: $12.00

Institutions:
U.S.A. and all other countries (in U.S. funds): $30.00

This periodical is indexed in the ATLA Religion Database, published by the American Theological Library Association, 300 S. Wacker Dr., Suite 2100, Chicago, IL 60606, Email: atla@atla.com, www: http://www.atla.com/; *Internationale Zeitschriftenshau für Bibelwissenschaft; Religious and Theological Abstracts;* and *Old Testament Abstracts*.

Please address all subscription correspondence
and change of address information to Wipf and Stock Publishers.

©2016 by Wipf and Stock Publishers
ISSN:
ISBN: 978-1-4982-9040-1

EX AUDITU

An International Journal for the Theological Interpretation of Scripture

Klyne R. Snodgrass, Editor
Stephen J. Chester, Associate Editor
D. Christopher Spinks, Associate Editor

North Park Theological Seminary
3225 West Foster Avenue
Chicago, Illinois 60625-4987
USA

Tel: (773) 244-6243
Fax: (773) 244-6244
email: ksnodgrass@northpark.edu
Web site: http://wipfandstock.com/catalog/journal/view/id/12/

EDITORIAL BOARD

Terence E. Fretheim, Luther Seminary, St. Paul, MN
Richard B. Hays, The Divinity School, Duke University, Durham, NC
Jon R. Stock, Wipf & Stock Publishers, Eugene, OR
Miroslav Volf, Yale Divinity School, New Haven, CT
John Wipf, Wipf & Stock Publishers, Eugene, OR

THE EDITORIAL BOARD MEMBERS AND CONSULTANTS represent various disciplines and denominations. Theological interpretation of Scripture is a task to be taken seriously by scholars who are committed to the Christian faith and tradition. However, as one editorial consultant stated: "Let people gradually get used to the idea that a sane hermeneutics is both oriented in advance toward agreement/consent and is simultaneously exigent, discriminating, critical."

EDITORIAL CONSULTANTS

Richard Bauckham
University of St. Andrews, Emeritus
St. Andrews, Scotland

M. Daniel Carroll R.
Denver Seminary
Denver, Colorado

Jan Du Rand
Emeritus, University of Johannesburg and Extraordinary Professor, North West University

Willie Jennings
The Divinity School
Duke University
Durham, N. Carolina

Robert Johnston
Fuller Theological Seminary
Pasadena, California

R. Walter L. Moberly
University of Durham
Durham, England

Kathleen M. O'Connor
Columbia Theological Seminary
Decatur, Georgia

Iain Provan
Regent College
Vancouver, B.C.

Anthony Thiselton
University of Nottingham
Nottingham, England

Augustine Thompson
University of Virginia
Charlottesville, Virginia

Marianne Meye Thompson
Fuller Theological Seminary
Pasadena, California

Kevin J. Vanhoozer
Trinity Evangelical Divinity School
Deerfield, Illinois

Geoffrey Wainwright
The Divinity School
Duke University
Durham, N. Carolina

Sondra Wheeler
Wesley Theological Seminary
Washington, D.C.

William H. Willimon
The Divinity School
Duke University
Durham, N. Carolina

N. T. Wright
St Mary's College,
University of St. Andrews, Scotland

EX AUDITU

CONTENTS

Announcement of the 2016 Symposium v

Abbreviations vii

Introduction ix
Klyne Snodgrass

North Park Theological Seminary Faculty Statement on Racism 1

"Racial Realism" in Biblical Interpretation and Theological Anthropology: A Systematic-Theological Evaluation of Recent Accounts 3
Elizabeth Y. Sung

Response to Sung 22
Valerie Landfair

Reimagining *Koinonia*: Confronting the Legacy and Logic of Racism by Reinterpreting Paul's Letter to Philemon 27
Lewis Brogdon

Response to Brogdon 49
Al Tizon

The Bible's Outrage at Blumenbach's Babel: An Antiracist Hermeneutic for White Followers of Jesus 53
Kyle J. A. Small

Enemies, Romans, Pigs, and Dogs: Loving the Other in the Gospel of Matthew 71
Love L. Sechrest

Response to Sechrest 106
Rebecca Gonzalez

Contents

The Lynching of the Suffering Servant of Isaiah: Death at the Hands of Persons Unknown   108
Bo H. Lim

Response to Lim   121
Evelmyn Ivens

What's Missing? Theological Musings on a Hermeneutics of Absence   124
Néstor Medina

Response to Medina   150
Bruce L. Fields

"Lost in Translation: Ethnic Conflict in English Bibles"—The Gospels, "Race," and the Common English Bible: An Introductory and Exploratory Conversation   154
Emerson B. Powery

Response to Powery   169
Michael O. Emerson

An Indigenous Reinterpretation of Repentance   172
Raymond Aldred

Response to Aldred   192
Mark Tao

Truth Be Told: A Necessary Funeral Dirge in the Middle of Our Conversation   200
Soong-Chan Rah

Annotated Bibliography on Race and Racism   207

Presenters and Respondents   221

Ex Auditu—Volumes Available

ANNOUNCEMENT OF THE 2016 SYMPOSIUM

North Park Theological Seminary in Chicago, Illinois, is pleased to announce that the thirty-second Symposium on the Theological Interpretation of Scripture will take place September 29–October 1, 2016. The symposium will start at 7:00 p.m. on September 29 in Nyvall Hall and will extend through a Saturday afternoon worship service on October 1. The theme in 2016 will be Science and Religion. The following persons have agreed to make presentations:

Paul Allen, Associate Professor of Theological Studies, Concordia University, Montreal, Canada.

Gerald Cleaver, Professor of Physics, Baylor University

Susan Eastman, Associate Research Professor of New Testament, Duke Divinity School

Johnny Lin, Senior Lecturer Computing and Software Systems Division, University of Washington Bothell and Affiliate Professor of Physics and Engineering, North Park University

Hans Madueme, Assistant Professor of Theological Studies, Covenant College

Iain Provan, Marshall Sheppard Professor of Biblical Studies, Regent College, Canada

Kara Slade, formerly with NASA (Ph.D. in Mechanical Engineering and Materials Science), PhD Candidate in Religion, Duke Divinity School

Michael Spezio, Associate Professor of Psychology & Neuroscience, Scripps College, Claremont, CA; Visiting Researcher, Institute for Systems Neuroscience, University of Hamburg Medical Center, Hamburg, Germany

Kirk Wegter-McNelly, Wold Visiting Professor, Union College (NY), who will preach at the worship service

Persons interested in attending the sessions should write before September 1 to:

Ms. Guylla Brown
North Park Theological Seminary
3225 W. Foster Avenue
Chicago, Illinois 60625

Meals may be taken at North Park and assistance can be provided in finding nearby lodging.

ABBREVIATIONS

All abbreviations are as specified in Patrick H. Alexander et al., eds., *The SBL Handbook of Style,* 2nd edition (Atlanta, GA: SBL, 2014). Bibliographical details and any abbreviations not listed here can be found there.

BibSac	*Bibliotheca Sacra*
CBQ	*Catholic Biblical Quarterly*
CEB	Common English Bible
CTM	*Concordia Theological Monthly*
ESV	English Standard Version
HKAT	Handkommentar zum Alten Testament
HTR	*Harvard Theological Review*
Interp	*Interpretation*
JBL	*Journal of Biblical Literature*
JSSR	*Journal for the Scientific Study of Religion*
JSNT	*Journal for the Study of the New Testament*
JTI	*Journal of Theological Interpretation*
JTS	*Journal of Theological Studies*
KJV	King James Version
NASB	New American Standard Bible
NET	The NET Bible
NICNT	New International Commentary on the New Testament
NIV	New International Version
NJB	New Jerusalem Bible
NLT	New Living Translation
NovT	*Novum Testamentum*
NRSV	New Revised Standard Version
NTS	*New Testament Studies*
SBT	Studies in Biblical Theology
TDNT	*Theological Dictionary of the New Testament*
ThTo	*Theology Today*
TS	Theological Studies

Abbreviations

USQR   *Union Seminary Quarterly Review*

ZNW   *Zeitschrift für die neutestamentliche Wissenschaft und die Kunde der älteren Kirche*

INTRODUCTION

When we somewhat innocently chose the topic Race and Racism, we had no idea the events would happen in Ferguson, New York, Baltimore, Mother Emanuel AME Church in Charleston, or that the video of the shooting of Laquan MacDonald in Chicago would be released. We intentionally wanted the discussion to be more than an African American and Caucasian discussion, and still do. Yet, at least in the United States, the racism between African Americans and Caucasians makes one weep. We can do better than this, and churches have to lead the way. Still, we must not forget other ethnic groups and the abysmal history of the treatment of Native Americans. There is work to be done in all arenas.

Watching the news can be hazardous to your health, especially your mental health and especially if you live in Chicago, as I do. The news reported demonstrators in Ferguson, MO, who said, "Black lives matter." After the murder of three students at the University of North Carolina, demonstrators said, "Muslim lives matter." After Baltimore, demonstrators in Annapolis said, "Blue lives matter," a statement in defense of the police. After a young woman was raped by four teenagers in New York, a female city official said, "The lives of women matter." DeMario Bailey was killed in Chicago on December 14, 2014, trying to defend his twin brother when four youths tried to rob them of a jacket. The twins' sixteenth birthday was three days later. There was no public protest after the death, except for a few members of his family who held up signs where he was killed proclaiming "All lives matter." It is not diminishing of racial issues to say "All lives matter," and it makes no sense for one group to say "Our lives matter more than yours." Of course, the matter is more complicated, as Soong-Chan Rah points out in his symposium sermon, because for a long time people said, "Black lives do not matter," especially in Missouri with the Dred Scott decision. According to CBS News on October 18, 2015, after another Chicago shooting, the mother of the victim asked "When are black lives going to matter to black lives?" After the killing of two white reporters near Roanoke, VA, by an African American reporter who had been fired, the father of the female victim said it should not be that hard to solve the gun control issue, but dealing with sin always seems simple on the surface. He did not want to take away all guns, just make it more difficult to get them. Cornell West, on August 27, 2015, the day after the killings of the reporters, said on CNN, "We are in a spiritual crisis. . . . What kind of

Introduction

people are we?" He used the words "rage" and "contempt" in speaking of race relations. Indeed, what kind of people are we?

Are we merely trapped in our history, or can we move forward, and if so, how? Several OT texts speak of the sins of the parents being visited on the third and fourth generation (e.g., Exod 34:7). We are already past the fourth generation since the end of the Civil War, and the sins have indeed fallen on us. Of course, new sins have been added. How long will this waterfall of sin keep going?

N. T. Wright described the root of the race problem by saying: "You are different from me, and I resent you for that,"[1] or maybe it is stronger—"I hate you for that." What divides us illegitimately, and what should we stand against, regardless of our race? How much is the problem a problem of arrogance—individually and culturally—and some sense that others should be like "me"?

No race sees itself in what others describe. Who are "they" describing? Further, the discussion of race is hardly the same in all places because of the simple fact that the distribution of races is not the same across the country. In some places people would not be sure what the conversation really was about and would have a hard time finding themselves in it. Nearly everywhere the discussion in the church or on the street is not what it is in the academic community. Many whites do not see themselves as the problem; they think they are just trying to make it. Whites may have an advantage in some contexts—certainly not others, and many whites do not feel privileged. Whatever one's race, it is easy to demean others, and attitudes of superiority and advantage get expressed on all sides, as if one's particular experience declared universal truth. We will never move forward until all of us stop seeing people of other races as the enemy or the cause of all the problems. Our history is plagued by sin, but are we trapped by our history? A great deal of humility is needed from all of us.

Race relations have improved since the early civil rights movement, but as one who was around in the 1960s, it does not seem to me that the *discussion* has changed that much. What sounds like a novel argument is novel only because people are unaware of earlier discussions or have forgotten. What can move the discussion forward? It will not be blaming; it will be, as several papers argue, when all of us take seriously the theological significance of humanity in the image of God, the specific love of people in front of us—love which God requires, a sense of the presence of the kingdom, and a sense of the Body of Christ.

The papers, however, do not treat all that must be addressed. Security and systemic issues were not treated, and sin was more presumed than treated. Culture was

---

1. *Bringing the Church to the World: Renewing the Church to Confront the Paganism Entrenched in Western Culture* (Minneapolis: Bethany House, 1992) 25.

an underlying current but was not discussed much. What is the relation of culture and race? How much of the race issue is primarily an urban and economic issue? Many of our problems are systemic and would not merely go away if all people were of the same skin color.

Predictions about the racial composition of the United States in 2050 suggest that no race will constitute even half the population. We will be a variegated society with whites constituting just under 47 percent, Hispanics 28 percent, African Americans 14.4 percent, Asian Americans just under 8 percent, and multiracial Americans almost 5.5 percent. Will we be better then, or will we still find a way to show that our tribe is superior to another?

Hermeneutics were always on the table, especially the relation of text and reader and the stance of the reader to the text, with all the implications of discussions of canon and the nature of Scripture. To what degree is it legitimate to read ourselves into the text rather than have the text read us and transform us? Is the former merely a way to control the text and conform it to our image? Are there controls to reading from the margins? Does the text even remain anymore? Reading ourselves into the text will never convince those who disagree with us. How do we get beyond preaching to the choir to engaging people for change?

Two items are included in the journal that were not part of the symposium. It did not seem right that no voice was given to one billion people from India who deal with a horrendous and unjust caste system. Therefore two songs are included from Pandita Ramabai, a scholar and Bible translator who came from the highest level of the Brahmin caste and who married a low caste man. I have also included a statement on race from the North Park Theological Seminary faculty.

At the symposium twice as much time is given to discussion of the papers as to their delivery, and the journal cannot reproduce the character of those discussions, which are always stimulating and enriching and perhaps the most important part of the symposium. People in attendance at the symposium include an interesting mix of faculty types, pastors, church leaders, students, and lay people. We are grateful to all who participated. Appreciation is especially expressed once again to all the presenters and respondents who made a significant investment in the life of North Park. The friendship of all the people involved is a gift we value deeply. The authors of papers were given a chance to edit their contributions after the symposium, but the responses are essentially as they were presented. As is obvious, the views expressed are those of the authors and not necessarily those of the journal or of North Park. Special gratitude is expressed to Hillary Bylund, a student at North Park, for her work on the bibliography, and especially to Guylla Brown from North Park's staff,

Introduction

without whom the symposium would be impossible. Anyone who has been to the symposium knows that is true every year.

Klyne Snodgrass
Emeritus Professor of New Testament Studies
North Park Theological Seminary

NORTH PARK THEOLOGICAL SEMINARY STATEMENT ON RACISM

As the faculty and staff of North Park Theological Seminary, we join our voices to those of our university, denomination, neighborhood, city, and nation and declare unequivocally: Black lives matter.

We affirm the dignity of every human being as made in the image of God, created to flourish physically, emotionally, spirituality, socially, culturally, and economically. As one body in Christ, if one part of the body suffers we all suffer; if one part of the body cannot breathe, none of us can breathe. The outcry heard on our campus and our streets demonstrates that the body of Christ cannot breathe. Violence against black lives without sufficient cause or accountability points to a broken system and demands justice.

We affirm the biblical witness that God desires justice on earth (Gen 18:19; Deut 16:19–20; Amos 5:15–24), that Christ himself is the servant who proclaims justice to the nations (Matt 12:18–21; cf. Isa 41:1–3), whose gospel puts to death hostility between races (Eph 2:14–16), and that the Spirit intercedes as we pray that equality before the law be realized (Rom 8:26–27). When our institutions, our churches, and especially our justice system do not align with these values, the systems, and not the values, are at fault.

As a seminary, we support nonviolent forms of civil disobedience that show solidarity with victims of power abuses and which refuse to perpetuate the very cycles of violence that spawn injustice. We commit to striving toward creating safe places for dialogue and conversation on the topic of racial justice in co-curricular activities, in our classrooms, in our community life. We, as the faculty and staff, acknowledge that the toil for justice is arduous and long. Nevertheless, Christians must not ignore any injustice; therefore we are committed in our vocations as educators to teach and embody God's heart for justice on our campus, in our city, and in the world.

"RACIAL REALISM" IN BIBLICAL INTERPRETATION AND THEOLOGICAL ANTHROPOLOGY: A SYSTEMATIC-THEOLOGICAL EVALUATION OF RECENT ACCOUNTS

Elizabeth Y. Sung

In the church and in the academy, as well as in society at large, discourse about "race"[1] is highly contentious, a condition due in large part to the use of supposedly commonsense notions, seldom-defined terms, and unexamined assumptions. Even in the domain of theological scholarship, exchanges are clouded by semantic ambiguity. Despite the apparently self-evident realities to which "race" refers, theological arguments often rely upon basic premises about "race" that are diametrically opposed, and hence they reach irreconcilable conclusions.

What is the status of human "races" with reference to ontological reality? Does "race" denote a basic aspect of the constitution of human beings, such that they cannot be satisfactorily comprehended apart from racial identification? Do racial categories accurately classify persons according to substantively different sets of traits at the level of biological structure? What are the theoretical and empirical bases for racial concepts? Moreover, does the practice of interpreting persons and groups qua "races" have biblical and theological warrant? That is, does modern racial reasoning comport logically with the social imaginary conveyed in Scripture and the patterns of biblical reasoning about the composition of humankind?[2]

Questions such as these comprise the point of departure for a specifically systematic-theological treatment of "race." Among its several tasks systematic theology seeks to clarify and to explicate what belongs to reality—what is real in Christ,

---

1. Here and subsequently, the expression "race" comprises the use of scare quotes to indicate the critical stance taken toward the prevailing assumption that the term denotes an empirically existent referent. This typographical convention seems to have originated with Julian Huxley and A. C. Cort, *We Europeans: A Survey of 'Racial' Problems* (London: Jonathan Cape, 1935), and some sociologists continue to employ it, e.g., Robert Miles, *Racism* (London: Routledge, 1989). However, with the adjectival form, the scare quotes typically are omitted.

2. "Social imaginary" refers to "the way ordinary people 'imagine' their social surroundings . . . not often expressed in theoretical terms [but] carried in images, stories, legends, etc." Charles Taylor, *A Secular Age* (Cambridge, MA: Harvard University Press, 2007) 171–72. Here, the term is used to indicate that the descriptions of the relevant phenomena in the biblical writings employ phenomenological language, as opposed to technical terms (philosophical or other).

sub specie aeternitatis—as informed by the Christian tradition, reason (the best knowledge available in the relevant extra-theological disciplines), and experience, all ultimately normed by what is divinely disclosed in Scripture. Because it confronts fundamentally ontological questions, a doctrinal account aims to render a normative statement concerning its subject matter. Systematic theology is essentially a normative mode of theological discourse, in that, as Gordon Lynch observes, ". . . it requires us to reflect on how we can speak truthfully or meaningfully about life in relation to [the] absolute [reference point of our existence], what it means to live our lives in a good or just way in relation to it, and what concepts such as evil, suffering, redemption, and beauty mean in the light of it."[3]

Evangelical systematic theologians set for themselves the goal of truthful discourse and assess the truth value of all proposals with respect to adequacy to metaphysical reality. On this view, truthful speech is that which proves to be internally coherent within a system of discourse and also corresponds to its referent, standing in a right relation to external reality as known, intended, and brought to spatiotemporal and eschatological actuality by the triune God, attested in the "one discourse" (*unus sermo*)[4] of Scripture (Augustine), the single story encompassing the creation of the cosmic order narrated in Gen 1 through the consummation of God's purposes for its redemption and flourishing depicted in Rev 22.

This normative criterion distinguishes systematic theological accounts from other forms of theological reflection, which are, arguably, primarily descriptive in character. That is, in the main, studies of "race" framed in other disciplines—biblical interpretation, historical theology, contextual theology, critical theology, theological ethics, practical theology—have tended to accept at face value and directly appropriate the symbolic resources of their subjects' cultural systems. The conventional cognitive categories, idiomatic vocabulary, and legitimation schemes of these local systems of knowledge and practice thereby are preserved in the theological reflections subsequently rendered.[5] In contrast, and in an ultimately complementary

---

3. Gordon Lynch, *Understanding Theology and Popular Culture* (Malden, MA: Blackwell, 2005) 94.

4. Robert L. Wilkens, *The Spirit of Early Christian Thought: Seeking the Face of God* (New Haven, CT: Yale University Press, 2003) 326n9.

5. The descriptive approach to theological formulation (as distinct from a normative one) is seen in the dominant practice of employing "race" as an accurate "master concept" in an objectivist, realist fashion. This largely descriptive mode of interpretation in theological disciplines other than systematic theology can be seen in the following exemplars: (a) in biblical studies, Wolfgang Stegemann, "Anti-Semitic and Racist Prejudices in Titus 1:10–16," in *Ethnicity and the Bible*, ed. Mark Brett (Leiden: Brill, 2002) 271–94; (b) in church history, Hilrie Shelton Smith, *In His Image, But . . .* (Durham, NC: Duke University Press, 1972); (c) in contextual theology, Bruce Fields, *Introducing Black Theology: Three Crucial Questions for the Evangelical Church* (Grand Rapids: Baker, 2001); (d) in practical theology, Curtiss De Young, Michael Emerson, George Yancey, and Karen Chai Kim, *United by Faith* (New York: Oxford University Press, 2003).

fashion, a systematic-theological approach to "race" submits these ordinary-language constructs and practices to rigorous conceptual analysis, evaluating them for accuracy with respect to their ontological implications and historical and empirical aptness as well as their commensurability with Scripture.

It is therefore crucial that—alongside biblical scholars, church historians, theological ethicists, practical theologians, and reflective practitioners addressing "race" and racism—systematic theologians come to grips with the concept of "race." The goal is analytical clarity which contributes to a specifically Christian account of humanity that is intellectually responsible and empirically valid "for the sake of action."[6]

Much of what follows here is a sketch of more extensive arguments presented in my dissertation,[7] which examines and clarifies "race" theories and ethnicity theories, and deconstructs the "race" concept by marshaling evidence from important studies in history—the history of science, human biology (from serology to genomic research), physical anthropology, human population variation, and cultural anthropology and sociology. Research within and across these disciplines, especially since the mid-twentieth century, has led to the conclusion in mainstream scholarship that discrete, biologically constituted "races" do not exist as such. Because of these findings, I argue, the "race" concept is untenable for biblical interpretation and for expounding the Christian doctrine of humanity. If the goal of Christian theology is to reform merely human (and in this case, false) patterns of reasoning and practice pertaining to humans in accordance with eschatological actuality in Christ as attested in Scripture, biblical interpretation and doctrinal accounts require reconstruction, employing an altogether different analytical concept—one that is empirically valid and proves to be logically compatible with "the logic of scriptural discourse."[8]

In fact, however, the overwhelming majority of exegetes and theologians, from the early modern era through the present, have subscribed to the belief that Scripture attests to the development of "races" in the course of world history as a fulfillment of

---

6. An Anselmic conception of theology ("faith seeking understanding") lends itself to the following characterization of philosophy logically contained within it: "Philosophy as an activity . . . revolves around asking certain basic questions the answers to which endeavor to establish the relevant connexions *for the sake of action*." See Graham A. Cole, "Thinking Theologically," *Reformed Theological Review* 48.2 (May–August 1989) 51–62, 55 (emphasis added).

7. Elizabeth Y. Sung, "'Race' and Ethnicity Discourse and the Christian Doctrine of Humanity: A Systematic Sociological and Theological Appraisal." Ph.D. dissertation, Trinity Evangelical Divinity School, Deerfield, IL (2011). Some of the material appearing in this paper will be published in a forthcoming monograph.

8. David Yeago, "The New Testament and Nicene Dogma: A Contribution to the Recovery of Theological Exegesis," in *Theological Interpretation of Scripture: Classic and Contemporary Readings*, ed. Stephen Fowl (Malden, MA: Blackwell, 1997) 87–102, 87.

the divine intention for humanity.[9] Whether they are racist or antiracist in aim and argumentation, all such interpretations treat the biblical presentation of humankind as if there were exegetical, canonical, and redemptive-historical grounds for subscribing to and endorsing the existence of "races" as such.

Accordingly, this essay draws attention to the widespread societal belief that human "races" are objectively existent natural kinds. This is a largely unrecognized problem that continues to characterize theological scholarship and churches' teaching about "race." The focus here is not on racism, but on the status of "race" concepts in relation to metaphysical reality generally and specifically to several common problems attached to the use of the "race" concept itself. This study examines and analyzes three contemporary accounts of "race" that exemplify the conflicting viewpoints in the realm of evangelical biblical and theological scholarship and pastoral reflection.

"Racial Realism" Defined

The view of "race" that overwhelmingly predominates in biblical and theological treatments is one that I have designated as "racial realism."[10] Racial realists believe that racial classificatory categories correspond to an objective state of affairs in the world of nature, namely "natural and separate divisions, akin to subspecies, exist within humankind."[11] On this view "races" denote discrete human groups possessing determinate, distinguishing traits rooted in biological constitution. Bodily features are but the most visible markers of the innate, natural endowments of the members of the respective races, which are fixed, not subject to alteration.

Historically, the vast preponderance of racial realists (or "race theorists") in the natural sciences, the humanities, and during earlier periods in the social sciences (including physical and cultural anthropology, sociology, economics, and the like) asserted that racial makeup is the fundamental determinant of the unique set of inborn qualities, capacities, cultural and moral proclivities, and other such characteristics possessed by individuals and groups. For various reasons, fewer scholars

---

9. See, e.g., Colin Kidd, *The Forging of Races: Race and Scripture in the Protestant Atlantic World, 1600–2000* (Cambridge: Cambridge University Press, 2000); Willie James Jennings, *The Christian Imagination: Theology and the Origins of Race* (New Haven, CT: Yale University Press, 2010); J. Kameron Carter, *Race: A Theological Account* (New York: Oxford University Press, 2008).

10. For a fuller treatment of the development of the "race" concept, spanning premodern European uses through late twentieth-century trends in the United States see Sung, "'Race' and Ethnicity Discourse," chs. 2 and 3.

11. Ibid., 60. The author framed this definition in a research paper commissioned by InterVarsity Christian Fellowship/USA: Elizabeth Y. Sung, "Culture, 'Race' and Ethnicity in Christian Perspective: Theoretical and Theological Foundations for Multi-Ethnic ministry" (Chicago: InterVarsity, 2001) 85.

publicly espouse the latter tenets today, but this kind of race-essentialist thinking continues to be propounded by theorists, of which the volume by Richard Herrnstein and Charles Murray, *The Bell Curve*, is an example.[12]

While the ideological arguments and racist aims of such works is overt and objectionable, it is also problematic that objectivist construals of "race" continue to predominate in scholarly writing as well as in church teaching and popular parlance. From a systematic-theological vantage point committed to truthful speech in accordance with the divine purposes in creation and redemption, which establishes eschatological reality in Christ, racial-realist, essentialist assumptions are an acutely problematic feature in theological discourse about humanity and about the church, even when it is directed toward antiracist ends.

Three comparatively recent books by evangelical writers—an OT exegete, a pastor-teacher, and theologian—are representative of the current state of conceptual confusion and disagreements concerning the meaning and validity of "race" concepts. It should be noted at the outset that all three writers make arguments that are antiracist in intention. Of prime interest is what they variously assume about "race" and how they employ it to interpret the scriptural testimony about human beings.

"Racial Realism" in Biblical Exegesis and Biblical Theology

J. Daniel Hays's OT monograph *From Every Tribe and Nation* in the "New Studies in Biblical Theology" series treats "race" and is a prime example of racial realism.[13] His study argues for the validity and value of racial and ethnic diversity within humanity and within the church by delineating two specific strands of teaching within Scripture.

First, Hays relates the concept of "races" to God's universal purposes for humanity. He does so by incorporating racial concepts into his sketch of the Abrahamic covenantal promise to bless the nations (Gen 12:3), the outworking of which is progressively realized in the course of Israel's history and is especially embodied in the inclusion of Gentiles in the people of God through incorporation into Christ.

Second, Hays retrieves the much-overlooked positive portrayals of Cushites (whom he designates "Black Africans")[14] in both Testaments. His treatment of the

---

12. Works by race theorists appearing in recent years include, e.g., Richard Herrnstein and Charles Murray, *The Bell Curve: Intelligence and Class Structure in American Life* (New York: Free, 1994); Vincent Sarich and Frank Miele, *Race: The Reality of Human Differences* (Boulder, CO: Westview, 2005); Gregory Clark, *A Farewell to Alms: A Brief Economic History of the World* (Princeton: Princeton University Press, 2007).

13. J. Daniel Hays, *From Every People and Nation: A Biblical Theology of Race* (Leicester: InterVarsity, 2003).

14. Ibid., 45; "The Cushites were clearly Black African people with classic 'Negroid' features," 36.

Cushites functions as a case study that supports the main thesis, which is the inclusiveness of the people of God and the equal status of the diverse members comprising it. It also highlights the fact that Phinehas, Ebed-Melech, and others are depicted in the biblical witness both as models of faithfulness to Yahweh and, indeed, as exemplary leaders.

Hays also argues—contrary to a variety of scholarly and popular interpretations of Numbers 12—that v. 1 indicates that Moses married "a Black Cushite woman from the Cushite civilization south of Egypt,"[15] and that Miriam and Aaron's opposition to this fact is not grounded in the "ban on intermarriage" with non-Israelites. He observes that "the foreigners that [Israelites] are allowed to intermarry [e.g., Deut 21:10–14; Num 12:1] are much more racially different than those whom they are prohibited from marrying. Obviously racial difference is not the issue; faith and theology are."[16] Indeed, the ensuing narrative and other instances in Scripture indicate divine approval of what Hays calls "interracial intermarriage" among believers: "Interracial intermarriage is strongly affirmed by Scripture."[17]

It is manifestly clear from this brief outline of the theses and the underlying structure of Hays's study that he presents an antiracist argument from Scripture for the dignity and equality of all people and a strong critique of racism in biblical scholarship, as well as in contemporary social practices within the evangelical church. In these respects, his study is salutary.

However, Hays interprets both Scripture and humanity within a racial-realist framework. That Hays believes that "race" denotes an accurate classificatory scheme that distinguishes among human groups on the basis of "physical appearance,"[18] i.e., "the colour of their skin,"[19] and "skin colour, facial features, hair,"[20] is seen, first of all, in the book's subtitle: *A Biblical Theology of Race*. Although the principal terms that the biblical writers employ to characterize the complex of humankind as a whole are "people" (*'am/laos*), "nation" (*gôy/ethnē*), and "tribe" or "family" (*mišppāḥāh/phylē*), Hays's choice to render the overarching biblical vision of humanity by recasting it in terms of "races" indicates that he regards it as an appropriate concept with which to explain humankind as presented in the biblical writings.

---

15. Ibid., 77.
16. Ibid., 78.
17. Ibid., 80.
18. Ibid., 29, 78.
19. Ibid., 81.
20. Ibid., 29.

The results of applying the presumed validity of the "race" concept to the analysis of Scripture are seen in the following interpretations of the creation accounts in Gen 1 and 2:

> From Genesis 1 comes the basic foundational premise for a theology of race: *all people are created in the image of God.* This gives every individual of every race in the world a remarkable status before God. It demolishes every theory of racial superiority or racial inferiority.[21]
>
> [T]he racially generic Adam represents all of humankind. All people of all races are thus created in the image of God. Blacks, Whites, and peoples of all other races are all created in the image of God. . . . All people of all races are created in God's image and therefore deserve to be treated with dignity and respect.[22]
>
> Adam and Eve are not Hebrews or Egyptians or Canaanites. It is incorrect for the White Church to view them as White or for the Black Church to view them as Black. Their "race" is not identifiable; they are neither Negroid nor Caucasian nor even Semitic. They become the mother and father of all peoples. The division of humankind into peoples and races is not even mentioned until Genesis 10. Adam and Eve, as well as Noah, are non-ethnic and non-national. They represent all people, not some people.[23]

What is especially notable in the latter statement is the assertion that according to Scripture, human races are a postcreational, postlapsarian, postflood development: "The division of humankind into peoples and *races* is not even mentioned until Genesis 10."[24] Hays states that human "races" objectively exist because Scripture attests (favorably) to their emergence as the result of divine providential action, recorded in the Table of Nations.

In addition to subscribing to the ontological reality of human "races," Hays apparently regards racial classificatory categories and concepts as valid descriptors and standards of reference with which to characterize both human beings in general, and those who inhabited the world of biblical antiquity and the world of the text. This belief is expressed in statements such as the following:

> For Anglo-European Christian readers, it is critical to come to grips with the fact that [the Semitic] people[s] were not blue-eyed, blond-haired Caucasians; they did not look like White Americans or White Britons. . . . If today's readers . . . want to find people of "Caucasian" appearance in the Old Testament, the Indo-European Philistines and Hittites are probably the closest. However,

---

21. Ibid., 62–63.
22. Ibid., 50–51.
23. Ibid., 47–48.
24. Ibid.

even the individuals from these ancient . . . groups probably resembled the people of modern Greece or Turkey more than [those] of modern England or mid-western America.[25]

Clearly the perception (conscious or subconscious) among many White Christians that the biblical story is a story about White people is wrong. The biblical story is full of different people of different ethnicities—and none of those in the Torah are Caucasian. As God's promise to Abraham in Genesis 12:3 (blessing to all peoples) unfolds, numerous different ethnicities are melded into the people of God in fulfillment of this promise. In the Torah, part of this melding process occurs through interracial marriage. Moses, the hero of the Torah, marries a Black woman with God's approval. Marriage across theological lines—that is, marrying unbelievers—is prohibited, but marriage to another of God's believing children, regardless of race, is affirmed.[26]

"Biological Racial Realism": An Assessment

Where "races" are thought to correspond to objective, naturally occurring systematic differences among groups and their members—differences rooted in underlying biological make-up, transmitted through heredity, and comprising the determinants of social and cultural behavior—there exists an instance of what I have called "biological racial realism."[27] This putatively scientific paradigm was introduced to and received elaboration in the United States from the 1780s through the 1870s.[28]

While biological racial realism continues to be the prevailing popular view, it is fundamentally flawed from the standpoint of research in human biology, particularly from the mid-to-late twentieth century onward, and especially confirmed in recent studies. For instance, among the findings reported by the Human Genome Project upon completion of the sequencing of the human genome in 2003 is the striking fact that—contrary to what phenotypic variation (observable bodily features) seems to suggest—human beings are 99.9 percent identical in genetic make-up.[29] In other words, the difference in genetic material carried by any pair of persons on the planet is one tenth of one percent, and these differences occur not between genes but at the level of alleles (i.e., the variations that occur in the expression of a gene due to mutations, either deleterious or beneficial).

---

25. Ibid., 34, 44.
26. Ibid., 86.
27. Sung, "'Race' and Ethnicity Discourse," 136.
28. Ibid., 135.
29. Francis S. Collins and Monique K. Mansoura, "The Human Genome Project: Revealing the Shared Inheritance of Humankind," *Cancer* 91 (2001) 221–25.

In addition, several major studies in human population variation have shown that many traits once regarded as fixed hereditary characters marking disparate racial groups occur independently of other traits, are subject to environmental pressures, and are distributed across population groups. In numerous cases mapping the incidence of genetic traits across continents displays a pattern not of clearly delineated populations with systematic differences akin to "natural kinds," but rather gradations of variation (clines) crossing geographic borders and overlapping the boundary lines of conventionally racialized groups.[30] At present no single trait or set of traits has been identified that is necessarily manifested by all members of a population group, nor have traits been found that are restricted to a single population group. For these and many other such reasons, most geneticists and biological anthropologists now concur with the view that biologically determinate "races" corresponding to traditional racial taxonomies do not exist.[31]

"Theological Racial Realism": An Assessment[32]

The expression of biological racial-realist beliefs and their employment in biblical interpretation produces a hermeneutic and a substantive theological position that I call theological racial realism. This view presents an ontologically objectivist account of human races as grounded in the original purposes of God, finding confirmation in biblical descriptions of its eschatological fulfillment. In Hays's work theological racial realism is deployed to criticize racism. His stance and the resulting study can be more precisely described as an expression of antiracist racial realism.

It is important to note that Hays's study is of particular value for refuting and correcting long-standing racist interpretations of scriptural texts and themes that continue to circulate in reprint editions of older scholarship. However, the problem that occupies us here is that his theological interpretation of Scripture assumes and asserts the ontologically real existence of co-equal human "races" that populate the world and the church in accordance with God's design, as attested in Scripture. The assumed validity of "race" apparently lies behind his choice to employ "race" as the organizing theme of his study.

---

30. Guido Barbujani, Arianna Magnani, Eric Minch, and Luigi Luca Cavalli-Sforza, "An Apportionment of Human DNA Diversity," *Proceedings of the National Academy of Sciences USA* 94 (April 1997) 4518.

31. Deborah Bolnick, "Individual Ancestry Reference and the Reification of Race as a Biological Phenomenon," in *Revisiting Race in a Genomic Age*, ed. Barbara A. Koenig, Sandra Soo-Jin Lee, and Sarah S. Richardson (New Brunswick, NJ: Rutgers University Press, 2008) 70–85; John Dupré, "What Genes Are and Why There Are No Genes for Race," in *Revisiting Race in a Genomic Age*, 39–55.

32. Sung, "'Race' and Ethnicity Discourse," 224.

However, Hays's descriptions of racial and ethnic phenomena in the biblical world behind the text and the world of the biblical text are frequently vague as well as inconsistent.[33] Most significantly, his actual interpretation of the Table of Nations ultimately falls far short of providing the promised evidence for the appearance of "races." (Remember his comment, "The division of humankind into peoples and *races* is not even mentioned until Genesis 10."[34])

"Race" versus Systemic Racism: An Assessment

It is significant that Hays consistently characterizes "the race problem"[35] as consisting in racial division and racial inequality, quoting from the work of Michael Emerson and Christian Smith in *Divided by Faith*: "[T]he race problem" is specifically "'the institutionalization of racialization—in economic, political, educational, social, and religious systems.'"[36] He also cites Bruce Fields's characterization of "the race issue" in *Introducing Black Theology* as "systemic sin."[37]

The political, economic, and sociocultural disparities that directly and indirectly impinge upon the agency, life-chances, and well-being of persons belonging to minority groups in our racialized society are numerous and grievous. They need to be rectified and redressed by sustained action on all fronts. However, the particular point of the present inquiry is that theological racial realism, funded by belief in biological racial realism, also comprises a serious problem for Christians concerned to acquire an empirically valid, conceptually accurate outlook on reality.

Racial realism is an example of uncritical reliance upon merely conventional social categories, in decided contrast to a framework built upon the best available analytical concepts based on empirical research. Racial realism weakens the positive substance, scope, and force of theological teaching that employs it. However well-intended the uses to which it is put, theological racial realism inhibits the recovery of truthful sight and speech which underlie appropriate action. Christian theological discourse needs to be reformed by the use of empirically valid concepts and categories that are commensurate with the normative biblical patterns of description, so that we accurately comprehend, convey, and appropriate in everyday living the

---

33. E.g., Hays, *From Every Nation*, 199.

34. For the interpretation of Gen 10, see Hays, *From Every Nation*, 63, 58; and for his earlier characterization of the text, 47–48.

35. "The race problem" (or "the race issue") is defined in Hays, *From Every Nation*, 17–22.

36. Ibid., 18, citing Michael Emerson and Christian Smith, *Divided by Faith* (New York: Oxford University Press, 2000) 170.

37. The expression "systemic sin" appears in Fields, *Introducing Black Theology*, 67–68; cited in Hays, *From Every People*, 18, n. 2.

wisdom embedded in scriptural discourse about humanity, human groups, and human identities.

"Racial Realism" and "Racial Nonrealism" in Practical Theology

Another book about "race," written by a prolific pastor-teacher with a wide platform and audience, requires attention. This treatment of "race" is not a scholarly work but a popular one: *Bloodlines: Race, Cross, and the Christian* by John Piper.[38] Several features are salient for our purposes of examining beliefs about "race" in the contemporary teaching of the church.

In contrast to the wholly unqualified racial realism that Hays's study expresses, this volume sets forth contradictory beliefs about racial realism. Piper simultaneously presents descriptions of racial realism and of its antithesis, a position I have called "racial nonrealism."[39]

On the one hand, in a prefatory "Note to the Reader on *Race* and *Racism*" (which is reproduced almost entirely verbatim in the Appendix, "Is There Such a Thing as Race? A Word about Terminology"), Piper writes:

> Believe it or not the existence of the reality of *race* itself is disputed. . . . I deal with this in appendix 1. And, of course, the term *racism* is ambiguous as well. It seems to me that it is a healthy sign to wish that the term *race* did not exist. It has not served well to enhance human relations. As we use it, it is not a biblical category. We may not be able to communicate in our day without the term, but we can at least try to show why it's a fuzzy term that has often been hijacked by ideology for racist purposes.[40]

There are three especially significant aspects of this statement. First, reflecting the increased attention and progress in research regarding race-related matters in the eleven years subsequent to the publication of Hays's book, Piper and his research assistant, Alex Kirk,[41] are cognizant that the term "race" itself is ambiguous and problematic, and that the objective facticity of "race" itself has been called into question. In the first Appendix (to which the reader is directed at the outset of the book for a discussion of the debate about racial realism), Piper reproduces a statement from the *World Christian Encyclopedia*, which defines "races" as "a biological concept":

38. John Piper, *Bloodlines: Race, Cross, and the Christian* (Wheaton: Crossway, 2011) 234.
39. Sung, "'Race' and Ethnicity Discourse," 332.
40. Piper, *Bloodlines*, 17; cf. 234.
41. Piper writes, "I am indebted to Alex Kirk for his research and insights in helping me clarify and document the issues in this chapter. If I have made any poor judgments, they are my own, not his." Ibid., 278, n. 2.

> In general, the term *race* has been used to signify "a biological concept referring to the taxonomic (classificatory) unit immediately below the species."[42]
>
> Thus . . . mankind or the human race today consists of a single surviving species, Homo Sapiens, and five surviving subspecies or races or racial stocks: . . . Australoid, Capoid, Caucasoid, Mongoloid and Negroid.[43]

This is a classic statement propounding biological racial realism, a fallacy the evidence for which is ample, accessible, and long-standing. As such, its inclusion by Piper is inexplicable.

On the other hand, Piper also draws extensively on and incorporates excerpts from Colin Kidd's historical treatment, *The Forging of Races: Race, Scripture, and the Protestant Atlantic World*.[44] These include the following direct quotations from Kidd himself:

> Tellingly, there has been no consensus among race scientists as to the number of races of humanity. The answers range from three to over a hundred races.[45]
>
> . . .
>
> Scientific observers of race have never been able to agree about the number of different races of humankind, nor about the characteristics that determine such groupings. Such disagreements do not mean that the scientific taxonomy of races is a holy grail which has still to be achieved, but that such a quest is, in fact, a fool's errand.[46]

What is important to note is that Piper merely reports that the opposing positions of racial realism and racial nonrealism exist and cites sources for each. He includes quotations of anthropologists' and historians' observations, all of which are racial nonrealist in substance, and distills them in the form of several basic points,[47] more so than with racial-realist statements, but he does not press further toward analytical clarity with which to judge between these rival positions.

Piper asserts that "the term *ethnicity* is more helpful and less destructive than the term *race* in marking human identity."[48] He cites two very generic descriptions of ethnicity. Anthropologist Eloise Hiebert Meneses's definition is presented first: "The

---

42. Ibid., 234, citing the *World Christian Encyclopedia: A Comparative Study of Churches and Religions in the Modern World AD 1900–2000*, ed. David Barrett (Nairobi: Oxford University Press, 1982) 207.

43. *World Christian Encyclopedia*, cited in Piper, *Bloodlines*, 278, n. 1.

44. Colin Kidd, *Race and Scripture in the Protestant Atlantic World, 1600–2000* (Cambridge: Cambridge University Press, 2006).

45. Ibid., 9.

46. Ibid., 10.

47. Ibid., 235–38.

48. Ibid., 235.

term *ethnicity* is usually used to stress the cultural rather than the physical aspects of group identity. Ethnic groups share language, dress, food, customs, values, and sometimes religion."[49] The second quotation is from a website: "Ethnicity refers to selected cultural and sometimes physical characteristics used to classify people into groups or categories considered to be significantly different from others."[50]

This conflation of a racial-realist conception of "race" and ethnicity is apparent in the following stipulation: "Unless I explicitly differentiate *race* and *racial* from *ethnicity* and *ethnic*, I would like you to think of both when I mention either—that is, *ethnicity* with a physical component and *race* with a cultural component.[51] He also writes:

> When you stand before a man who is manifestly different from you in skin color, hair type, and facial features, and you want to respectfully and intelligently take his significant differences into account in your interaction, it is generally more helpful to know that he is a Korean-American-third-generation-born-in-Philadelphia than to know that he belongs to the Asian race. Or if you are an African American standing before a "white" man whom you would like to interact with in an intelligent and respectful way, it will probably be more relevant to know that he is a Danish-international-student-studying-urban-trends than to know that he belongs to the Caucasian race.[52]

In the span of this paragraph Piper employs racial-realist description ("he belongs to the Caucasian race"), likewise describes a geographic group category as a "race" ("the Asian race"), possibly indicates he regards the term "white" as questionable by placing it within quotation marks, and employs descriptors that properly pertain to ethnicity and nationality.

"Racial Realism" and "Racial Nonrealism": An Assessment

Taking these representative statements together, it appears that, despite the inclusion of multiple citations of the racial nonrealist studies by Kidd and Meneses, Piper did not directly investigate the considerable evidence presented in those works or the extensive scholarship and the mainstream interdisciplinary consensus elsewhere

---

49. Ibid., 235. The quotation is found on p. 34 of Eloise Hiebert Meneses, "Science and the Myth of Biological Race," in *This Side of Heaven: Race, Ethnicity, and the Christian*, ed. Robert Priest and Alvaro Nieves (Oxford: Oxford University Press, 2006) 33–46.

50. Online: http://anthro.palomar.edu/ethnicity/ethnic_1.htm, emphasis added. Piper, *Bloodlines*, 278n4.

51. Ibid., 239, emphasis original.

52. Piper, *Bloodlines*, 234.

which led Kidd to conclude that the search for a "scientific taxonomy of races is . . . a fool's errand."[53]

Instead, Piper's repeated use of merely conventional racial categories and terminology ("the Caucasian race," "white") and reference to the associated symbolic markers ("skin color, hair type, and facial features"), at best leaves readers in a state of ambiguity and confusion about the actual ontological status of "races," i.e. whether they comport with biological facts. In view of the power and operation of socialization and institutionalization, this practice perpetuates the purported objectivity of the pseudoscientific concept of biological racial realism.

"Race" versus "Racism": An Assessment

A related and significant feature in Piper's argument is his explicit definition of "racism," and the distinction he draws between "race" and "racism," as seen in the subheading "Racism Values One Race over Another."[54] In this section, he employs a statement issued by the Presbyterian Church of America (PCA) to define racism: "Racism is an explicit or implicit belief or practice that qualitatively distinguishes or values one race over other races."[55] He elaborates on this assertion:

> The focus of this definition is on the heart and behavior of the racist. The *heart* that believes one race is more valuable than another is a sinful heart. And that sin is called *racism*. The *behavior* that distinguishes one race as more valuable than another is sinful behavior. And that sin is called *racism*. This personal focus on the term *racism* does not exclude the expression of this sin in structural ways, for example, laws and policies that demean or exclude on the basis of race.[56]

The Presbyterian Church of America definition that Piper propounds gives expression to racial realism: racism is construed as preference for "one race" over against "other races." Lacking a disclaimer of biological racial realism or other qualifying distinctions, the statement employs the term "races" as if it refers to objectively existent, ontologically distinct groups. Piper's assertion that ". . . [race is] a fuzzy term that has often been hijacked by ideology for racist purposes"[57] draws a

---

53. Kidd, *Forging*, 10.

54. Piper, *Bloodlines*, 239.

55. Ibid. Cf. full citation, 279n14: "Committee on Mission to North America, Pastoral Letter on Racism," approved at the March 2004 MNA Committee Meeting as the Committee's Recommendation to the Thirty-Second General Assembly," http://www.pca-mna.org/churchplanting/PDFs/RacismPaper-Final%20Version%2004-09-04.pdf.

56. Piper, *Bloodlines*, 239–40.

57. Ibid., 17, 234.

distinction between "'race'" and "racism." On this description, "racism" exists when racial concepts are (illegitimately) coopted and put to ideological use. This statement suggests that Piper (like J. Daniel Hays) regards "race" itself as a valid, fundamentally neutral concept that can be employed for positive purposes.

However, neither this construal of "race" nor the posited ethical distinction between "race" and "racism" evinces interaction with the great body of scholarship available in the humanities, the social sciences, the history of the philosophy of science, and in recent theological treatments of "race." This scholarship demonstrates that modern "race" constructs were from the very beginning expressly created to legitimize domination and exploitation. Writing in the tradition of intellectual histories of "race" by scholars such as Ivan Hannaford[58] and critical race theorists such as Richard Delgado and Jean Stefancic,[59] theologian Willie James Jennings demonstrates that in the history of European colonization and missions, the concept "black" (and its implied antithesis, "white") was originally devised by Christian intellectuals in accounts invoking divine providence and soteriology as a rationale for exploration and conquest, the expropriation of lands and profitable goods, and especially the enslavement of the peoples encountered in regions beyond Southern and Northern Europe. In this quintessentially modern remapping and re-creation of the existing world *qua* "races," the ruling powers, merchants, missionaries, and others positioned the concept of whiteness as central and naturalized separatist arrangements within a hierarchical social order. This contravened all that the Christian doctrines of creation, humanity, Christology and ecclesiology stood for.[60]

Theologian J. Kameron Carter traces the origins of the pervasive concept of white supremacy to Immanuel Kant's vision of the new, modern world order, articulated in his writings in speculative anthropology, theology, and especially his political-philosophical program for the nation-state.[61] Both Jennings and Carter treat the "Christian-colonial way of imagining the world"[62] as ultimately predicated on theological supersessionism.

---

58. Ivan Hannaford, *Race: The History of an Idea in the West* (Baltimore, MD: Johns Hopkins University Press, 1996).

59. Richard Delgado and Jean Stefancic, *Critical Race Theory: An Introduction* (New York: New York University Press, 2001).

60. Willie James Jennings, *The Christian Imagination: Theology and the Origins of Race* (New Haven, CT: Yale University Press, 2010). Space constraints preclude further discussion of Jennings's study, but see Elizabeth Y. Sung, "Willie James Jennings: *Theology and the Christian Imagination*," *Themelios* 39.3 (November 2014) 585–88.

61. J. Kameron Carter, *Race: A Theological Account* (New York: Oxford University Press, 2008). For a review of this study, see Elizabeth Y. Sung, "J. Kameron Carter: *Race: A Theological Account*," *Themelios* 40.1 (April 2015) 156–58.

62. Jennings, *Christian Imagination*, 208.

What is immediately relevant to the point at hand is that the concept of discrete natural "races" that underlies the racialized social imaginary of the church and society at large is a basic example of ideology *par excellence* in the Marxian sense: knowledge in the service of power. In view of the copious evidence readily available to the general public, the continued use of "race" in an unqualified, nondeconstructive fashion preserves a falsifying and reductionistic organizing system with which to interpret human beings and the social world.

While more exists to be queried,[63] it is clear that Piper's treatment of the meaning of "race" itself is a thin description, and his construal of the ontological status of human "races" is inconsistent. His account repeatedly vacillates regarding the truth-value of the contradictory views of racial realism and racial nonrealism. No attempt is made to arrive at a logically coherent set of conclusions vis-à-vis their respective relations to ontological reality, ultimately in the light of eschatological actuality in Christ as conveyed in Scripture. Over against a truly systematic-theological treatment, it is an ad hoc, practical theology reflection which does not offer a resolution for these mutually exclusive positions.

"Racial Nonrealism" in Systematic Theology

Douglas Sharp, a systematic theologian, likewise treats "race" and asserts that both "race and racism challenge the Christian faith and contradict the gospel of Jesus Christ because they are expressions of human sin."[64]

Sharp deconstructs the commonsense logic of racial realism by drawing on theories in the sociology of knowledge—specifically, concepts from Peter Berger and Thomas Luckmann's seminal study, *The Social Construction of Reality*[65]—to illumine the process by which racializing (read "racist") practices historically became embedded and continue to be maintained in societies like the United States. He concludes that "[r]ace and racism are inherently oppositional and disruptive of human

---

63. Note Piper's statement (*Bloodlines*, 239): "If, as we have defined it, ethnicity includes beliefs and attitudes and behaviors, we are biblically and morally bound to value some aspects of some ethnicities over others. There are aspects of every culture, including our own, that are sinful and in need of transformation." While the second sentence is a commonplace, the first calls for explication. Specifically, which ethnicities are to be valued over others, and what are the biblical and moral grounds for doing so?

64. Douglas Sharp, *No Partiality: The Idolatry of Race and the New Humanity* (Downers Grove, IL: InterVarsity, 2002) 11.

65. Peter Berger and Thomas Luckmann, *The Social Construction of Reality: A Treatise in the Sociology of Knowledge* (New York: Anchor, 1967).

community because they express differential status and power relations and require that human beings identify with one group over against another."[66]

Sharp also proposes that the positive alternative to "race and racism," i.e., racializing practices, is racial reconciliation. He articulates this Pauline theme as follows:

> Jew or Gentile, male or female, slave or free, black or white, brown or yellow—all these are socially constructed ways of defining and expressing ourselves *over against* others, and as such they *contradict* God's purpose for humanity, the purpose of cohumanity with and for one another, as disclosed in the one new human, Jesus of Nazareth.[67]

"Racial Nonrealism": An Assessment

In conspicuous contrast to Hays's unqualified racial-realism and Piper's fundamental equivocation between racial realism and racial nonrealism, Sharp stoutly asserts the racial nonrealist position. Furthermore—contra Piper and Hays—not just "racism" but "race" itself is ideological since both "express differential status and power relations."[68]

Notably, Sharp rightly criticizes "inherently oppositional" forms of identity and difference. However, casting as inherently divisive all of the varying forms of social identification and community claimed by humans—especially the "Jew or Gentile, male or female" categorical pairs and what they signify—results in a reading of Scripture that is too truncated and thin.

Instead, as I argue elsewhere, a theological account that does justice to the biblical presentation of humanity and to the new humanity in Christ requires the employment of alternate conceptual resources of two kinds. Following the Augustinian approach, the first analytical concept must be both adequate in relation to the external reality to which it refers and logically consistent with scriptural discourse about humanity in order to be adaptable for Christian doctrine. Specifically, I develop a theological exegesis of the principal passages of Scripture that constitute the relevant "canonical pattern of judgment."[69] I show that the analytical usefulness of

---

66. Sharp, *No Partiality*, 272.
67. Ibid., 274, emphasis added.
68. Ibid., 272.
69. A "canonical pattern of judgment" refers to "the implicit rationality presupposed in the 'patterns of judgment' that individual biblical texts and the canon as a whole display." Sung, "'Race' and Ethnicity Discourse," 231, citing concepts employed to describe the canonical-linguistic approach to theology, which attends to the "patterns of judgments" that "subsist *in* the particular [biblical] texts and their particular literary and historical contexts," i.e., "patterns of communicative action." See Kevin Vanhoozer, *The Drama of Doctrine: A Canonical-Linguistic Approach to Christian Theology* (Louisville, KY: Westminster John Knox, 2005) 341.

the particular sociological conception of "ethnic groups" put forward by Richard A. Schermerhorn surpasses that of other known concepts. His approach enables the more precise characterization and further clarification of those features pertaining to the world's peoples that are favorably depicted in the canonical outlook.[70]

The second analytical concept is relevant to racialized settings and must enable people residing in a social world where "race," racial realism, and racism have been institutionalized to recognize and accurately reframe racial realism and racism in their various forms. Such an analysis underlies responsible corrective action. To this end, I propose a carefully qualified technical designation that assists in the diagnosis, deconstruction, and dismantling of "race" as a discursive formation in its manifold expressions.[71]

Theology Reforming Ideology: Seeing Truthfully in Scripture's Light

In the course of this brief treatment I have pointed to three objections pertaining to the position of theological racial realism, which is expressed in the use of the concept of "race" and racial categories to render the scriptural presentation of humanity and to describe humankind and the church (the new humanity). Two objections attach to the objectivist conception of "race" itself: its historical provenance as a paradigm case of ideology and its status as a pseudoscientific theory. As noted earlier, it is therefore unsurprising to find that racializing theological readings of Scripture and of humanity prove to have no exegetical basis whatsoever. Thirdly, there is no textual or logical warrant within the scriptural account of humanity for depicting or classifying individuals or groups in racial terms. Such terms are fundamentally reductionistic and profoundly misleading regarding the human constitution and the complex psychosocial, cultural, and religious aspects of human identities.

Theological reflection that is antiracist in aim ultimately is best served by a threefold strategy: (1) thoroughly deconstructing the illusion of biological fact that continues to be ascribed to "race" concepts; (2) by employing a more nuanced conceptual-linguistic variant of the designation "race" for the purposes of engaging in critical analysis which informs the antiracist action to be taken; and (3) by appropriating an entirely different master concept that is accurate and adequate to scriptural discourse to depict its favorable outlook on the variations that arise from descent, culture, historical experience, and other such factors. In combination, these

---

70. Schermerhorn's concept and the evidence for its aptness for theological interpretation of Scripture—along with critique of other concepts employed by exegetes and theologians—is set forth in Sung, "'Race' and Ethnicity Discourse," 221–343.

71. For a summary of this pair of analytical concepts, see Sung, "'Race' and Ethnicity Discourse," 348–51.

efforts will better advance the cause of truthful speech and practice as we endeavor to bear witness to the gospel in word and deed that God in Christ through the Spirit is reconciling the world to himself and its peoples to one another in union with Christ, bringing eschatological reality in Christ—already taking hold with the inbreaking of the reign of God in this age—to fully actualized existence in the life of the world to come.

RESPONSE TO SUNG

Valerie Landfair

I appreciate Elizabeth Sung's contribution to the conversation regarding race and racism. She provides a brief synopsis of a sampling of "race" theories, critiques their empirical validity, and evaluates their appropriation of race in their theological engagement of Scripture. She argues that often scholars and lay theologians, because of their presuppositions, employ "racial realist" lenses in their attempt to dismantle racism and in their appropriation of race in their interpretation of Scripture.

She argues racial realists assume that racial classificatory categories correlate to an objective state of affairs in the world of nature: an order of "races," akin to subspecies, exists within humankind. This approach sees "races" as discrete human groups possessing determinate, distinguishing traits that are rooted in the biological constitution. Bodily features are but the most visible markers of the innate, natural endowments of the members of the respective races, which are fixed, not subject to alteration.

Sung proposes a twofold corrective for racial realism: deconstruction of racialized terms and formulation of alternate ethnic terms more in alignment with Scripture.

In my response I will provide a brief critique regarding Sung's focus only on the topic of race, and I will address her interpretation of J. Daniel Hays's *From Every People and Nation: A Biblical Theology of Race*.

I am curious how her proposal for formation of alternate ethnic terms would eradicate or diminish ethnic labels and slurs in public discourses regarding African Americans, Latinos/as, Native Americans, and Asian Americans in light of the contemporary reality of racialized disharmony in respect to these communities. Sung's article compels me to dissect the present realities of responsive movements such as the black lives matter movement and to recognize the possibility of a new reality. For example, she proposes we eliminate the reductive binary framework of race, particularly white/black, for what she argues would be more biblically accurate racialized categories. I appreciate her engagement with various voices in dialogue with God's universal purpose for humanity. I am indebted to her work for recognizing and presenting a new reality of engagement regarding race.

Valerie Landfair — Response to Sung

I wonder how a contemporary theologian deals with race without addressing the issue of racism. Is it possible for Sung to approach objectively the challenge of current models of racial categorization while suspending her discourse on the topic of racism within this paper? If we agree that Sung has shown that racialized categories serve to sustain racism, then does not the very lack of a framework for dismantling racism serve to exempt the church? An unintended consequence of tabling racism within a theological discourse on race leads to premature foreclosing of the possibilities of healing of wounds sustained from embattled racialized traumas. Moreover, minimizing or muting the naming of racialized sins delays the dismantling of racist principalities, power, systems, and structures, and I propose renders prayers of lament and prayers of repentance unessential.

Sung is in concert with Hays's critique of European Western race constructs as nonexistent in the Bible. The two agree that Scripture identifies people groups by their ethnicity. However, Hays states that the names of certain ethnic groups translate into descriptive terms, as, for example with Ethiopian: burnt faces equate to black people. Nevertheless, I concur with Hays that categories of ethnic groups in antiquity appropriate a descriptive framework to distinguish Israelites and non-Israelites. For Sung, Hays's treatment of "physical appearance," i.e., "the colour of their skin," and "skin colour, facial features, hair," imputes race into biblical writings thereby supporting racist dogma.[1] However, would the adoption of racialized ethnic categories lead to more accurate narratives regarding the presence in Scripture and in church history of non-Europeans and especially Africans? Jesus is usually portrayed with European skin pigmentation in movies and historical documentaries.[2] How one speaks English, the clothes one wears, and the food one eats have all been racialized. Lydia Hernández observes, "Indigenous people speak what is known as a 'dialect,' not a language."[3] I am unsure how the eradication of racial realism eradicates racism. In my view racism will continue to flourish within any framework that does not daily affirm, teach, and live out a life-giving theology of truth that all of humanity is created in the image of God—African, African American, Arab, Asian, Latino/a, Native American and more. The good news is that there is no partiality with God (Rom 2:11). In the Christian tradition God loves us first and commands us to love our neighbors as ourselves (Mark 12:31). Is this not a sign and an embodied

---

1. J. Daniel Hays, *From Every People and Nation: A Biblical Theology of Race* (Leicester: InterVarsity, 2003) 29, 78, 81.

2. *The Bible Series* premiered on the History Channel in 2013; *Ben Hur: A Tale of the Christ* in 1959; *Jesus* in 1999; *Jesus of Nazareth* in 1979; and *The Passion of the Christ* in 2003.

3. Lydia Hernández, "Even Today What Began Five Hundred Years Ago," in *New Face of the Church in Latin America: Between Tradition and Change*, ed. Guillermo Cook (Maryknoll, NY: Orbis, 1994) 14.

witness to the transforming power of the triune God? However, the implication of racism excludes certain individuals and communities from being one's neighbor.

To discuss the image of God I propose a life-giving theology of truth about "Spirit baptism in divine love."[4] The Azusa Street revival, even if for a brief moment in history, influenced the ways in which social, racial, and economic barriers were nullified within the church. This is no small point, for one of the primary and most persistent critiques against Pentecostalism is its emphasis on the individualistic, self-absorbed, and hyper-emotional reception of charismatic gifts, which is often linked to self-gratification.[5] In an ironic twist, a multicultural ministry was birthed under the leadership of African American William Joseph Seymour during Jim and Jane Crowism.[6]

Estrelda Alexander builds upon the scholarship of Walter Hollenweger and Leonard Lovett[7] who emphasize that the roots of American Pentecostalism were in African spirituality and slave religion.[8] The social implications for the first three years of the revival, 1906–1908, are clear: "Though most worshipers were from the

---

4. I surveyed *The Apostolic of Faith* newspaper of every use and formation of the word "love." Testimonies of divine love are where the believer described her or his Spirit baptism as one of being filled with divine love or the love of God. Their testimonies included an internal change in their heart and/or spirit that had outward manifestations.

5. Cecil M. Robeck, Jr., *The Azusa Street Mission and Revival: The Birth of the Global Pentecostal Movement* (Nashville: Thomas Nelson, 2006) 23.

6. Rodney Woo maintains "A multiracial congregation is by nature and definition a place of contrast; this moves us out of our comfort zones and forces us to trust in the God of all peoples." See his *The Color of Church: A Biblical and Practical Paradigm for Multiracial Churches* (Nashville: Broadman & Holman Academic, 2009) 49. I appropriate Ed Stetzer's definition of multiracial and multicultural churches. He states a multiracial church is a church with "persons of color" in attendance. "A multicultural church is not simply about skin tone, but about the intentional engagement of cultures. So a multicultural church will not simply have people who are African-American, but will engage to some degree in African-American cultural contexts. I offer that a multicultural church reflects ethnic diversity of leadership and economic distribution. Leadership in the Azusa Street revival in its inception crossed gender and racial lines. See his "Thinking Through the Multicultural Church," *Christianity Today*, accessed November 20, 2015, http://www.christianitytoday.com/edstetzer/2013/december/thinking-through-multicultural-church.html. See Richard N. Pitt, "Fear of a Black Pulpit? Real Racial Transcendence versus Cultural Assimilation in Multiracial Churches," in JSSR 49 (2010) 218–23. Note on p. 222: "Multiracial churches, in spite of their composition, retain mostly white characteristics even when whites are outnumbered by other racial groups."

7. Walter J. Hollenweger, *The Pentecostals; The Charismatic Movement In the Churches* (Minneapolis: Augsburg, 1972); Leonard Lovett, "Perspective on the Black Origins of the Contemporary Pentecostal Movement," *Journal of the Interdenominational Theological Center* 1 (1973) 36–49.

8. Estrelda Y. Alexander, *Black Fire: One Hundred Years of African American Pentecostalism* (Downers Grove, IL: InterVarsity, 2011) 16. Karla F. C. Holloway wrote "More than four thousand African Americans were lynched between 1882 and 1942" and "The evidence of our history continued to argue for some association between color and death, much as one might have wished it to be otherwise." See her *Passed On: African American Mourning Stories* (Durham: Duke University Press, 2002) 58, 60.

lower and working classes, there were no stratifications either by class, race, gender or age in involvement or leadership in the services."[9]

This connects with Paul's description of spiritual gifts in First Corinthians. As Gordon Fee rightly points out, the greatest theological contribution to the Christian faith is Paul's understanding of the church's "visible expression in the local community of redeemed people."[10] Such a visible expression, as the temple of God, requires them to live counter-culturally to the life that surrounds them (1 Cor 5:1; 6:7; 10:32; 14:23).[11]

Certainly the church is united in the body of Christ and is the temple of the Holy Spirit (10:17; 11:29; 12:12–26), a visible expression of "one body" consisting of diversity in nationalities, genders, ethnicity, social, and economic locations, but they are united in Christ. Paul's imagery of unity within the various manifestations of "one Spirit" reflects God's presence. Paul's understanding is that "When God's Spirit is manifested among them by prophetic utterance, pagans will have their hearts searched and judged and they will recognize that God is among his people (1 Cor 14:24–25)."[12] Rather than being unbiblical or out of touch with authentic Christianity, radically egalitarian worship corresponds closely with first century Christianity's ethos.

"Spirit baptism in divine love" overflows in the believer's heart, words, and actions. As a consequence these very attributes will not only dwell in the recipient's heart as an inward witness but will manifest themselves as a visible witness in a person's daily living by loving the other. Perhaps more important is the fact that once one is submerged in the love of God, that person is now empowered to suffer alongside and with the other, whether African American, Native American, Arabic, or whatever, in a spirit of humility. Spirit baptism empowers the believer to be gentle, meek, and humble. Moreover, this Spirit baptism in divine love is a sign that there

---

9. Alexander, *Black Fire*, 121. In August 1906 W. E. B. DuBois hosted the Niagara Movement, a black civil rights movement seeking the enforcement of the principles outlined in the Declaration of Independence and the Constitution regarding the right to vote, elimination of segregation in public accommodation, access to interracial friendships, equality in laws enforced and education, and freedom of speech. The Niagara Movement's manifesto is, in the words of Du Bois, "We claim for ourselves every single right that belongs to a freeborn American, political, civil and social; and until we get these rights we will never cease to protest and assail the ears of America." W. E. B. DuBois, "No Cowards or Trucklers," in *In Their Own Words: A History of the American Negro: 1865–1916*, ed. Milton Meltzer (New York: Thomas Y. Crowell, 1965) 150. Mass racial violence in the United States during the first three years of the Azusa Street Revival occurred in 1906 (Little Rock, AR; Atlanta, GA), 1907 (Bellingham, WA), and 1908 (Springfield, IL). See Philip Dray, *At the Hands of Persons Unknown: The Lynching of Black America* (New York: Modern Library, 2002).

10. Gordon D. Fee, *The First Epistle to the Corinthians*, NICNT (Grand Rapids: Eerdmans, 1987) 25.

11. Ibid., 18–19.

12. Ibid.

is one body of Christ, which includes educated, uneducated, rich, poor, male, and female, but they are one nonetheless in Christ. It is apparent that the repercussions of these effects of the Holy Spirit result in social renewal and protest against all forms of unjust societal structures, both within and outside of the universal church.[13]

In conclusion, I label myself as an African American woman created in the image of God and joint-heir with Jesus. My roots connect me to Christianity in Africa before the European missionaries and African enslavement, the civil rights movement, the black empowerment movement, and the Black Lives Matter movement. The only way to eradicate racism is a lived out "Spirit baptism in divine love" that daily aligns one's words and deeds to critique prophetically the one body of Christ in harmony with the Scripture. How can you love God whom you have not seen and hate me whom you have seen? (See 1 John 4:20.)[14]

---

13. David Barrett affirms Pentecostals and charismatics are found in "9,000 ethnolinguistic cultures, speaking 8,000 languages covering 95 percent of the world's total population." See "The Worldwide Holy Spirit Renewal," in *The Century of the Holy Spirit: 100 Years of Pentecostal and Charismatic Renewal*, ed. Vinson Synan (Nashville: Thomas Nelson, 2001) 383. On the social engagement of Pentecostal and charismatic churches see David D. Daniels III, "Future Issues in Social and Economic Justice," in *Spirit Empowered Christianity in the 21st Century*, ed. Vinson Synan (Lake Mary, FL: Charisma, 2011) 339–55; and Yolanda Nicole Pierce, "Woman-tology and the Future Face of Pentecostalism" in *ThTo* 68 (2012) 381–82.

14. Korie L. Edwards provides a sociological analysis of her Midwest church's disappointment regarding "how race manages to control, infuse, and reorganize human relations such that whites remain dominant, even in places that embrace racial diversity." See her *The Elusive Dream: The Power of Race in Interracial Churches* (New York: Oxford University Press, 2008) vii.

REIMAGINING *KOINONIA*: CONFRONTING THE LEGACY AND LOGIC OF RACISM BY REINTERPRETING PAUL'S LETTER TO PHILEMON

Lewis Brogdon

The Tragedy at Mother Emmanuel and What It Means for the Church

On June 17, 2015, Dylann Roof, a white male, attended a Bible study at Emmanuel AME Church. One of the survivors said that they "welcomed" him to their church. Later that evening he opened fire on the participants, killing nine people. Among the victims was Rev. Clementa Pickney, the pastor of the church and a state senator in South Carolina. It was reported that while he was shooting members of what many call Mother Emmanuel, he yelled "You're raping our women. You're taking over and you have to go." This statement is instructive because it reveals something about the mentality of a racist and, more importantly, the logic of racism.[1]

Why did he say, "You're raping our women and you're taking over"? Everything he did that night was calculated, and I believe he said this statement for a reason and left a victim alive so she could report what she saw and heard. His reference to rape reflects his belief that interracial relationships between black men and white women were wrong. He used the stark language of rape to describe this kind of relationship. The statement "you're taking over" was a clear reference to African Americans becoming leaders and contributing members of society that some white Americans have to see, work with, and respect to some degree. Roof murdered nine African Americans because of racist beliefs, and these beliefs were an inescapable part of this tragic event.

---

1. I summarize the logic of racism accordingly: (1) human beings are members of three or four biological races; (2) humans have physical (bodily) differences that do not change and are inherited; (3) blacks are the most inferior race and are inferior intellectually, socially, and morally because they are violent, hyper-sexual, and emotional; (4) whites are the superior race; (5) every racial group has a place in a divine social order or racial hierarchy that leads to a harmonious society, in which blacks are cursed and called by God to be slaves or servants and to serve other races; and (6) the races should be divided. Marital, familial, social, and religious intercourse is forbidden, defended by legal and religious law, and often reinforced with violence.

Crossing Lines of Race Today and Signs of the Continuance of Racism

Roof's horrible actions and inflammatory words that night are very revealing. America was forced to witness racism, the evil that many so vociferously denied still exists. However, his actions were another troubling sign that racist beliefs are more widespread among white families and communities than we would care to admit. We would like to think that Roof was an extremist whose beliefs in no way resemble beliefs shared by mainstream white Americans. I would respond to this by saying that he grew up in a Lutheran church in Columbia, South Carolina. He is a product of white Christianity, which means part of his views on race has been influenced by white Christians. It is worth noting that not a single member of his immediate family or anyone from his home church has publicly renounced Roof's actions and racist beliefs. They have been largely silent and indirectly complicit in fostering racism. Roof was also influenced by white supremacist and nationalist groups online, so there were other influences. The church he attended may not have overtly supported racist thinking, but it is clear that it did little to disrupt and deconstruct the logic of race and racism. This thinking was allowed to fester and grow resulting in the deaths of nine innocent black people inside the sacred walls of a Christian church.

Roof's beliefs were not exceptional but rather shared by many white Americans who believe it is wrong for whites and blacks to worship God in the same space and to love and to raise families together—the language often is it is "better" not to. The logic of racism claims that there are certain levels of relationships that are off limits, namely blacks and whites dating and marrying one another.[2] It also reflects

---

2. There are numerous examples that this belief is widespread. In the early 1990s, during a sermon at his church in Broken Arrow, Oklahoma, Ken Hagin, Jr., told his church that he taught his children that "we" can be friends with them but we do not date or marry them. He used this statement to teach the young people at his church that it is wrong for young white Christians to marry people of other races. When news of this reached his longtime friend Pastor Fred Price and Hagin Jr. refused to publicly repent from such thinking, a national controversy erupted. See Frederick K. C. Price, *Race, Religion and Racism* (Los Angeles: Faith One Publishing, 1999) 3–65. In March of 2000, Bob Jones III, president of Bob Jones University, a large "Christian" university in South Carolina, dropped the school's five-decade ban on interracial dating, which was rooted in their belief that God created people differently. Jones did this in the wake of a national controversy over George Bush's visit there and later rebuke of their policy, calling it bigotry. It was not until 2005 that the university apologized for these and other racist policies. More recently, a Pew study on interracial marriage found that evangelicals are more opposed to it than most Americans and have the most negative view of interracial marriage. They actually believe it is bad for society. In addition to this, not only do white evangelicals think that it is a bad thing for whites and blacks to marry, they are largely against integrating churches. A recent phone survey of 1,000 churchgoers found that only thirty-seven percent wanted to see their churches more ethnically diverse. The Southern Baptist Convention is the largest Protestant denomination. Of its 51,000 congregations, only one percent are multiethnic. See Tobin Grant, "Opposition to Interracial Marriage Lingers Among Evangelicals," *Christianity Today*, http://www.christianitytoday.com/gleanings/2011/june/ opposition-to-interracial-marriage-lingers-among.html; and Tom Boggioni, "Two-Thirds of Evangelicals Resist Integrating their Churches" *Raw Story*, http://

deep anxieties and fears about the high rates of social intercourse that are happening between blacks and whites. Some believe that there is too much "race-mingling" occurring today. After all, we are only five decades from Jim and Jane Crow segregation. These families and individuals may concede that blacks and whites can be friends but not family and definitely not lovers. The fact that this belief has not been challenged, exposed, and expelled from their imagination is both shameful and instructive. There is much work that needs to be done to exorcise such thinking from the minds of Christians in America. Roof's ideas are a product of white churches' racist beliefs about dating, marrying, and worshipping with people across the sinful and socially constructed lines of race that run contrary to the radical teachings of the gospel of Jesus Christ.

How does one understand this thinking which is still so pervasive among white Christians? It is best to begin with Howard Thurman's classic *Jesus and the Disinherited* because he argues that racism has been a perennial problem for Christianity in America and says:

> Why is it that Christianity seems impotent to deal radically and therefore effectively with the issues of discrimination and injustice on the basis of race? Is this impotency due to a betrayal of the genius of the religion, or is it due to a weakness in religion itself? The question is searching, for the dramatic demonstration of the impotency of Christianity in dealing with the issue is underscored by its own inability to cope with it within its own fellowship.[3]

These words were penned in 1949, and these probing questions have visited my thoughts every year since reading this text as a seminary student in Louisville, Kentucky, in 2003. Why is Christianity unable to address race and overcome or stymie racism in any way in America? Is the problem that American Christians betray the true genius and power of Christian faith, or is the problem the Christian religion itself? There are no easy answers to this question, but I tend to believe it is because we betray the genius of our religion. We compromise the core of what it means to be a Christian. The fact that racist thinking and racist ways of relating to others continues still makes it difficult to answer these questions.

In the past three years I have repeatedly turned to two African American theologians who wrote on the issues of race and Christianity. They have helped me understand both why and how this kind of thinking continues to permeate Christian churches. These works are Willie Jennings's *The Christian Imagination*, and Brian Bantum's *Redeeming Mulatto*.[4] These theologians unravel the complicity of

---

www.rawstory.com/2015/01/two-thirds-of-southern-baptists-resist-integrating-their-churches-poll/.

3. Howard Thurman, *Jesus and the Disinherited* (Boston: Beacon, 1976) preface.

4. Willie James Jennings, *The Christian Imagination: Theology and the Origins of Race* (New Haven,

the church and its theology in Christianizing race. They expose the fact that the church was an integral part of promoting the belief in humans as racial beings. The church at every juncture has supported racialized ways of relating between whites and blacks and have made very little progress in deconstructing the logic of race and racism in its families and churches. Where European and African American Christians live, where they go to school, who they befriend, love, and marry are more informed by race than their commitment to the gospel of Jesus Christ. Nowhere is the belief more evident than the historic and current practice of whites mostly worshipping with whites and blacks mostly worshipping with blacks. The eleven o'clock hour continues to be the most segregated hour of the week.

The deeper problem when this line of thinking is not corrected is that, though only one part of the logic of racism, it feeds other aspects of this logic and opens the possibility for persecution, alienation, and violence when these socially constructed lines of relations are crossed. American Protestantism has to do more than hide behind barriers and walls of race and racism. In order to do this we have to learn how to think and talk differently about the effects of racism in our churches. For example, Jennings says the most common way to narrate this historical reality is to speak of different forms of Christianity, white and black, or different cultural expressions of Christianity.[5] This belief supports those who claim it is better for whites and blacks not to worship and love across the lines of race or those who believe whites and blacks have different cultural expressions of Christian faith. The belief that it is better for white and black Americans to segregate is very weak. What does "better" really mean, and who is it really better for? Furthermore, while I concede that Christian faith has many different cultural expressions, I do not accept cultural expressions that are deeply segregated and racialized as a legitimate reason to maintain separate churches and families. These are not good reasons for social segregation. There are deeper beliefs that sustain the logic of segregation and exclusion, and Jennings exposes it. Beyond different "cultural" expressions of Christian faith, the real problem is "a diseased social imagination."[6] What enables Christians to live and worship in separate spaces is an idolatrous acceptance of a social vision of racialized people who in turn racialize God, Jesus, and the church universal as either white or black. Jennings and Bantum helped me to think about racism as a form of idolatry that captivates our imagination. Churches need to deconstruct and rebuke such thinking and in the words of Paul "take captive every thought to make it obedient to Christ"

CT: Yale University Press) 2010; Brian Bantum, *Redeeming Mulatto: A Theology of Race and Christian Hybridity* (Waco, TX: Baylor University Press, 2010).

5. Jennings, *The Christian Imagination*, 6.
6. Ibid.

(2 Cor 10:5). Doing this opens the door for us to reimagine how to live together as people created in the image of God and called to fellowship with one another in Christ.

Racism as a Distorted Understanding of Koinonia

Many white Christians have a distorted understanding of *koinonia* because they think and live according to the logic of racism. They live separated from people with whom God has called them to experience *koinonia* in meaningful ways. The logic of racism wants to divide people in ways that are inconsistent with the gospel vision of God's family and create congregational and familial spaces where prejudice, hatred, and racial hostility can fester. This only concretizes the divide and prevents any possibility of experiencing reconciliation, intimacy, and fellowship across lines drawn by societies past and present.

One of the primary reasons white Christians and their churches hold such sinful views is because they have not been taught to deconstruct the logic of race and racism, drawing on the resources of the Bible, Christian tradition, and the experience of marginalized persons. The process of deconstructing racism is lifelong and must begin in the mind and extend to intimate spaces like one's families, circle of friends, and places of worship. White Christian Americans need to deconstruct racist theologies that separate them from non-whites and construct theologies that help us experience relationship in ways that are consistent with the principles of the gospel. This is some of what I attempt to do in my research on the letter to Philemon. In this small letter, I see ideas that sought to radicalize the gospel in the first century and ideas that can disrupt the logic of racism in our churches today. Interestingly, this letter was used to support exclusionary practices and had a role in the history of racism in America. It is a letter that, if read differently, can help the church chart a new path.

In this letter I found a special term—*koinonia*. *Koinonia* denotes participation and fellowship. *Koinonia* is often translated as "fellowship" in texts such as Acts 2:42; 1 Cor 1:9; Phlm 6; and 1 John 1:3. Paul uses the term *koinonia* thirteen times in his letters to denote the religious fellowship or participation of the believer in Christ and for the mutual fellowship of believers.[7] I translate *koinonia* as fellowship in Philemon and have found this term to be incredibly insightful when thinking of ways to address both the legacy and logic of racism. *Koinonia* means fellowship, but there is also a deeper meaning that I want to explore.

---

7. See "κοινωνία," *TDNT* 3:797–809.

Koinonia is a spiritual bond that Christians share with God through his Son Jesus Christ, the Holy Spirit, and fellow believers, and it is extended to those not in Christ. It is a spiritual reality, activated and made effectual by faith and knowledge that can transform how Christians see and treat people. This reality manifests itself in concrete acts of kindness, generosity, hospitality, and love. In a NT passage exhorting believers to "share good things" with teachers, Paul demonstrates the extent of *koinonia* when he said, "As we have opportunity, let us do good to all people, especially to those who belong to the family of believers" (Gal 6:10). Christian fellowship is not just being members of the same denomination, attending church dinners or other "get togethers," or that we meet in the same building every Sunday and Wednesday for worship and prayer. This is often the extent of some Christians understanding of fellowship. *Koinonia* is much deeper than denominational labels, dinners, and worship services with people with whom we are comfortable. Fellowship is an important part of what it means to be a Christian, and because too many Christians ignore this term, there is confusion about NT teachings on salvation and the church. Being saved does not just mean you make a confession of some sort and start attending a church. It means you enter into a living relationship with God and people, and there are significant implications about the nature and ethics of these relationships.

First, NT texts teach that fellowship is rooted in a bond with God made possible by Jesus Christ. In 1 Cor 1:9 believers are called to fellowship with the Son, which refers to our spiritual communion with him. This suggests that people interact with, learn from, and follow Jesus in a way that transforms their lives—the way they see the world, the things they value, and the things for which they are willing to suffer. *Koinonia* changes us in profound ways. In Phil 3 Paul considered fellowship with Christ to be the most valuable thing to him. His achievements and worldly accruements paled in comparison to the knowledge of Christ that he gained through fellowship. He considered them "refuse" when compared with the knowledge he gained in Christ, and like Christ in 2:5-8, Paul divested himself of worldly things, even things related to his ethnicity and culture. He described his quest in life this way: "that I may know him, and the power of his resurrection, and the fellowship of his sufferings, being made conformable to his death" (Phil 3:10).

This understanding and experience of *koinonia* is clearly lacking in our churches that are mired in the logic of racism and segregated from one another. The reason many white Christians are still captivated by the logic of racism and our churches are so segregated is because they do not understand and are not experiencing fellowship with God and his Son Jesus Christ. They go to church, sing hymns and praise songs, and hear sermons, but they have not experienced fellowship in a way that transforms how they interact with people society labels as "others" and unworthy of fellowship. They are too beholden to labels, ethnic, and cultural markers that denigrate and dehumanize African Americans.

Second, *koinonia* is multidirectional in that it speaks both to one's vertical relation to God and horizontal relations with all people. The bond with God and his Son Jesus transforms horizontal relations with people. *Koinonia* begins with Christ, but it extends outward to fellow believers and all people. While "fellowship" is the term often used for *koinonia*, it carries other meanings that shed light on how believers relate to one another. *Koinonia* can also mean "communion," "generosity," a "gift" or "contribution," and "sharing."[8] The fact that *koinonia* is linked to Communion is significant (1 Cor 10:16). Communion is a ritual sharing bread and wine in remembrance of the death of Jesus. It became a sacrament or an ordinance that is practiced by Christians for centuries. Partaking in communion calls us to remember the death of Jesus and to examine how we treat one another as members of Christ's body. The latter part has been grossly neglected by the church. An important dimension of *koinonia* is recognition of our oneness in Christ and critical reflection on how we treat one another. To partake in holy communion is to give serious consideration to our relationships. *Koinonia* reflects deep Christian practices like generous giving and sharing what one has with others. Acts 2 and 4 chronicle this kind of fellowship. When one recognizes Christian "oneness," acts of kindness, generosity, and love should result. What I have is yours and what you have is mine. It is a very radical concept. Both the ordinance of communion and practices like giving and sharing are based on our common faith and participation in the ministry of Jesus.

Koinonia is radical and goes against the thinking of the world that is characterized by hatred, bigotry, selfishness, and selective relationships. *Koinonia* calls the church to relationships and communities that are characterized by love, generosity, and sharing regardless of one's class status, race, or gender. The church today needs both to understand and practice *koinonia*. We need a different kind of spirituality, different motives for giving, deeper relationships, compassionate outreach, genuine hospitality, improved race relations, and shared blessing. *Koinonia* provides a new center of meaning, one that transcends earthly boundaries and categories like race.

Exclusion in the New Testament

The idea and practices surrounding *koinonia* emerged as early Christians struggled to embody the radical vision of inclusion inherent in the message of the gospel.

---

8. Walter Bauer, William F. Arndt, and F. Wilbur Gingrich, *A Greek English Lexicon of the New Testament*, 2nd ed. (Chicago: University of Chicago Press, 1979) 438–39.

Often what prevailed among early Christians was the human and sinful tendency to exclude people who are different from fellowship. Churches that were endowed with charismatic gifts and prominent apostles practiced selective exclusion with those who fell outside their fellowship base. For example, the schisms, divisions, and practices of exclusion in worship at the church at Corinth, as well as Peter's withdrawal from gentile Christians in Antioch, are relevant for interpretations regarding social tensions latent in early churches. In both instances early congregations were not models of inclusion but struggled to resist social practices of exclusion and to reflect the radical inclusiveness of the gospel that transcends social status.

Exclusion from fellowship was a recurring problem and created opportunities for theological development in early churches. I argue in my book *Not a Slave But a Brother* that exclusion was a perennial issue for first-century churches and the main issue in Paul's letter to Philemon.[9] However, this is not the dominant reading of the letter. The slave-flight reading predominates the imagination of white Christians, which is one reason why they cannot address racism in its families and churches. They read and interpret the Bible in ways that sustain such thinking.

The Traditional Interpretation of Philemon

Philemon is a small Pauline letter that is often ignored and rarely read closely, so I will briefly summarize this important text. The letter was written by the apostle Paul sometime around 60 CE from a prison in Rome or Ephesus.[10] Philemon, a leader in the church at Colossae, was committed to the work of the gospel (v. 1). Paul heard how beneficial Philemon had been in the church "refreshing the hearts of the saints" (vv. 4–7). The letter was delivered to Philemon by Onesimus, a slave of Philemon, who for reasons unknown left his master and found his way to Paul (vv. 10, 15). Paul reported that Onesimus had been converted and was helpful to him in prison (vv. 10–12). Onesimus was so helpful that Paul desired to keep him but would not impose apostolic influence without Philemon's consent (vv. 13–14). More importantly, he believed that somehow God was at work in Onesimus's separation. He was separated so Philemon could experience a different kind of relationship with his slave Onesimus. Paul sent him back and asked that Philemon receive him back "no longer as a slave but more than a slave, as a beloved brother in the flesh and in the Lord." He also promised, if Philemon had been wronged, he himself would

---

9. Lewis Brogdon, *Not a Slave But a Brother: An African American Reading of Paul's Letter to Philemon* (Saarbrucken, Germany: Scholars, 2013).

10. Joseph Fitzmyer, *The Letter to Philemon* (New York: Doubleday, 2000) 9–11; Markus Barth and Helmut Blanke, *The Epistle of Philemon,* Eerdmans Critical Commentary (Grand Rapids: Eerdmans, 2000) 122–23.

repay him upon being released from prison (vv. 16, 19, 22). It also appears that Paul mildly suggested that Philemon allow Onesimus to return to continue helping Paul in prison or even manumit him (vv. 16, 20–22).

It is important to note that the letter was written not only to Philemon but also to the church that met in his house. Paul assumed that the letter would be read publicly to the church.[11] Although the letter was addressed to Philemon, the situation it addressed was not handled in a private manner. He informed Philemon that six people outside the household were also aware of the situation (vv. 1, 23–24). In the opening and concluding verses Paul greeted Philemon, Apphia, Archippus, the church that meets in Philemon's house, Epaphras, Mark, Aristarchus, Demas, and Luke. The letter was more than a personal letter to a friend. It conveyed a public issue that compelled the church to explore theologically what it means to live out the radical demands of the gospel.

Most people today when reading Philemon think of a runaway slave who met an imprisoned apostle and became a Christian. Paul, knowing the law regarding runaway slaves, wrote a letter to his master, Philemon, to accept his runaway slave back as a Christian brother. This prevailing interpretation in both the wider church and in biblical scholarship is commonly referred to as the slave-flight hypothesis. This theory can be traced to interpretations employed by prominent figures in the Christian tradition such as John Chrysostom, Jerome, Ambrosiaster, Theodore of Mopsuesta, and Thomas Aquinas. Reformation figures, such as Martin Luther and John Calvin, also held the slave-flight hypothesis. The slave-flight reading served to buttress proslavery interpretations of Scripture during the antebellum era. Today the slave-flight interpretation is still the predominant theory of the letter's occasion. Many NT introductions, and English, French, and German commentaries use the slave-flight hypothesis as the basis of their interpretations of the letter. Even a recent African Bible commentary uses the slave-flight hypothesis.

The slave-flight hypothesis argues the following. Onesimus, was a slave of Philemon but not a particularly good slave. In fact, scholars argue that he was a useless or unprofitable slave (v. 11). Onesimus robbed his master (v. 18) and fled (v. 15), hence the runaway slave hypothesis. Onesimus found his way to Paul who converted him to Christianity (v. 10). Onesimus was transformed and became useful to the imprisoned apostle (vv. 11–12). In this interpretation Paul sent him back with this letter requesting that Philemon forgive him and accept him as a brother in the Lord (v. 16). This interpretation suggests that Paul promised to repay Philemon for whatever Onesimus may have stolen (v. 18) and was confident that Philemon will exceed

---

11. Sarah C. Winter, "Paul's Letter to Philemon," *NTS* 33 (1987) 1–15.

Paul's request (v. 16, 21). Paul intended to visit the church after his release, likely to follow up on this matter (v. 22).

In the twenty-five verses in Philemon Paul does not actually state that Onesimus ran away from the house of Philemon, but scholars infer flight based on their prior understanding of the events that supposedly led to the flight. Scholars make three arguments to defend the slave-flight hypothesis. First, some interpret the phrase "he was separated" in v. 15 as a euphemism for flight.[12] Second, when scholars account for the absence of any reference to flight in the letter, they reason that Paul intended to divert attention from the fault.[13] The failure to refer to the fault improves Paul's chances of effecting forgiveness and reconciliation. Third, scholars turn to Greco-Roman culture and argue that slaves often ran away from masters.[14] For example, John Nordling examines extrabiblical texts that mention runaway slaves and Roman law which give precedent and context for what is allegedly being reported in the letter.[15] In varying ways these arguments are deployed to support the slave-flight hypothesis.

This reading of Philemon has a painful history in the church that I fully document in my book. I found that Christian interpreters failed both to challenge social beliefs and practices linked to slavery and to apply a liberating hermeneutic to this letter. In some instances interpreters explicitly endorsed a "Christianized" version of slavery and held problematic beliefs about the enslaved. Some commentators argued that Christianity makes better slaves. For over a century the letter's theological value was inextricably linked to the practice of Christianized slavery. The troubling legacy of this letter was particularly difficult for enslaved Africans during the antebellum era. Philemon was used to defend slavery from the Bible and discourage flight as being against God's will. There is a historic link between the slave-flight hypothesis and the suffering of enslaved Africans in America that is an inescapable part of the legacy of this letter in the church. Enslaved Africans were captured and returned to the abuse of their masters in the South as a result of the Fugitive Slave Act, and some churches were resistant to help fugitive slaves because they were taught it was antithetical to the teachings of the Bible. This is the legacy of the slave-flight reading of Philemon.

---

12. John G. Nordling, "Onesimus Fugitivus: A Defense of the Runaway Slave Hypothesis in Philemon," *JSNT* 41 (1991) 97–119.

13. John M. G. Barclay, "Paul, Philemon, and the Dilemma of Christian Slave-Ownership," *NTS* 37 (1991) 161–86, 164.

14. T. Wiedemann, *Greek and Roman Slavery* (Baltimore: Johns Hopkins University, 1981); Nordling, "Onesimus Fugitivus," 99.

15. Nordling, "Onesimus Fugitivus," 109.

The slave-flight argument not only has a problematic history, but it is also culturally offensive. John Knox characterizes this interpretation as a stereotype.[16] Allen D. Callahan argues that the slave-flight hypothesis "buys into the stereotype of the thieving, indolent slave which is a part of all slave-holding societies."[17] In a later response to NT scholar Margaret Mitchell's critique, Callahan provides an assessment of what is actually influencing interpreters. He says, "the fugitive slave hypothesis put forward by Chrysostom and others reflects the interests of a class of interpreters as opposed to a historically defensible reconstruction of the original *Sitz im Leben* of the letter" that is "propped up with a reconstructed narrative" and is "saturated with the kind of hostile stereotypes of the slave purveyed by the master class in all slave regimes."[18] African American biblical scholars refer to this as Eurocentric interpretations of the Bible. Because scholars of European descent dominate the field of biblical studies and because they have failed to recognize the influence of their context in how they interpret the Bible, they have transmitted perspectives that are culturally incompatible for African Americans and all modern Christians. Eurocentric interpretations not only reflect their cultural context, but they also ignore the effect of these interpretations on minority people and race relations in general. The slave-flight hypothesis utilizes master-slave ideology in inappropriate and deeply problematic ways. Surely this is not the way the letter to Philemon should be read in the church as American Christians continue to struggle with issues of race and racism. There is a serious need for an alternative and liberating reading of this text, and such a reading is found by focusing on the issue of exclusion and the use of *koinonia* in Philemon.

Reinterpreting Philemon

Instead of this letter addressing a pilfering runaway slave who is returned to his good master, I offer a back story that is both consistent with the text and a better grounds from which to address theologically issues of exclusion like race and racism. A different historical occasion, like the one I provide below and refer to as the "exclusionary *koinonia*" hypothesis, can open the letter to Philemon in many helpful ways.

While Philemon was a leader in the church and committed to the work of the gospel, his understanding of fellowship was limited because he did not extend it to

---

16. John Knox, *Philemon Among the Letters of Paul* (Chicago: University of Chicago, 1935) 10.

17. Allen D. Callahan, "Paul's Epistle to Philemon: Toward an Alternate Argumentum," *HTR* 86 (1993) 361.

18. Allen D. Callahan, "John Chrysostom on Philemon: A Response to Margaret M. Mitchell," 88 (1995) 149–50.

his slaves. In the eyes of Philemon slaves are useless, only fit for miscellaneous tasks in his household. Philemon occasionally mistreated and even abused his slaves for not performing duties properly. It is clear that Philemon had little regard for slaves in the household. Onesimus was strong-willed and disliked the treatment that his fellow slaves received at the hands of Philemon. Much to the dismay of his fellow slaves, Onesimus even confronted Philemon about the issue but it did not change how Philemon viewed and treated his slaves.

Over the course of time the relationship between Philemon and Onesimus became contentious. Onesimus felt that Philemon was hypocritical in showing generosity to the saints and not to his slaves. In fact, while some slaves had become Christians, Onesimus refused to accept this distorted form of religion and told his friends that Christianity was a sham. One particular afternoon Christians from the community gathered to share the bread and cup. Philemon had the slaves prepare the meal but forbade them from participating with the others. After seeing this Onesimus became angry and again confronted Philemon. Being embarrassed by the confrontation Philemon threatened to punish his slave severely. Fearing punishment, Onesimus left (possibly taking money to facilitate travel) and sought out Paul in the hope that the imprisoned apostle would intercede on his behalf. Onesimus knew of Paul through Philemon, Apphia, and Archippus. Onesimus shared his story with Paul. Much to his surprise, he found Paul to be loving and welcoming. For the first time he felt respected and accepted as a person, and not just a slave. Days later, in a cold prison, God's love finally broke through the social barriers of the day and touched his wounded heart. Shortly thereafter Onesimus became a Christian and received the bread and cup from the apostle himself. Inspired by God's work in his life, he immediately began to help Paul. The imprisoned apostle became extremely fond of the sincere zeal, energy, and giftedness used to meet the apostle's needs as he served other churches.

Knowing that Onesimus was legally bound to return to his master and also wanting to effect reconciliation, Paul penned this mediatory letter which was to be delivered to Philemon by Onesimus. He had two primary concerns in mind: to offer some word concerning Onesimus, and more importantly, to speak a word to Philemon and the church at Colossae about the kind of *koinonia* that can transform this broken relationship between master and slave. Paul requested that Philemon's capacity for fellowship be expanded so as to include the slaves in his household and Onesimus who has returned with the letter. Paul also requested that Philemon welcome Onesimus as a beloved brother and no longer only as a slave. Furthermore, he promised that if Philemon had been wronged, the apostle himself would repay him when next they meet. It also appears that Paul mildly suggested that Philemon allow

Onesimus to return to Paul to continue helping him in prison or even manumit him altogether. Paul was confident that Philemon, who had already demonstrated a capacity to refresh the hearts of saints, will do this and more, especially considering how God had worked to give him a broader understanding of *koinonia*.[19]

The Master's Other Side

To interpret this letter in a way that speaks to issues of inclusion, one has to shift the orientation away from patting the master on the back for being good to actually challenging the master for not living up to the Christian vision of *koinonia*. Such an interpretive move begins with looking at Paul's prayer for Philemon differently. Verses 4–5 indicate Paul had heard of Philemon's good works. Paul said that he had demonstrated love and faithfulness to all "the saints." One may ask, "How can Philemon be accused of selective exclusion when Paul commends him in vv. 4–7?" These verses suggest that Philemon did things that are good. However, his commendation should not be understood to mean that Philemon was above duplicity. Philemon could practice generosity toward some and exclude others. Yet, scholars interpret the statements, "I thank my God because I hear of your love and faith," and "because the hearts of the saints have been refreshed through you," to imply that Philemon's character is beyond question.[20] For example, John Koenig interprets Paul's commendation as affording to Philemon "high honor," and that the reference to "all" in v. 5 "indicates that Philemon has not been prejudicial about his hospitality but has welcomed everyone who comes in the Lord's name."[21] Similarly, William Barclay boasts that "Philemon was clearly a man from whom it was easy to ask a favor. He was a man whose faith in Christ and love to the brethren all men knew, and the story of them had reached Rome." He even went as far as saying that "his house must have been an oasis in a desert."[22] Both are exaggerations to some extent.

At this juncture in the letter, a letter that will be read publicly, it is both necessary and strategic to be complimentary and not overtly confrontational. So Paul gave thanks for Philemon's faith and love for the saints. It is no surprise that Paul commended Philemon for his love because this is a practice he used in other letters,

19. Brogdon, *Not a Slave But a Brother*, 117–18.

20. Fitzmyer, *The Letter to Philemon*, 94; James D. G. Dunn, *The Epistles to the Colossians and to Philemon* (Grand Rapids: Eerdmans, 1996) 315–17, 320–21; Eduard Lohse, *Colossians and Philemon: A Commentary on the Epistles to the Colossians and to Philemon*, trans. William Poehlmann and Robert J. Harris (Philadelphia: Fortress, 1971) 92–95; Marvin Vincent, *A Critical and Exegetical Commentary on the Epistles to the Philippians and Philemon*, ICC (Edinburgh: T. & T. Clark, 1902) 177–81.

21. John Koenig, *Philemon* (Minneapolis: Augsburg, 1985) 194.

22. William Barclay, *The Letters to Timothy, Titus, and Philemon* (Philadelphia: Westminster, 1975) 278.

but one can scarcely find a church that perfectly exemplifies love. Paul used love as a goal or measure by which to spur the churches toward more mature expressions. It is here that most exegetes miss the subtlety of the overall intent of this prayer. This point is important because it provides a hint that Paul's commendation might not be the result of Philemon's perfect obedience, but more a way to encourage and challenge him to grow in this area.

It is not a stretch to think that Philemon could be very hospitable to social peers and abusive to his household slaves. Such behavior was common in the first century, and it is likely that Philemon behaved this way too. Paul's commendation does not preclude the possibility that Philemon was capable of the kind of hypocrisy and duplicity that slaves throughout the Roman Empire and enslaved Africans witnessed for centuries at the hands of Christian masters, who otherwise appeared to be models of Christian piety. It is important to note that some commentators believe that Philemon may have been in the wrong and could have mistreated Onesimus. Instead of the lazy and pilfering slave doing wrong, as argued by the slave-flight hypothesis, they see evidence in vv. 4–6 that Philemon is the perpetrator of wrong.[23] Paul wrote hoping that Philemon would draw on the capacity of love for Onesimus.

The Exclusion of Onesimus

Why did Paul address the issue of *koinonia* in this letter? He did so because Onesimus experienced exclusion, and this becomes a matter Paul used to instruct the church about the nature of fellowship. In v. 6 Paul expressed his desire for Philemon to expand his fellowship base to include house slaves. He prayed that the "fellowship of (Philemon's) faith may become effective through the knowledge of every good thing which is in you for Christ's sake." One scholar comments that "hidden in the lauds and thanksgiving he is heaping upon Philemon and the church, Paul targets Philemon with a left jab in disguise."[24] He interprets Paul's prayer for the fellowship of faith to become effectual as a reflection of ineffective efforts on the part of Philemon. Once Paul gave Philemon knowledge that fellowship in the gospel should be extended to house slaves, people he may view socially inferior to him, his potential to extend fellowship to Onesimus would become effectual. What does "effective" mean in this verse? I believe it means expanding his circle of fellowship and extending fellowship to a slave. This is Paul's prayer for him. Unless Philemon's base was expanded, he would not be able to extend fellowship to those who were outside

---

23. Markus Barth and Helmut Blanke, *The Letter to Philemon*, 138–39, 143–44; Robert H. Van Dyke, "Paul's Letter to Philemon," *Sewanee Theological Review* 4 (1998) 392.

24. Van Dyke, "Paul's Letter to Philemon," 392.

his circle or base of fellowship. What made his later request in v. 16 possible is the critique here in v. 6.

Paul emphasized the role of knowledge in this verse. One's capacity to live out Christian ethics is largely dependent on knowledge, which again is the occasion for Paul writing this letter. Knowledge of God activates or makes one's faith effectual and enhances fellowship, which Paul expects will change the dynamics of the relationship between Philemon, Onesimus, and the church that gathers in the house of Apphia and Archippus. This is done for Christ's sake because *koinonia* is always both the result of the salvific work of Jesus Christ and the grounds for shared unity in the church. Paul's understanding of *koinonia* points to new realities that transform relationships. Christian fellowship implies shared unity and equality, and the implications are quite radical because it transcends social boundaries. This is why knowledge is important. Knowledge of what God has done in Christ causes earthly relationships to take on new meaning. This is what Paul wants Philemon to understand, and it is only by understanding this that Philemon cam move from exclusion to inclusion in his fellowship with his slave Onesimus.

The Conversion of Onesimus

In v. 10 Paul appealed to Philemon on behalf of Onesimus, a departed slave. Interpreters employing the slave-flight hypothesis miss the significance of this conversion outside the house of Philemon. This is a point that many commentators surprisingly ignore. For example, Eduard Lohse's classic commentary in the Hermeneia series ignores this possibility when he comments, "Onesimus had been a slave of a Christian master, but was not yet a member of the Christian community."[25] The fact that Onesimus was not a Christian but belonged to a master who is known to "refresh the hearts of the saints" is significant. Lohse failed to explore reasons for this, which would open new doors for exegesis and theological reflection.

Because this is ignored as an exegetical and theological issue, the impact of the conversion of Onesimus is lessened. Instead, great emphasis is given to Philemon's benevolence and the return of a wayward slave. For slave-flight interpreters the conversion of Onesimus was the incident that ensures the return of a better slave. As a result Philemon was encouraged to forgive Onesimus and accept him as a Christian brother. This is both a distorted and limited reading of the letter. In my reading of Philemon exclusion and its role in the unconverted condition of a house slave are important exegetical and theological issues. I believe that Onesimus departed and was not a Christian because of Philemon's practice of selective exclusion, a problem

---

25. Lohse, *Colossians and Philemon*, 199.

prevalent in other churches Paul served. The conversion of Onesimus served as an indictment against Philemon and the church. In addition, the return of Onesimus as a Christian takes on a different kind of significance than what is argued by slave-flight interpreters.

Onesimus is referred to in the most favorable light as Paul's son. Paul was accustomed to speak of his converts as children: Timothy in 1 Cor 4:17; Titus in Titus 1:4; the Corinthian Christians in 1 Cor 4:14; and the Galatian Christians in Gal 4:19.[26] Because of Onesimus's conversion in prison, Paul refers to him as his spiritual son. The father and child image was sometimes employed in rabbinic Judaism to describe the relationship between a teacher and a student whom he had instructed in the Torah.[27] In addition, the reference to Onesimus as a son fits the extensive use of familial language in this letter. What Paul reports in this verse is the most significant matter to take into consideration. Onesimus had become a Christian. In a real sense, Onesimus's becoming a Christian is an important part of his forging a new identity, one not completely defined by his condition of enslavement.

Onesimus is no longer simply an estranged slave of his master. He is now a Christian brother. Paul's careful, heartfelt appeal presented this truth to bear upon Philemon and the church at Colossae. Paul, Philemon, and Onesimus's mutual understanding of the gospel will have everything to do with how this problem is worked out. The dynamic of the entire situation has now changed. Great care would be taken to mediate the new parameters of their relationship.

Onesimus was Useless?

Onesimus experienced exclusion in the house of Philemon and the reason for it is partly due to the way Philemon thought about house slaves. Verse 11 is an integral component of this belief and discloses the language of exclusion. Greek philosophers like Aristotle taught that slaves were tools or objects to be used. This belief was held by many in the first century. In v. 11 Paul refers to Onesimus as one who was "formerly useless" to Philemon. What is meant by the words "useless" and "useful" is of critical importance. It is obvious that Paul used Onesimus's name to make an important point, but by asking new questions we may reach a new understanding of what Paul may be implying.

The mention in v. 11 of Onesimus's uselessness is probably a reference to Philemon's belief. The name Onesimus means "useful." In v. 11 Paul remarked that

---

26. F. F. Bruce, *The Epistle to the Colossians, to Philemon and to Ephesians* (Grand Rapids: Eerdmans, 1984) 213.

27. Lohse, *Colossians and Philemon*, 200.

Onesimus was formerly useless. Upon becoming a Christian, Onesimus had become useful. This verse supposedly puns the meaning of Onesimus' name and how useful he had become now that he was a Christian. The first clause referred to him as formerly useless. Some commentators interpret the clause to possibly correspond to the time when Onesimus was a worthless runaway slave before Paul had met him.[28] Others understood the phrase to imply that earlier Onesimus might have been a useless slave to his master.[29] It is obvious that Paul is using his name to make an important point.[30] However, if different questions are being asked, then it is possible to take a different look at what Paul may be inferring.

Verse 11 provides insight into the preconversion relationship between Philemon and Onesimus. It also puns the meaning of Onesimus's name and how useful he had become now that he was a Christian. The first clause refers to him as formerly useless. If Onesimus and other slaves were being excluded and marginalized by first-century Christians, then the phrase he was "formerly useless" takes on new meaning. Paul could be suggesting that this is how Philemon viewed Onesimus. Again commentaries fail to pick up on this nuance or interpretive possibility. Paul's assessment needs careful analysis. He said "formerly he [Onesimus] was useless to you," then added that after his conversion he has become "useful to you and to me." It is possible to infer that Onesimus was useless to Philemon for some reason, such as not diligently working or consistent failure to complete assigned tasks. His "useless" condition could have been because slaves were not given the same treatment that the "saints" received in v. 7. "Useless" is strictly a reference to Philemon's perception of slaves. Masters view slaves through a utilitarian lens. Slaves' value was tied to assigned duties and social invisibility. It is likely that Philemon assigned this kind of worth to Onesimus. He was someone whose worth is tied to his utility. Because of this, Philemon did not see the need to include Onesimus in his fellowship. Onesimus possibly left Philemon's household because he was treated like chattel. He was "just a slave." While Philemon refreshed the hearts of saints, slaves were treated like property. Paul's phrase supports at least considering this as a viable possibility.

In vv. 11–13 Paul remarks how helpful Onesimus had become, serving him in his imprisoned state. Beyond the worth of Onesimus as a slave, Paul referred to this slave as his very heart, expressing deep love for him. Paul loved this slave. This is a radical statement and a challenge to privileged masters such as Philemon. While hearing this letter read, Philemon would be surprised and convicted to hear Paul speaking of a slave in such a way. One who was formerly useless to him has become

---

28. Vincent, *The Epistles to the Philippians and Philemon*, 185.
29. Lohse, *Colossians and Philemon*, 200.
30. David Garland, *Colossians and Philemon* (Grand Rapids: Zondervan, 1998) 330.

the "very heart" of the imprisoned apostle. Paul referred to Onesimus in this way to help Philemon make the shift in his mind and heart to see Onesimus in a different way. He also does this to move him from a posture of exclusion to one of inclusion that fully embodies the depth of Christian *koinonia*.

Eradicating "Slave Status" in the Church

Koinonia, as radical mutuality, has the potential to undermine inequitable and broken relationships like the one that compelled Onesimus to leave the house of his master. "Through knowledge of every good thing which is in you" (v. 6), Philemon can extend *koinonia* to his departed slave. In v. 16 Paul makes a radical suggestion and a bold move by suggesting that Philemon receive Onesimus "no longer as 'just' a slave, but more than a slave, a beloved brother." Commentators tend to think that this verse is the most significant in the letter.

Verses 15b–16a should be read together because they are results of God's work in this situation. In this verse in particular Paul reinforces the earlier tendency of Philemon toward exclusion by insisting that Onesimus return "no longer as a slave." I prefer to translate it as "no longer as just a slave," which better reflects Paul's intent. Some commentators agree with this. Markus Barth and Helmet Blanke argue, ". . . through the eyes of Philemon and of the church members in the Colossian house . . . that man (Onesimus) had been and still was nothing but a slave . . . certainly not a brother to his master."[31] When one is just a slave or worse yet chattel in the social structure, it is not a stretch to conclude that this resulted in exclusion. Verse 16 implies that Onesimus was "just a slave" to Philemon. This belief caused Onesimus to be excluded and because it was held by one who was so generous to the saints Onesimus left the house and sought out Paul.

Paul's concern was not that Onesimus be welcomed back in his status as a slave but rather as a beloved brother. Philemon should receive Onesimus back, and more importantly he should no longer consider him as "just a slave but as a dear brother in the flesh and in the Lord." This clearly means that he should be included in the *koinonia* of faith. The phrase "more than a slave" implies "over and above, and designates that which excels or surpasses."[32] Onesimus was not only to be received and welcomed; he was to be given a new status in the church. J. B. Lightfoot comments, "The no more as a slave is an absolute fact, whether Philemon chooses to recognize it or not" and that it implies "the termination of Onesimus former status."[33] This is

---

31. Barth and Blanke, *The Letter to Philemon*, 418.

32. Friedrich Blass and Albert Debrunner, *Greek Grammar of the New Testament*, trans. Robert Funk (Chicago: University of Chicago Press, 1961) 121.

33. J. B. Lightfoot, *St. Paul's Epistles to the Colossians and to Philemon* (London: Macmillan, 1904)

why I argue that Paul called the church to eradicate the "status" of slave. He did not take on the *institution* of slavery, but he did call the church to transform how they relate to one another within the world. Relationships in Christ transcend social distinctions even if they are not abolished in the social world in which Christians live.[34] Vincent's comment on this verse captures the power of Paul's request: "whether Onesimus shall remain a slave or not, he will no longer be regarded as a slave but a beloved brother."[35] This is a bold request made by Paul that connects with his prayer in v. 6 that Philemon's capacity for *koinonia* expand to include one formerly thought of as a useless slave.

Paul made a radical claim by instructing Philemon not to view Onesimus as a slave but a brother. From v. 8 to v. 16 Paul had been encouraging, even modeling to Philemon, how to respond to a situation that is so personal. Paul had repeatedly made references to doing the right thing. The right thing in this context is the eradication of the status of slave which led to the exclusion of slaves in the church. This eradication is possible because of the transformation that the gospel has accomplished in the situation. Giving all persons, including slaves, new status in the church is an idea communicated to the church at Galatia and Corinth. Galatians 3:28 levels ethnic, gender, and social status in Christ while 2 Cor 5:16–17 removes worldly distinctions among Christians. In Christ all participate in the new creation as children of God. Therefore, one can believe that Paul was not only drawing on Jewish and Greek ideas but also was drawing upon the revelatory truths given him by God to speak to Christian slaves.

Summary and Relevance

The departure of Onesimus, his conversion through the ministry of Paul, and the letter that Onesimus brought back to Philemon all seem to indicate that exclusion and *koinonia* are the central issues in the letter. I interpret Paul's commendation of Philemon as a way to address his understanding and practice of *koinonia*. Onesimus was not a Christian in Philemon's house because of the duplicity of his master in welcoming social peers and mistreating slaves. There is evidence of this in vv. 10–11. Both the fact that Onesimus was not converted while a slave in Philemon's household and Paul's pun of "useless" seem to indicate that Philemon excluded and marginalized Onesimus due to his status as one enslaved. Paul called him to change his thinking and to receive Onesimus back as a brother, as one who he is equal with

---

139.

34. Ibid., 334.
35. Vincent, *The Epistles to the Philippians and Philemon*, 189.

him in Christ and one with whom he shares Christian fellowship. Paul ended the letter confident that Philemon will do this and more.

Philemon and the Issue of Race and Racism

Paul's letter to Philemon speaks to issues of race and racism in profound ways when read through the lens of exclusion. It can speak a word of meaning and hope to this nation as it continues to cope with what happened in that church the night of June 17. I conclude this paper with five ways this letter speaks to issues of racism today.

First, in the same way Philemon demonstrated duplicity in his dealing with the "saints" and house slaves like Onesimus, too many white Christians are duplicitous in their beliefs and practices. Many are very kind and hospitable to fellow white Christians. They help them when there is a need and have no problems with marriage and family within the "sacred" boundaries of race. Like Philemon was known to do, they refresh the hearts of white saints and send mission dollars to other countries. They enjoy fellowship among themselves and easily identify themselves as brothers and sisters. Yet too many do not want to fellowship with African Americans and other ethnic minorities. Many refuse to integrate their churches and institutions to any degree under the racist belief that the races should remain separate. They do not want to share a pew with a black person or family. They do not want to see blacks leading their churches and pastoring them. They do not want to break the bread of communion with them, and they certainly do not want to see their son or daughter bring a minority home as a future or current spouse. This duplicity is not new in the church. It goes back to this small Pauline letter. There are many like Philemon in today's church who need a more inclusive vision of Christian *koinonia*.

Second, in the same way Onesimus was excluded by Philemon white Christians are excluding too many African Americans from their churches and families. Their vision of *koinonia* is distorted and racialized. They believe they are not called to share fellowship with blacks. They continue to view blacks as different kinds of humans and a different kind of believer. They do not see blacks as brothers and sisters in Christ with whom they have all things in common. They concretize difference and hide behind walls that keep us separated.

Third, in the same way Onesimus was not converted to the faith because of his experience of selective exclusion, many black and white people today have turned away from Christianity because it is so deeply racialized. Many do not believe in the power of God and the transformative power of the gospel because they see so many "Christians" bound by the demonic and idolatrous power of race and racism. Like Onesimus they flee racialized homes and churches, wrongly thinking that

Christianity is the problem instead of realizing that its present form is a poor witness of which many Christians are guilty. Some find solace in more inclusive Christian churches and communities. Others abandon the Christian religion altogether. One can only hope that more of them encounter Christians with a radical understanding of *koinonia* like the one Paul modeled before Onesimus and which led to Onesimus's conversion. Maybe then we will not lose a generation to secularism, agnosticism, and atheism.

Fourth, Onesimus was considered "useless" by Philemon and excluded from the fellowship. Philemon accepted Greco-Roman social norms concerning the enslaved and did not subject these beliefs to the liberating truths of the gospel. The same things are happening today. The only difference is the different connotation of "useless." The logic of racism still predominates in too many white churches. There are still too many Christians who view African Americans as "others" or less human than white Americans. Mean-spirited labels, insulting names, racial categories, and other stereotypes still pervade the imagination of too many white Americans and influence reasons they choose to exclude, disassociate themselves from others, and not see that love can be experienced across racial lines.

Finally, it seemed that Paul was attempting to eradicate the status of slave in Christian congregations instead of seeking to abolish slavery in the Roman Empire. He sought to call Christians to establish fellowships that were egalitarian and united. This was not the first time he did such a thing. In the Galatian letter, he wrote there is "neither Jew nor Greek, there is neither slave nor free, there is neither male nor female, for you are all one in Christ Jesus" (Gal 3:28). In both Philemon and the earlier letter to the Galatians, he argued that the gospel transcends social categories. This idea is significant in addressing the identity forming and social organizing power of race. Paul's belief challenges the logic of race and status in profound ways. The gospel challenges Christian disciples not to define relationships by the social norms of the fallen world. Churches should embrace *koinonia* in Christ as our primary organizing principle and power. Christian relations should be characterized by our identity in Christ. In this way social norms lose their efficacy in the fellowship and the communion of the saints. This was what made the shootings at Emmanuel AME Church so tragic. Nine members of that church opened their doors to a young white male with no hesitation. His race did not preclude them from opening their hearts to one who had come to murder them. Even though their hospitality opened the door to death, the nation was greatly impacted by the manifold manifestations of *koinonia* modeled that night and the days following. Their actions drank deeply from the well of Christian thought and spirituality.

Philemon's Relevance for Christian Theology and the Church

This small letter invites the church to a level of theological reflection that can yield transformative results because it calls us to wrestle with the hard realities of this world. The letter to Philemon teaches us that injustices like racism will always be a part of this fallen world, but the church can offer the world an alternate vision and space for justice and equality, a new fellowship rooted in Christ. The church should model fellowship so that Christians view one another as persons who have been made new in Christ and the Christ reality transcends and predominates social categories and distinctions rooted in this "present evil age" from which Christians have been delivered (Gal 1:4). In an important way what Paul suggested in v. 6 has implications for the church as a social model and manifestation of the new creation mentioned in 2 Cor 5:20. Paul said, "I pray that the sharing of your faith may promote the knowledge of all good that is ours in Christ Jesus." This prayer expressed Paul's desire for this church. This is a desire that I too have for the church, especially for white churches like the one Dylann Roof attended for many years. Paul wanted Philemon and the church at Colossae to expand their fellowship base to include those on the margin such as slaves. Is this not also the call for all "Christ followers," especially the many whose minds and hearts are closed to the possibility of experiencing fellowship across the lines of race and whose silence on racial inclusion and continuing objection to inclusion allow minds already distorted by the power of sin possibly to repeat similar horrifying acts against African Americans.

I believe the letter to Philemon could be a great theological resource for the church in the coming years as we grapple with issues of difference and inclusion. I sincerely hope that my work on Philemon will encourage others to mine this letter anew and explore ways for us to reimagine fellowship.

RESPONSE TO BROGDON

Al Tizon

I have always found it a helpful exercise to paraphrase Scripture that I happen to be studying to help clarify my own interpretation of any given passage. I figure that if I do not try to publish paraphrases as new translations or some such thing, I am not crossing too many lines. I mention this because after reading Brogdon's paper several times, I was inspired to rewrite Paul's letter to Philemon. So if you'll allow me:

> Greetings, Phil. I hope you're doing well, my friend. I'm so thankful for you, because of your strong faith and your love for everybody. You can't know how much that encourages me while I sit here in prison, knowing that you're leading the faithful in your house with truth and love.
>
> That's why I'm writing to you in confidence about a subject you probably don't want to talk about, but we simply must. It's about Onesimus. You may or may not know that he found his way to me, so I know what went down between you two. You'll be happy to know though that while he was here with me, he has become a committed, zealous follower of Jesus.
>
> Now I know what the world thinks of slaves—that they're mere property, and furthermore, that defiant slaves are useless property. But Phil, I'm writing to tell you that Onesimus is beginning to live into his name, which, as you know, means useful and beneficial. I'm not talking about useful and beneficial as a slave, but as a brother in the Lord and a servant of the gospel just like us. In fact, I was tempted to just not say anything to you and keep him here, but I thought better of it.
>
> Based on his genuine faith and usefulness in the gospel, my strong request is that you not only welcome him back, but that you welcome him back as part of the family of God. I know what I'm asking goes against everything the empire tells us, but let's "stick it the man" and show the world the power of the gospel! Indeed the gospel of Christ creates the kind of fellowship in which both slave and free worship together and in which they treat each other with dignity and respect. I'm confident that you of all people can grasp this truth. Please share this letter with the rest of the church, so that you can together practice the radical *koinonia* that the gospel calls us to.
>
> Oh, and whatever Onesimus did to have been rendered useless by you or if he owes you anything, I'll take care of it. Do you remember when you said that you owe me everything? If you meant that, then give me this one thing, that you welcome Onesimus into genuine fellowship and thus start a new kind

of community that demonstrates to the world the equalizing power of the gospel. I hope to join you soon in that beautiful community I am imagining even now in your house. In fact, make a bed for me. I'm coming!

Meanwhile, our mutual friends in prison here with me say hello. Take care of yourself, Phil, and God bless you all. Paul

I do not paraphrase Scripture without being inspired. Though academic papers do not usually have that effect on me, Brogdon's paper did. It was brilliant in many ways, not the least of which is the fact that it enlivened the book of Philemon. This unassuming letter, consisting of only twenty-five verses located toward the back of the Bible, can easily be overlooked by the church. In light of Brogdon's treatment of the text, for the church to neglect it would be a travesty. Who knew that this mini-memo from Paul to Philemon—and the church that meets in his house—offers such a treasure of theological gold to help God's people achieve deep, intercultural, interclass *koinonia*?

We thank Dr. Brogdon because the church desperately needs guidance today, as racism has made a vicious comeback—not that it ever left the scene entirely. In light of the tragedy at Emanuel AME Church, the church burnings that occurred immediately afterward, and the many other hate-based crimes that plague the news today, we can say that racism has reared its ugly head again in the ugliest of ways.

It is sobering and deeply disturbing to think that the traditional interpretation of the book of Philemon—based on the "slave-flight hypothesis"—has done its part in justifying the institution of slavery, or at least keeping intact the logic and structure of racism that makes slavery possible. If I understand it correctly, the "slave-flight hypothesis" refers to a reading of the text that basically views Philemon as the good guy whom Paul asks to take back Onesimus, the runaway, criminal slave (i.e., the bad guy) by virtue of Onesimus's newfound faith in Christ. Such an interpretation of the text, which has been the accepted interpretation, offered no challenge during slavery's heyday; worse, it encouraged the Christianization of slavery, that is, the idea that slaves would be more hard-working, obedient, and compliant if they were Christian slaves. Though the institution of slavery in America is no longer, the slave-flight hypothesis interpretation of Philemon is still the dominant one, and thus continues to cultivate racism, which in today's volatile times will increasingly result in the likes of the Charleston tragedy.

All the more why Brogdon's paper must be circulated (which today means published, blogged, facebooked and even cut up into hundreds of tweets), for it has rescued the letter of Philemon from its racist, yet generally-accepted interpretation by offering a fresh rendering that is more consistent with the God whom we have come to know and love as the God of justice. By using the "exclusionary *koinonia* hypothesis," Brogdon turns the tables. What if Onesimus was "the good guy," who ran away from duplicity, oppression, and abuse at the hands of a Christian master who just did not get it, whose understanding of fellowship did not extend to the slave community and therefore fell short of the truth of the gospel? What if Paul wrote this letter ultimately to challenge Philemon's racism by admonishing him to take the newly converted Onesimus back, no longer as a slave, but as a brother?

This rendering of the text has Paul calling for something that the NT, if not all of Scripture, calls for—a community of the redeemed where "there is no longer Jew or Greek, slave or free, male and female, for all of us are one in Christ Jesus" (Gal 3:28). Indeed biblical faith calls the people of God not to conform to the world, which means in large part not to submit to the social, hierarchical stratification of people according to race, ethnicity, and caste. Instead, we are to model an alternative community, a counter culture that forms relationships characterized by justice, equality, and reconciliation by the power of the gospel. Paul called Philemon to model this kind of all-inclusive fellowship by welcoming Onesimus (and other slaves perhaps owned by other Christians in the church) as part of the family of God. Through this living letter the Spirit continues to call Christians in positions of power and dominance to regard the powerless and marginalized as sisters and brothers in Christ, and thereby subvert racism, oppression, and other unjust systems of this world.

Practical Questions

As an Asian-American teacher and denominational leader in international mission, I want to raise a few practical questions in response to the paper. First, as an Asian-American, who has also experienced being on the wrong side of racism, I had difficulty locating myself in the argument because of the black-white binary that framed it. Indeed, most discussions on race in America are literally black and white, and there are valid reasons for this. Nonetheless, it cannot be overstated that to achieve the kind of radical *koinonia* this paper calls for requires language that includes everyone. How can we prophesy against racism, as well as champion justice, reconciliation, and radical *koinonia* in such a way that includes all tribes, nations, peoples, and tongues?

Second, as a teacher-practitioner of holistic mission, which includes the ministry of reconciliation, I am persuaded that both sides of the race issue have a part to play in eradicating racism. I wanted to hear more about what Onesimus can teach African Americans and others who have been on the short end of the stick of racism. While the paper demonstrates what people like Philemon must do to overcome racism, what can be learned from Onesimus's example to instruct racism's victims?

Third, as a teacher of Bible and theology, I am inspired by this paper to interpret and teach Scripture from the margins by being more open to fresh, liberating readings that promote justice, peace, salvation, and reconciliation, but not at the expense of honest exegesis. This paper shows that the angle from which we read can change everything. What hermeneutical tools are needed to remain true to the text, while always advocating for the poor, oppressed, and marginalized in our use of the Bible?

Lastly, as a denominational leader in international mission, I could not help but apply this paper to the relationship between Western missionaries and the indigenous population, raising all sorts of postcolonial issues that range from how to purge ethnocentrism and paternalism from the hearts of outgoing missionaries to what genuine ministry partnerships should look like to the ethics of hiring the indigenous as maids and gardeners. What would missionary training curricula look like that addresses these kinds of issues?

I suspect that we will never read Philemon the same way again, and we should be grateful for that. Part of the definition of a good academic paper is its usefulness, i.e., its ability to evoke practical questions such as the ones that I have posed. Now our task is to live into the answers.

THE BIBLE'S OUTRAGE AT BLUMENBACH'S BABEL: AN ANTIRACIST HERMENEUTIC FOR WHITE FOLLOWERS OF JESUS

Kyle J. A. Small

"White America is largely unconscious and mute, unable to address the question of its identity as white. Power normally does not have to give an account of its own basis of operation."[1]

"Whites today cannot separate themselves from the culture that lynched blacks, unless they confront their history and expose the sin of white supremacy."[2]

Introduction

Recently, after participating in a large church conference, I received an email asking me to complete a survey assessing the success of the event. The evaluation asked the typical questions. The final questions were demographic in nature, and with regard to race/ethnicity, I expected to scroll down and select "white." The option was not "white" but "Caucasian," and it was first on the list.

I began asking white colleagues, students, and friends if they knew the history of the word "Caucasian." Almost no one knew from where the term emerged or why. The search for its emergence became the basis for this essay and for the recognition that "Caucasian" signifies a world that upends Pentecost, distorts Babel, and confuses theological interpretations of Scripture.

This essay seeks to name white consciousness as white supremacy and to sustain a discomfort for myself, as the writer, and for white followers of Jesus. This is an attempt to give a socio-theological account for my basis of daily operation. The essay traces one layer of the social architecture of whiteness and wrestles with Johann Friedrich Blumenbach's eighteenth-century science experiment that antagonizes God's work at Pentecost. I recognize that my ability to fail in this project is higher

---

1. James W. Perkinson, *White Theology: Outing Supremacy in Modernity* (New York: Palgrave MacMillan, 2004) 1.
2. James H. Cone, *The Cross and the Lynching Tree* (Maryknoll, NY: Orbis, 2011) 165.

than my ability to succeed, for I do not have a double consciousness,[3] even as I seek recovery from supremacy and privilege. My white body has a particularity to it and a universality to it that communicates to others domination. I wonder if my white body can mean differently, and if my own person can be white without supremacy and privilege? This essay is a personal deconstruction of my whiteness, first for my own journey toward understanding supremacy, and second as an offering to other white folks willing to enter the struggle to destroy the racism present in white space.

This essay will feel *oppositional* in many places as it seeks to offer a way forward that does not uphold a master-slave hermeneutic or a false sense of servanthood (as is often considered in servant leadership)[4] but seeks a theological form of friendship (John 15) that participates in outrage on behalf of people and bodies of color and on behalf of freeing the captivity of the white consciousness. The *opposition* will be against the abuses of appropriating Scripture to oppress God's many-hued image bearers[5] and to continue white supremacy. These are central scaffolds to the social architecture of race, both in eighteenth-century science and in present day theology.[6] The *opposition* is also toward hope.[7] Lament and confession may be better liturgical

---

3. W. E. B. DuBois, *The Souls of Black Folk* (New York: Barnes and Noble, 2003) 8. "It is a peculiar sensation, this double-consciousness, this sense of always looking at one's self through the eyes of others, of measuring one's soul by the tape of a world that looks on in amused contempt and pity. One ever feels his two-ness, an American, a Negro; two souls, two thoughts, two un-reconciled strivings; two warring ideals in one dark body, whose dogged strength alone keeps it from being torn asunder. The history of the American Negro is the history of this strife—this longing to attain self-conscious manhood, to merge his double self into a better and truer self. In this merging he wishes neither of the older selves to be lost. He does not wish to Africanize America, for America has too much to teach the world and Africa. He wouldn't bleach his Negro blood in a flood of white Americanism, for he knows that Negro blood has a message for the world. He simply wishes to make it possible for a man to be both a Negro and an American without being cursed and spit upon by his fellows, without having the doors of opportunity closed roughly in his face."

4. See Jacquelyn Grant, "Sin of Servanthood and Deliverance of Discipleship" in *A Troubling in My Soul: Womanist Perspectives on Evil and Suffering,* ed. Emilie Maureen Townes (Maryknoll, NY: Orbis, 1993) 199–219.

5. I am indebted to Denise Kingdom-Grier for this term; the language of color is complex, and my use of the race categories "black, brown, yellow, and red" participates in a history that does an ongoing injustice.

6. Michael O. Emerson and Christian Smith, *Divided by Faith: Evangelical Religion and the Problem of Race in America* (New York: Oxford University Press, 2000). Enlightenment-era science and philosophy are not the central point for the emergence of racism; however, enlightenment-era pursuits solidified racism within new legitimacy structures and serve as an important starting point for understanding racism in the Evangelicalism of the United States.

7. I join James Cone in pursuing hope. He said, "I speak out against white supremacy not because I have lost hope, but rather because I too have found it. Hope, for me, is found where two or three small groups of people—blacks, whites and other people of color who believe in Martin's vision of the beloved community—become willing to bear witness to the Gospel's transcending racial bonding and move toward human bonding. We need some signs of that transcending. Where will they come from if not from the church? And how will these signs be expressed, except by preachers and priests

avenues for comfort on the topic of racism and race, yet comfort is not what I seek; discomfort is one avenue to hope even if contrary to most Christian piety.

Willie Jennings invites theological institutions to enter the racializing conversation and to discover the social architecture of race.[8] I receive Jenning's call similar to the way a generation of white scholars before me received James Cone's call for a theological engagement with whiteness.[9] This essay seeks to name the power of white supremacy, which is a more explicit word for "whiteness," and means primarily the rise of white consciousness as a domineering perspective that decentralizes, marginalizes, and tries to eliminate all other consciences.

Redeeming Race?

Race was not a science, construct, or category in the scope of God's work in the beginning. In other words, race is a social and demographic construct about which God was ignorant at creation. Race was born of a white devil as a way to remove people from the garden and dislocate them from the land in order to possess them. Race science, developed by Johann Friedrich Blumenbach (1752–1840) and made more radical by Christoph Meiners (1747–1810), was one way to bring hell to earth and stratify people against one another. Race science, as documented later in the essay, developed according to the operating assumptions in Europe that white skin is superior to black. The science lacks a critical apparatus and fails the scientific methods central to the field. In order to understand race and its purpose one must initially go to hell to understand it. The good news is that God in Christ has traversed the gap, entered into hell, and on the third day rose from the dead redeeming that which was foreign and divisive to the life-giving work at creation.

God is liberating race (not eradicating it) in ways that defeat the devil and the ongoing abuses of racism.[10] Racism complicates the space and creativity that

---

and rabbis?" from George M. Anderson, "White Supremacy and Theology: An Interview with James Cone," *America: The National Catholic Review*, November 20, 2006 (http://americamagazine.org/issue/592/article/theologians-and-white-supremacy).

8. Willie James Jennings, *The Christian Imagination: Theology and the Origins of Race* (New Haven, CT: Yale University Press, 2010).

9. Perkinson, *White Theology*, 2.

10. Race has changed since the eighteenth century, yet it has not gone away. The future of race-talk is unruly to track, yet American news cycles prove that we are not a post-racial society, desirous as it may be for some. How then do we discuss race today? Race is fluid and flexible, albeit complicated to know its ebbs and flows. Race identity, as a self-described identity, is generative for cultural creativity that has emerged amidst racial oppression. Race is not a system of stratification that deems some more human or more pure than others. The latter is what is finally being broken and also redeemed into something new that is generative. Racism, with its clearer and more agreed upon definitions, is the devil's work that makes understanding the gifts of race all the more complicated.

emerges from racial identities. The liberation of race is recognizing the emergence of cultural particularities, histories, and creativities within racialized identities. The liberation is slowly fracturing the supremacist assumptions that degenerate people based on skin color. Shalom is and will come from God who has redeemed race and who continually speaks outrage to racism.

I want to enter the hell that has been created by comparative science, not to develop a unitive science or unitive theology, for that too is a white supremacy claim, recently seen in the switch from #BlackLivesMatter to #AllLivesMatter. The hell that white Christians must enter is one that has shaped our reading of Scripture through a misconstrued science.

Johann Friedrich Blumenbach and the Architecture of Caucasian Beauty

Johann Friedrich Blumenbach (1752–1840) was a medical scientist in Göttingen, Germany, and accomplished his doctorate with a fifteen-page dissertation on comparative science and the natural varieties of humankind.[11] He quickly became an extraordinary professor of science and popularized the "degeneration hypothesis" and single-origin theory. He gave birth to these myth-gone-scientific-facts that for more than 125 years were without challenge.[12] His research legitimated white supremacy as a scientifically proven perspective for the whole world. I am not an expert on natural science or anthropology, but one can read Blumenbach's thesis and recognize how sexualized preoccupation with white bodies, namely female bodies identified from the Caucus Mountains, became the scientific method of his work and the social architecture of race science. One can identify his preconceptions that led to his observations and framed the three editions of his dissertation, *On Natural Variety of Mankind* (1775, 1781, and 1795).[13]

Blumenbach specialized in medical science and became an avid collector of skulls, which served as the basis of his comparisons in developing the variety of races. He named his collection *Golgotha* and hobnobbed with princes, travelers, and well-to-do businessmen to acquire skulls from far off lands.[14] His treasure seekers invested in Blumenbach's work for its participation and amplification of the legiti-

11. His dissertation is a fascinating read on the biased nature of Enlightenment science. I include extensive quotations from the third edition of the dissertation to highlight the bias and tenor of race science as developed by Blumenbach.

12. Nell Irvin Painter, *The History of White People* (New York: W.W. Norton, 2010) 327–42.

13. Johann Friedrich Blumenbach, *On Natural Variety of Humankind*, in *The Anthropological Treatises of Johann Friedrich Blumenbach*, ed. Thomas Bendyshe (London: Longman, Green, Longman, Roberts, and Green, 1865).

14. Ibid., 8. There is little documented regarding how Blumenbach acquired more than sixty skulls from far-away lands, but it takes little imagination to understand how these were gained.

macy of the economic slave trade. Blumenbach himself did not travel much, which gave him the appearance of objectivity rooted in observation of skulls. Even so, his writings articulate a deep knowledge of the world and its many lands.

Blumenbach was pretentious and elitist, albeit with a populist rhetoric. His spirit as a teacher and rhetorician conjures images of Donald Trump.[15] The method to his science was loose but convincing, as he adopted the popular interpretations of European history to make meaning out of his scientific observations.

Blumenbach's science argued that the older the artifact or source, the purer the knowledge and truth.[16] Blumenbach's logic was eventually borrowed by Kant, and the whole of the Enlightenment adopted race science as a framework for modern philosophical understanding, namely *that the primeval source is the purest and most beautiful form.*

It is also important to note the sexualizing and objectifying nature of Blumenbach's scientific methods. In discussing the uniqueness of the human skeleton, he discusses the pelvis of male skeletons and the vagina of female skeletons. This sexual preoccupation with white women became important to the manner in which Blumenbach cast the woman from the Caucus region (the Caucasian) as the most beautiful, pure, and premiere primitive of humankind. Blumenbach's sexual obsession is most evident in his explanation of the distinctive human practice to walk erect: "according to the same direction of the female vagina [an erect direction], that question must be settled which has been often discussed form the time of Lucretius, what position is most convenient for man to copulate?"[17] What does this question have to do with his hypothesis or his science on human variety? He has a fascination with women's bodies and is constantly reflecting on his dissection of them for the purpose of scientific discovery. Later in his dissertation, following his classification of races, he returns to the description of body parts, including breasts, hymen, and genitalia, and here he also takes up the size of the male penis.[18]

---

15. Karl Marx, a colleague of Blumenbach, writes in what reads like a eulogy, "He made the results of his own persevering researches intelligible and agreeable to every educated person who was anxious for instruction, and understood very well how to interest the upper classes of society in them, and even to excite them . . . . He knew how to select whatever would arouse or sharpen conversation, to give a clear prospect of what was in the distance, and to clothe the practical necessities in a pleasing dress." From K. F. H. Marx, "Memoir of J. F. Blumenbach by Prof. Marx," *The Anthropological Treatises of Johann Friedrich Blumenbach*, 6–7.

16. Ibid., 13; "Blumenbach was thoroughly penetrated with the truth, that we are only then in proper position to understand the appearances of the present, when we attempt to clear up as fast as possible their condition in the beginning, and from early times down to the present. He considered archaeology and history not only as the foundations of true knowledge, but also as the sources of the purest pleasures." This logic has even imposed itself onto biblical and theological studies.

17. Blumenbach, *On Natural Variety of Humankind*, 169.

18. Ibid., 246–51.

What then is his assessment of the primeval source from which the purest and most beautiful human form emerges?[19] Blumenbach's sexual fantasies drive his sense of causation, and his lust constructs an evil. His argument seems to flow quickly to skin color based on his fixation with women from the Caucus region. He then oddly argues that since mucous is the membrane closest to the skin, and the mucus is clear or a thick, milky white, then the purest and most original form of skin, which is most integrated with the membrane, is white. Anything other than this is degeneration.[20]

This turn from mucous to skin color is the move made for classifying or stratifying populations, the first of which is white.

> All mankind, as far as it is at present known to us, seems to me as if it may be best, according to *natural truth*, be divided into the five following varieties: Caucasian, Mongolian, Ethiopian, American, and Malay. I have allotted the first place to the Caucasian . . . which make me esteem it the primeval one.[21]

These differences in skin color are due to several factors, including climate, diet, mode of life, hybrid generation ("different varieties come to copulate together"), and hereditary peculiarities from diseased temperament.[22]

---

19. Ibid., 194–202. Blumenbach developed the "formative force theory" (a clear demonstration of the Enlightenment mentality seeking unity and pure source). The theory asserts the following: "The genital liquid is only the shapeless material of organic bodies, composed of the innate matter of the inorganic kingdom, but differing in the force it shows, according to the phenomena; by which its first business is under certain circumstances of maturation, mixture, place, etc. to put in the form destined and determined by them; and afterwards through the perpetual function of nutrition to preserve it, and if by chance it should be mutilated, as far as lies in its power to restore it by reproduction." Blumenbach identified several variables that weaken the formative force to repair and preserve the destiny of genital fluid and leads to the degeneration of the species. These degenerative factors result in human beings having different skin colors and forming varieties.

20. Ibid., 208. "Seat of the colour of skin. The mucous, commonly called the cellular membrane, about whose most important function in the economy of the human body we have spoken above, affords as it were a foundation of the whole machine. It is interwoven with almost all parts alike, even to the marrow of the bones, and is collected on the outermost surface of the body into a thick white universal integument called the corium. By this, the rest of the body is surrounded and included; and above all it is penetrated by a most enormous apparatus of cutaneous nerves, lymphatic veins, and finally with a most close and subtle set of sanguiferous vessels. . . . Besides, each of these allied strata of integuments so make up the *seat of colour*, that in clear-complexioned men, where they are strained with no pigment, they permit the natural roseate whiteness of the corium to be seen through."

21. Ibid., 264, emphasis mine.

22. Ibid., 214. Blumenbach noted the causative effects of these external variables for human varieties, "Unless I am mistaken, we must look for the reason why colored nations who feed copiously on animal oil not only smell of it but also contract a dark colour of skin; while the more *elegant* Otaheitans [Tahitians] on the contrary, *who try to be of a pale colour*, live every year for some months on the bread-fruit alone, to the use of which they attribute great virtue in whitening the skin, although part of that effect must be attributed to the fact that during the same period they remain at home, covered with clothes, and never go out. How great an influence abstinence from the free and open air has in giving whiteness to the skin, our own experience teaches us every year when in spring very elegant and delicate women show a most brilliant whiteness of skin, contracted by the indoor life of winter."

The climax of race science occurs at the *end* of the third edition of the dissertation versus midpoint in the first and second editions. Blumenbach detailed the five races with the final race being the Caucasian, the people who are the source of humanity and evidence true beauty. He identified Europeans with "Caucasian" because they are people who have "no strain of pigment."[23] The revision develops a rhetorical movement that corroborates with the theological work before it.

Blumenbach's description of the Caucasian, which was largely generated from one female skull and several hand-painted pictures, is explained: "... in general, that kind of appearance which, according to *our* opinion of symmetry, we consider most handsome and becoming."[24] Who is this "*our*" he mentions but the recipients of his third edition, Sir Joseph Banks and the Royal Society of friends. Blumenbach adopts Caucasian for the color of whiteness displayed by the people from the region of the Caucasus Mountains:

> For in the first place, that stock displays, as we have seen, the most beautiful form of the skull, from which, as from a mean and primeval type, the others diverge by most easy gradations on both sides to the two ultimate extremes (that is, on the one side the Mongolian, on the other the Ethiopian). Besides, it is white in colour, which we may fairly assume to have been the primitive colour of mankind, since, as we have shown above, it is very easy for that to degenerate into brown, but very much more difficult for dark to become white, when the secretion and precipitation of this carbonaceous pigment has once deeply struck root.[25]

Blumenbach declared the beauty of whiteness from lustful opinion, which he then attempted to factualize through his method of observation.[26] At the end of describing the Caucasians, he continued his descriptions of the other races, labeling certain antagonistic emotions and behaviors to skin color (most of which he had never seen or experienced due to his lack of traveling experience). In his later writing, *Contributions to Natural History*, Blumenbach argues for the presence of God, the Creator, in his theoretical model, and ties the formative force hypothesis and the degenerative hypothesis "to the great mutability in nature . . . and to the

---

Emphasis mine.

23. Ibid., 210.
24. Ibid., 265.
25. Ibid., 269.
26. As Alisdair MacIntyre says, "fact is in modern Western culture a folk-concept with an aristocratic ancestry" quoted in Lesslie Newbigin, *Foolishness to the Greeks: The Gospel and Western Culture* (Grand Rapids: Eerdmans, 1986) 76. Or to borrow from my colleague and mentor, Dr. Tom Boogaart, who gives more candor to Macintyre, "Facts are simply opinions that linger too long."

active and wise determination of the Creator."[27] Blumenbach associated the geography of Adam and Eve with the Caucus regions, declaring that the origination of humankind, as understood by theology for some time and now by science, was from the white-skinned region of the Caucuses.[28] Now faith and science agree that whiteness is righteousness, and the term "Caucasian" is born supreme for Enlightenment rationalities.

Jennings clearly notes the impact of Blumenbach's science: "Eighteenth century scientific investigations of the new worlds yielded an even more viciously derogatory portrait of the black intelligence. These classificatory schemas drew the entire known world into grand metanarratives of development."[29] *By the late twentieth century Blumenbach's science was considered invalid, yet the social psychology of the science was clearly embedded in the white consciousness of supremacy and has yet to be discarded from the psyche of Western and white dominant cultures.* Blumenbach, Linnaeus, and Meiners are "examples of classificatory systems that place the comparative practices of the previous centuries on a new level of philosophical and theological speculation."[30]

From Divine Pentecost to Blumenbach's Babel: Narrative Divergence

In the multicultural event of Pentecost (Acts 2:1–13) the nations are gathered as a common participation of humanity and a *parody* of the world at Babel (Gen 11:1–9). The differences or varieties in Acts 2 were stark, and political, economic, and social dynamics were noticeably present. Yet divine agency brought the cacophony into a melody that was participatory in nature and divine in source. The particularity and variety are not diluted in the unity but amplified, celebrated, and continued for God's missionary movement. The Pentecost movement was a divine reframing of Babel.[31] Here God is making a name for himself, and humanity is a full participant.

Theological interpretations of Pentecost have argued that God *reverses* Babel through the coming of the Holy Spirit. Joel Green considers the stories parodies

---

27. Johann Freidrich Blumenbach, *Contributions to Natural History, Part I*, in *The Anthropological Treatises of Johann Friedrich Blumenbach*, 277–314, 290.

28. M. Flourens, *Memoir of J. F. Blumenbach*, in *The Anthropological Treatises of Johann Friedrich Blumenbach*, 47–64, 60. The unity hypothesis and theory was clarified after Blumenbach's death by Flouren's saying, "According to [Blumenbach's] doctrine, all men are born, or might have been born, from the same man. He calls the negroes, our black brothers. It is an admirable thing that science seems to add to Christian charity, or, at all events, to extend it, and invent what may be called human charity."

29. Jennings, *The Christian Imagination*, 193.

30. Ibid.

31. Joel B. Green, *Seized By Truth: Reading the Bible as Scripture* (Nashville: Abingdon, 2010) 27–31.

not reversals.[32] In both Gen 11 and Acts 2 divine power is scattering and gathering humanity. Babel is only partially punitive in nature, countering the idolatry that humanity was practicing for its own glory. Additionally, Babel was a continuation of the creation story to scatter humanity to populate the earth (Gen 1:28).

Pentecost is related to Babel, not as a reversal, but as a rehearsal. Pentecost begins with a unity (Acts 2:1 and 2:42–47), which is not defining a people as a pure source but as a *koinonia* (plurality in unity) that emerges from the power of the Holy Spirit with the same divine purpose as Babel, to scatter the people (Acts 1:8). Human scattering occurs in both stories through tragedy, yet divine purpose is at work. For Babel it is the act of idolatry that allows God to scatter and populate the earth; in Acts it is the tragic stoning of Stephen that scatters the people from Jerusalem to the ends of the earth. Each, however, has a larger and more creative divine purpose.

Enlightenment science generally, and Blumenbach's race science specifically, disorder the Babel and the Pentecost narratives. Indeed Enlightenment science is a reversal (an undoing) of divine purpose. Modern developments allowed agents of Christendom empires (kings, princes, explorers, scientists, etc.) to travel the earth and discover the peoples scattered at Babel. Instead of discovering brothers and sisters separated at Babel, they discovered what they deemed degenerations of the original peoples. These displaced people needed to be brought home, to Europe, to be restored to their *original* identities as Caucasian sons of Adam. The science believed that being relocated to the original peoples, Caucasians (Europeans), would eventually restore all of humanity to flourish in its *purest* form. Degenerations or degradations of people would no longer be a problem; everyone would eventually return to a white skin color and Caucasian identity. Obviously, less than two hundred years later, when dominant white nations could no longer subdue degenerate races, genocide and holocaust became the way to eliminate degradation and preserve original humanity.

Blumenbach's science produces babble that is punitive and disruptive to the actual Babel impact; Blumenbach's Babel destroys the divine narrative and contributes to a history of misinterpretation of Babel and Pentecost. His science misinterprets what was an extension of the creation blessing (Gen 1:28). It results in actions that disrupt "filling the earth" to subdue and having dominion over the *land*. Instead, Blumenbach scientifically subdued God's people. Blumenbach's Babel is that his science believes that everyone must be brought back to the *original* location of humanity's birth, a land that *he* has established and that *he* (and his people) will use to force submission and practice domination. The practice of race science encourages

---

32. Ibid., 29.

Europeans (and white Americans) to treat brothers and sisters as objects of creation who should be subdued and dominated. This is a theological practice of white supremacy.

Too often common day readings of Babel and Pentecost (and Revelation) adopt hints of this same logic. Reading Babel (Gen 11) as a dissolution of "one language" or Pentecost as the restoration of "one language" is an adoption of the social architecture of race science. Joel Green prophetically reminds interpreters of the NT that the myth of "one language" is "a metaphor in the Ancient Near East for the subjugation and assimilation of conquered peoples by a dominant nation."[33] Borrowing the one-language interpretation is a participation in modern empire practices, a tradition that plagues the church even today. *This* theological interpretation of Scripture—and Jennings dedicates a significant portion of his opus to this argument—participates in white consciousness and continues readings that oppress and that do not liberate. In this way the tradition of interpretation trumps the text. The story of Pentecost and Babel are toward *koinonia*. Pentecost is a participation in human-human *koinonia*; Babel is participation in human-land *koinonia*. Green says it well, "*Koinonia* is not the consequence of political domination, and unity is not instituted at the expense of distinctions among human communities."[34] Through the two narratives *koinonia* is an ongoing human participation across the earth of brothers and sisters with a variety of cultures in the ongoing practice of creation, namely flourishing the land through creative participation.

What happens when we understand Babel as a participation in creation blessing? God's gathering is towards a scattering. God's creativity in scattering is a promise of God's identification with people in their particular land and context. When God scatters, he is not dislocating the people but establishing each in a new land, a home, in creation that will prosper life (Ps 65). When God gathers his people, he is not inviting us to become alike, as an empire necessitates, but is inviting hospitality, understanding, embrace, and love, indeed, *koinonia*.[35] The stories of Babel and Pentecost demonstrate the importance of land for identity and the importance of plurality for unity. Blumenbach's Babel disallowed for unity with plurality and assumed the empire's perspective of exact sameness (*idem*).

---

33. Ibid., 30.

34. Ibid., 30–31.

35. Jennings, *The Christian Imagination*, 266. "Nothing is as humbling as learning the language of another in which the very rudiments of daily life must be identified in the signification system of another people. Such learning inevitably involves learning either directly or indirectly the land out of which the language came to life in the operation of everyday practices. Language is bound to landscape as the essential context of identity."

Divine agency spoke creation into being and formed humanity from it as an invitation into participation with God. God continued this invitation by scattering humanity across the earth. Through his promise of our participation, divine agency reconciled all things through Jesus Christ and the Holy Spirit as witnessed in the Pentecost event. Alternatively, scientific agency in the eighteenth century tried to undo the very agency of God through comparative race science and the *unitive* Adam principle whereby one only becomes fully human by becoming Caucasian—only by being born in a certain place. Blumenbach's science is an episode in human history whereby *scientists* proclaim, "Come, let us make a name for ourselves."

An Antiracist Hermeneutic for White Followers of Jesus

Blumenbach's science and the philosophical works that follow him have shaped the white consciousness for sameness as sanity. Some white people (the news cycle makes it impossible to say most) did not wake up and decide to accept this supremacy logic, yet it is the organizing framework for white consciousness.[36] What has become a result of a supposedly objective science is finally under investigation. Critical race theorists are exposing the myths of a unifying conceptual framework in favor of a plurality of frameworks that understand the narratives and stories that inform theories of dominant cultures. Mai-Ahn Le Tran, a theological educator, explains how critical race theorists examine unifying frameworks and expose fallacies. She exposes the weakness of the work of Blumenbach and others and shows that a unifying framework is a myth "sustained by misconceptions, misrepresentations, and lack of nuanced empirical data." Everything is contingent. She goes on to give an example of how complex human variety is and how one ethnic variety is not a degeneration of another,

> The broad racial construct of Asian American or Asian Pacific Islander in educational research obfuscates vast ethnic differences, socioeconomic disparities, and the significant under-educated percentage in AAPI populations in the U.S. A multiple passport holding executive from Hong Kong, a Korean grocery stop owner, a Filipino doctor, a Laotian refugee in middle Tennessee, a migrant from the U.S. territory of American Samoa, and an Amerasian child of biracial heritage would all be homogenized under the "Asian or Pacific Islander" racial category.[37]

---

36. Jennings, *The Christian Imagination*, 25. "Slowly out of these actions, whiteness emerges, not simply as a marker of the European but as the rarely spoken but always understood organizing conceptual framework."

37. Mai-Anh Le Tran, "When Subjects Matter: The Bodies We Teach By," in *Teaching for a Culturally Diverse and Racially Just World*, ed. Eleazar S. Fernandez (Eugene, OR: Cascade, 2014) 45.

For Blumenbach all of these populations would be considered "yellow" and subsumed under his limiting scientific descriptions of behavior, climate, and ability.

Critical race theory and antiracist practices are too often developments by people of color; the absence of white authors continues the oppressive thought that race problems are "those" people's problems. It is time to recognize the place of global (cosmopolitan) citizenship, or even more, theological participation for white followers of Jesus. Race problems are our problems. James Perkinson invites me and white theologians to reengage James Cone's invitation for white people to speak against privilege and supremacy. As white theologians engage, no one should have a quick expectation of reconciliation.[38] The deformities of white Christian identity and of our practices of intimacy are too offensive for some to expect quick solutions. The deformation is what I am trying to demonstrate in the Blumenbach narrative. I think Jennings is right, "In truth, it is not at all clear that most Christians are ready to imagine reconciliation."[39]

I want to reengage a theological interpretation of Scripture not initially for practices of racial reconciliation but for a theological understanding of whiteness. I desire only to pursue reconciliation by first working out my own theological understanding of whiteness. This is a long journey in a painful direction. This will require a new canon for the conversation. The common biblical canon for engaging questions of racism and race includes Rev 4 and 7; Gal 3:28; John 17:20–23, and other quick-to-rush-to biblical texts. These are not unhelpful to the conversation but too often become a quick fix toward reconciliation and pass over the Scripture's prophetic outrage at oppression and privilege, which are practices of white consciousness and supremacy.

The following antiracist practices arise from a hermeneutic borrowed from James Perkinson.[40] The difficulty of offering a hermeneutic or set of practices for white followers of Jesus is that what is recommended can continue into just another universalizing theory that constructs the very race/racism predicament that currently shapes our theological imagination. The importance of the hermeneutic is that it does not center on the theoretical model, universally, but plunges white people into particularity. This hermeneutic and following set of practices are initial questions and categories which invite white followers of Jesus to remain present

---

38. Jennings, *The Christian Imagination*, 10. "I am convinced that before we theologians can interpret the depths of divine action of reconciliation we must first articulate the profound deformities of Christian intimacy and identity in modernity. Until we do, all theological discussions of reconciliation will be exactly what they tend to be: a) ideological tools for facilitating the negotiations of power; or b) socially exhausted idealistic claims masquerading as serious theological accounts."

39. Ibid.

40. Perkinson, *White Theology*, 217–48.

to the fight, struggle, and pain in a particular place with a particular people for a greater engagement in a heterogeneous world. This is an assumption of cosmopolitan citizenship—not that we would abandon particularity, but embrace it as a way to understand our participation toward justice in the larger world.

Perkinson provides a three-fold hermeneutic for entering the struggle and outrage to understand white consciousness and supremacy. This is a theological engagement of apostasy, exorcism, and initiation. I adopt his hermeneutic and amplify it, offering it to my white colleagues and co-laborers as we partner in the work to destroy supremacy and recognize the power of redeemed race identity. God has traversed already the gates of hell and redeemed the races of people who have been and always will be fully formed identities in the kingdom of God. Now it is time for white people to stop being obstacles of ambivalence and self-preservation and instead to participate in God's ongoing liberation.

Apostasy

Apostasy is about forsaking the myth of objectivity as true method and dispassion as true virtue; apostasy is about taking up a passionate outrage when people of color are defamed, displaced, dislocated, or dead. The venture into apostasy is toward the venture to apostolicity. This is the development of a white double-consciousness, "a lived tension between what is and what could be, that is carried with both indignation and forgiveness and crafted into a persona politics of resilient vitality."[41] Apostasy is forsaking an exclusive kinship to your own and embracing a cosmopolitan kinship with communities who are being butchered, beaten, and mistreated. Apostasy is not the too often recommended practices of being patient and listening to people of color, as if we cannot see injustice when child immigrants are detained, black men beaten by police, or Asian women over-sexualized for profit.

How then do we live? Do we join the apostle Paul and the early Christians in the face of the Roman Empire? Do white men and women *risk* the ostensible comforts of our pensions, the safety of our children, or the promise of a career to participate in the outrage needed to transform supremacy and privilege? Are we willing to pay for our opposition (and face crucifixion) or play with the dominance of the white world (and enjoy security)? These questions are not rhetorical but mournful, as entering these questions results in loss.

God engages apostasy through outrage at the sight of injustice. God gives up dispassionate orthodoxy and takes up outrage and anger when he sees those who hurt children, when he recognizes hypocrisy from the Pharisees, when the poor are

---

41. Ibid., 235.

not fed, the naked not clothed, and the sick not visited. God is outraged when the people of the Lord forsake him and make a name for themselves or form an idol to manage their insecurity.[42] The impact of God's anger is not parental discipline or shock and dismay; it is earth shattering, ground-breaking outrage that impacts the earth and all of its creation;

> Then the earth reeled and rocked; the foundations also of the mountains trembled and quaked, because he was angry.
> Smoke went up from his nostrils, and devouring fire from his mouth; glowing coals flamed forth from him.
> He bowed the heavens, and came down; thick darkness was under his feet.
> He rode on a cherub, and flew; he came swiftly upon the wings of the wind.
> He made darkness his covering around him, his canopy thick clouds dark with water.
> Out of the brightness before him there broke through his cloud hailstones and coals of fire. (Ps 18:7–12)

The post-white apostle knows when and why God expresses outrage and joins this apostolic task. The apostle emerges from apostasy by "dreaming big, acting relevant, celebrating small, raging with a purpose, and weeping without regret."[43] Imagine if the rage spent on worship styles would have been poured into antiracism.

Exorcism

Racism is a polyvocal demon that haunts white followers of Jesus and needs exposure. Exorcism is the exposure of the legion and the transformative delivery of a new whiteness (Mark 5:1–13). Exorcism occurs following an emotional moment, an exposure, where racism rears its head beyond the scope of sight, whether in an offense, conversation, or objectification. These events occur every day in white space, yet most white followers of Jesus are either desensitized to the violence or captured by acedia. Exorcism occurs when white people recognize the limits in speech, time, and quotidian practices, otherwise known as "codes of whiteness." Without an ability to name one's codes and see them, the demons of supremacy and privilege live in white consciousness and white embodiment. Without recognizing the codes, any experience that challenges these codes creates fear. We cross the street, grab our purses, look past bodies, and disengage from multicultural conflict with a false objectivity.

Exorcism requires moving in and out of the white constructs of success, space, and security that are so essential to our white control and privilege. White followers

---

42. See *Ex Auditu* 24 (2008) which focuses on "The Idolatry of Security."
43. Perkinson, *White Theology*, 236.

of Jesus can personally experience naming the demons that haunt our mundane lives.[44] Equally as important is to understand the deeper structures that shape our consciousness that we have been unaware as white bodies. Ignorance of the deeper structures of our consciousness results in personal defenses (for example, I never owned slaves) and flight. As white evangelical followers of Jesus, exorcism invites us to confess and lament stories from *our* faith communities, owning the oppression of people of color within *our* histories. Jennings does this over and again in his work, but white followers of Jesus need to tell these stories and not rely on people of color to show the way.[45] My willingness to accept stories that others inherently see

44. Several years ago, I had an experience that showcased my white consciousness. Following dinner at a global market, I hit a car driven by a Latino male, Abraham, who spoke little English. I, who speak no Spanish, backed into his car, and fortunately a black woman witnessed the accident. I immediately ran to his car, asked if he was okay, and then proceeded in a manner of white procedures. Should we call the police and request a Spanish-speaking officer? Would you like my insurance information? I asked a series of questions rooted in legal order, hoping that I could do everything to help Abraham.

Within minutes I realized I was all wrong. The assumptions made by a white male in khaki pants, shiny black shoes, and a sport coat were embedded in white space and ignorant that other space was invisible to me. For him police and insurance were words of danger. He immediately called a friend who spoke English, and this friend assured me that police and insurance were unnecessary; the accident was not that bad. The female witness was quick to tell Abraham to give me very little information, saying to him, "Give only phone number and first name, no address." My physical appearance and my manner was "whiteness" with its assumed knowledge, perspective, and power fully unveiled for the watching world, and I was doing my best to be aware. That which counts me trustworthy in my own community figured me untrustworthy in this *new* community.

In the end I realized that this man wanted nothing from me, and anything that I could offer would require him to go public with his own identity, which did not come with the security of knowing whether or not *his* identity would be believed. The risk of self-identification carries too potent a fear. In return I gave him a token one hundred dollars in cash, knowing that the formal channels would have cost me significantly more. This experience is an exorcism, for which I am still in process.

45. The social architecture of American Evangelicalism is one story that many white followers of Jesus either do not know or refuse to accept. American Evangelicalism found its home in modern enlightenment reason, including Blumenbach's universalizing framework. American Evangelicalism's historical origin arises during American slavery and white domination of First Nation people. It adopted exceptionalism and taught that dominant white culture was the culture determined at creation. One result of this teaching is that for white people the fall results from not living into your dominant culture identity of spotless and sinless participation with God. Sin is therefore an individual failing. The fall, however, is systematized for people not classified as white, who as a population were always considered more sinful as part of a degenerated variety. In other words, American Evangelicalism adopted modern race science as a theology and equated dark skin with sin regardless of individual identity.

Evangelicalism promises quick redemption for white people, namely race science proves that all white people are part of the original and chosen people of Israel; this is "gentile forgetfulness." American Evangelicalism continues the logic of race science and structures redemption for black people only through their accommodation to the white system. In other words, for dark skin to be redeemed, it must belong to an individual who practices Christian identity as a white person or it must become "white."

This is part of the social architecture and DNA of the American Evangelicalism, even as some Evangelicals participated in the liberation of slaves and the demise of slavery as an acceptable system.

attached to my body arises from a discipleship that understands privilege as a root of sinfulness, personally and systemically. However, if I cannot accept privilege in my own self, then I cannot recognize the inherently racist system in my faith tradition.

Initiation

Finally, initiation serves as the identification marker for renewal. With regard to the old being, my former NT professor used to proclaim, "Drown the rascal." Initiation is not a sentimental bringing forth of a child to the church but a downright experience in death to life. We are being initiated into a new whiteness that is not supreme or privileged, even while white bodies must be aware that our bodies will bear the marks of supremacy and privilege long beyond a personal and cultural transformation.[46]

In the Evangelical Covenant Church the baptism liturgy shares with other traditions a final question, "Empowered by the Holy Spirit, will you do all in your power to participate fully in the life of this congregation, *to do justice, to love kindness, and to walk humbly with your God*?"[47] This question begs a deeper engagement than simply, "I do" or "We do." At this moment candidates, infants included, should stop the service and ask, "What in hell does this mean?"

Initiation into an antiracist hermeneutic, namely to do justice, as a white follower of Jesus will require an understanding of entering hell and returning to heaven. The baptismal question begs our wondering "What is doing justice?" or " What would be required for whites to have formed within themselves the kind of vital ferocity necessary to struggle lifelong against the powers and privileges that whiteness constantly leverages in and around them?[48] This is too long of a question for the liturgy, but Micah 6:8 points the direction in this question.

The requirements of doing justice, loving kindness, and walking humbly, as a white follower of Jesus, is a passionate, full-bodied struggle. Salvation is a war and a feast. Race in the United States is a war.[49] The struggle is against both principalities and powers *and* flesh and blood. Retelling the stories of ancestors that have enslaved, abused, and ignored nonwhite bodies is a hell-bent exercise that puts one's DNA

This social architecture results in an inherently racist system of Christian practice and has shaped public policy related to police enforcement (brutality), prison systems, and educational inequity. Telling this story and my participation in it is a first step in allowing the Holy Spirit to exorcise the demons of privilege and supremacy of my whiteness and in uprooting systems of oppression that are larger than my own personal decisions.

46. Perkinson, *White Theology*, 239–42.
47. *The Covenant Book of Worship* (Chicago: Covenant, 2003), 143, emphasis mine.
48. Perkinson, *White Theology*, 242.
49. Ibid., 220–21.

under investigation. White followers of Jesus will mourn when we recognize that those we love, including ourselves, have seeded supremacy and privilege for another generation through our quotidian practices, personally and in our institutions. However, at baptism, when white followers of Jesus agree to do justice, we agreed *at baptism* to become angry along with God. David Whyte reflects on the redemptive power of anger,

> Anger truly felt at its center is the essential living flame of being fully alive and fully here; it is a quality to be followed to its source, to be prized, to be tended, and an invitation to finding a way to bring that source fully into the world through making the mind clearer and more generous, the heart more compassionate and the body larger and strong enough to hold it.[50]

Going to hell, where Jesus Christ himself ventured to go on our behalf, is one manner in which we join divine action with the trust that divine action will bring us through to new life, a new whiteness.

Coming up from the turbulent waters of initiation is new life; indeed, a white person with a white body can participate differently. Rising from the drowning, ascending from hell, is a rejection of Caucasian as an identity marker. The word is drowned in the depths and will not return. The initiation is a participation in something other than whiteness currently understood. The journey to hell exposes the fullness of white privilege and supremacy practiced by white followers of Jesus. The journey down discloses the full white consciousness. The pain, misery, and shame that will occur to a white body that enters hell will emerge from the depths out of breath and seeking help from divine participants who are image-bearers-of-many-hues.

The ascent from hell is an invitation to life; this is a transformation toward reconciliation. The resurrected, antiracist white body is one that will be invited to a feast only as it rediscovers a Christian theology of belonging, desire, and intimacy for which it is not the source or substance. The white (male) body that is raised from the dead will find many-hued-image-bearers willing to welcome him to the table. Do not expect the invitation right away; your body still has marks of the devil. Once he enters hell and sees that before being grafted into God's election and prior to being raised from the dead, he was a stranger and foreigner in most lands, only then can he be raised. He will recognize that he has no land, except that which he stole, and his only location/space is through his interdependence with people of color. This is *kenosis* (Phil 2). This interdependence will welcome him into participation with the many-hued manifestation of the Spirit at Pentecost. Rising from death, the

---

50. David Whyte, *Consolations: The Solace, Nourishment, and Underlying Meaning of Everyday Words* (Langley, WA: Many Rivers, 2015). Taken from http://www.brainpickings.org/2015/05/15/david-whyte-consolations-anger-forgiveness-maturity/.

table can *begin* to be set, and the Host will be present with us, and he will have marks in his hands.

How will this post-racist white body look in a war-torn racialized world, whereby white uniformed bodies are witnessed as beating black and brown bodies, is yet to be seen.[51] However, apostasy, exorcism, and initiation welcome white bodies and white people into kinship with colorful bodies and people of color. This upholds difference while recognizing intimacy and belonging through journeys of suffering—suffering which can be shared through testimony but will never be shared in common experience.[52] This new kinship will redefine science, Christian imagination, and quotidian practices.

Conclusion

The hermeneutic for white followers of Jesus is offered by this white male, who has taken up antiracism and redeeming race as a lifelong journey of action and participation. The three practices have been experienced accidentally. Through friends of color and white allies my accidents are being made purposeful. I invite others to journey in these ways, experiencing outrage that is not orthodox, exorcism that is obnoxious, and initiation that is a death that leads to life.

---

51. I am growingly assured that it will not look like the story of former NAACP leader, Rachel Dolezal, even as this story is showing the complexity of racialized identities. Race will remain, albeit dynamically understood, constructed, and enacted. I think that the *action* of alliance from Dolezal to the black community is a practice of advocacy and liberation, yet its *form* and *expression* are complicated and unsettling. See Chanequa Walker-Barnes, "Race Matters and So Does Racial Fraud" https://drchanequa.wordpress.com/2015/06/17/race-matters-and-so-does-rachels-fraud/.

52. See Miroslov Volf's comments on embrace as an act for difference but which yet engenders belonging, intimacy, and forgiveness in his *Exclusion and Embrace: A Theological Exploration of Identity, Otherness, and Reconciliation* (Nashville: Abingdon, 1996) 140–47.

ENEMIES, ROMANS, PIGS, AND DOGS: LOVING THE OTHER IN THE GOSPEL OF MATTHEW

Love L. Sechrest

In my interdisciplinary work at the intersection of critical race theory[1] and NT interpretation, I have become fascinated with the tension that modern life poses between ethnoracial identity[2] and Christian identity. This tension is one not often understood or acknowledged by the vast majority of scholars in the Christian academy, given its overwhelming whiteness. In the United States, whiteness is normed and thus invisible, but not so with respect to the identities of people of color. Yet, as a female African American NT scholar who is well read on the dynamics of race and gender in American society, I sometimes find that my engagement with critical theory in race and gender collides with what may be for some an uncomplicated embrace of the imperatives of the gospel. For example, how should a woman who is stereotyped as a nurturing mammy who owes tender concern to her superiors embrace the gospel's self-sacrificial regard for the other? Should she embrace the self-effacing stereotype even though it has been a form of oppression, or should she reject the forced subordination of her own God-given agency and need for self-protection as someone created in the image of God? It is one thing to exhort the privileged and comfortable to surrender their privileges on behalf of a lost humanity, but it is an altogether different matter to charge the downtrodden with further abasement that ends up redounding to benefit of the oppressor. Thus, the centrality of loving, cruciform, suffering in the way of Jesus in the Christian message becomes enormously

---

1. The study of race and ethnicity is a large and unwieldy matter, spanning multiple disciplines in the humanities and social sciences such as cultural anthropology, sociology, literary studies, ethnic and racial studies, education, philosophy, and more. Technically, Critical Race Theory refers to the examination of race, ethnicity, and social justice within legal studies, but I use it here as an umbrella term describing the study of race across all of these disciplinary areas and refer to this broad body of work with lowercase type as a way to differentiate it from the narrower concerns in legal studies. For more on Critical Race Theory, see, e.g., Kimberlé Crenshaw, et al., eds. *Critical Race Theory: The Key Writings that Formed the Movement* (New York: New Press, 1995).

2. I use the term "ethnoracial" instead of talking about ethnicity and/or race as a way of signaling that these terms are difficult to disaggregate. For more on this terminology see Denise Kimber Buell, "Rethinking the Relevance of Race for Early Christian Self-Definition," *HTR* 94 (2001) 449–76, 450 n. 3; Denise Kimber Buell and Caroline Johnson Hodge, "The Politics of Interpretation: The Rhetoric of Race and Ethnicity in Paul," *JBL* 123 (2004) 235–51, 236.

complicated for historically oppressed peoples and especially for those who have experienced one or more of the evils of racism, sexism, genocide, colonialism, or imperialism as Native Americans, African Americans, Latino/as, Jews, women, and others have.

In American society the word "racism" is culturally loaded and evokes images of bigotry such as Wallace's legendary stand barring the doors of integration at the University of Alabama, Rush Limbaugh's in-your-face use of gangster stereotypes when describing the heavy concentration of African Americans in the NFL and NBA, and Don Imus's characterization of the Rutgers University women's basketball team as "nappy headed hos."[3] Despite the fact that racism inhabits institutions in ways that implicate many sectors of society, if you are not using a fire hose to rebuff peaceful demonstrations for civil rights, then in this country you are not a racist. Thus when Dylann Roof executed nine black people on June 17, 2015, at Emanuel African Methodist Episcopal church in Charleston, South Carolina, he instantly became an iconic image of white supremacist racism. This singular example of the conflict between Christian regard for the other and a lived history of racism, sexism, and other forms of oppression can be found in the various responses to the Charleston massacre.

In the immediate aftermath of the shooting, one common response involved speculation about Roof's mental health on the reasoning that only someone suffering from mental illness could have gunned down Christians at prayer in a house of worship after spending an hour with them in a Bible study.[4] On the one hand, this compassionate response can give rise to a helpful discussion about the inadequacies of American institutions for mental illness,[5] but on the other hand it raises questions about why the media eschews alternate and more appropriate characterizations of the Charleston killer that better reflect Roof's stated motivations. Why not use labels like "terrorist" or "white supremacist"?[6] Another kind of response, born out of over-

---

3. Rush Limbaugh: see Simon Maloy, "The 20 Worst Racial Attacks Limbaugh's Advertisers Have Sponsored," blog on MediaMatters for America, March 7, 2012, http://mediamatters.org/blog/2012/03/07/the-20-worst-racial-attacks-limbaughs-advertise/184776; Don Imus: see Judy Faber, "CBS Fires Don Imus Over Racial Slur," CBS News April 12, 2007, http://www.cbsnews.com/news/cbs-fires-don-imus-over-racial-slur/.

4. Matthew Lysiak, "Charleston Massacre: Mental Illness Common Thread for Mass Shootings," *Newsweek*, June 19, 2015, http://www.newsweek.com/charleston-massacre-mental-illness-common-thread-mass-shootings-344789.

5. E. Fuller Torrey, "Ronald Reagan's Shameful Legacy: Violence, the Homeless, Mental Illness," excerpt from *American Psychosis: How the Federal Government Destroyed the Mental Illness Treatment System* (New York: Oxford University Press, 2014), cited in *Salon*, September 29, 2013, http://www.salon.com/2013/09/29/ronald_reagans_shameful_legacy_violence_the_homeless_mental_illness/.

6. The early framing of Roof's actions in terms of mental illness was seen by some as a refusal to admit to racial motivation or as a way of exonerating or mitigating the heinousness of the crime, but

whelming grief, reached back into the psalms of Israel to pray imprecatory prayers about the massacre. Surely the most astounding response was one born from the gospel of Jesus Christ as some members of the victims' families forgave Dylann Roof when they had the chance to face him in a bond court hearing, at a time when their pain at the wrenching shock of the murders was still raw (cf. Matt 18:21–22). Yet another response from black church leaders in South Carolina attempted to straddle the gulf between lament and forgiveness: "You cannot be the thing you hate. You cannot become the evil you seek to eradicate. Forgiveness is not the same as ignoring the facts. We want justice."[7]

This last response illustrates the tension between an uncompromising love of enemies that represents the apex of Christian ethics in Matt 5:43–48 and the cries of the suffering wounded who find in that same Gospel succor for a persecuted and trampled *imago Dei*. How should the downtrodden give love to enemies and how should the dominant be loving as enemies in times of ever-increasing racial tension? In this paper I share a framework from the Gospel of Matthew that can be useful in navigating the borderlands of conflict and love. It turns out that it will be helpful to look at how Jesus's enemies are depicted in the Gospel and to observe how these interactions demonstrate love for enemies. We will focus not so much on Jesus's own actions but more on the character of the enemies' interactions with him. We will examine Matthew's depictions of enemies, both in the ideal and in the ignoble, to help imagine how we ourselves might be transformed from enemies to friends. In other words, we will try to construct a Christian ethic of allyship. I begin with a survey of scholarship about being allies before looking at Gentiles as enemies in the Gospel of Matthew. We conclude by developing a gospel-centric synthesis on the nature of allyship.

"Love" in Other Words: From Enemies to Allies

It will not be surprising to learn that there is little discussion involving explicitly Christian ideas about loving the enemy in the theoretical literature about race and

---

such framing seems less frequent when the actions of people of color are involved. See Anthea Butler, "Shooters of Color Are Called 'Terrorists' and 'Thugs.' Why Are White Shooters called 'Mentally Ill'?" *Washington Post*, June 18, 2015, https://www.washingtonpost.com/posteverything/wp/2015/06/18/call-the-charleston-church-shooting-what-it-is-terrorism/.

7. Wade Goodwyn, "Charleston's Black Leaders Want to See Justice As Much As Forgiveness," *NPR*, July 2, 2015, http://www.npr.org/2015/07/02/419405863/charlestons-black-leaders-want-justice-as-much-as-forgiveness. For a survey of Christian responses to the Charleston massacre, see Kate Shellnutt, "A Lament for Charleston: What Makes This Mass Shooting Different," *Christianity Today*, June 19, 2015, http://www.christianitytoday.com/gleanings/2015/june/lament-for-charleston-what-makes-this-shooting-different.html.

racism; such categories are simply not deemed relevant outside of an explicitly Christian worldview. Indeed the rarity of acts of love towards enemies in the public imagination perhaps explains the swift and decisive action of those who lobbied to remove the Confederate flag from state houses across the south in the wake of the Charleston massacre. The "astonishing" act of forgiveness offered to Dylann Roof after he went into that AME church to find blacks he could kill in fulfillment of his white supremacist delusions acted as a moral prod against a revisionist history that had for decades successfully painted the Confederate flag as a symbol of Southern culture instead of the battle flag of a republic that fought and lost a war for the right to enslave blacks.[8] Yet one area of inquiry that may serve as an approximation of this kind of discourse in critical theory is one that discusses the identity and habitus of allies for racial justice. "Allies" are those from dominant or privileged groups who engage in activism in support of social justice by helping to dismantle systems of oppression and unfair advantage in favor of increasing access to social goods for all.[9]

The term may have originated in LGBT activism against heterosexism in the 1990s,[10] but it also appears in discourse about social justice work and critical whiteness studies.[11] According to frequently cited definition a social justice ally is "a person who is a member of the 'dominant' or 'majority' group who works to end oppressions in his or her personal and professional life through support of, and as an advocate with and for, the oppressed population."[12] These activists acknowledge their unearned privileges and the power that their social identities grant them as they act to dismantle the structures in society that support privilege and power. They may be motivated to be allies by a sense of responsibility regarding the acknowledg-

---

8. An interesting fact that emerged in the daylight of the renewed debate to take the Confederate flag down from state houses in the South was that the flag became a symbol of Southern culture almost one hundred years after the end of the Civil War, notably, during the Civil Rights movement in the 1950s and 1960s. See Amber Philips, "Why is the Confederate Flag Still a Thing Even Though the South Lost the Civil War?" *The Washington Post*, July 10, 2015, http://www.washingtonpost.com/news/the-fix/wp/2015/07/10/why-is-the-confederate-flag-still-a-thing-even-though-the-south-lost-the-civil-war/.

9. Ellen M. Broido, "The Development of Social Justice Allies during College: A Phenomenological Investigation," *Journal of College Student Development* 41.1 (2000) 3–18, 3. A participant in a study of white female antiracist allies suggests that an ally is "someone who had reflected on being called a racist and admitted personal racial shortcomings" (Kim A. Case, "Discovering the Privilege of Whiteness: White Women's Reflections on Anti-racist Identity and Ally Behavior," *Journal of Social Issues* 68 [2012] 78–96, 84).

10. Broido, "The Development of Social Justice Allies," 3.

11. Viraj S. Patel, "Moving toward an Inclusive Model of Allyship for Racial Justice," *Vermont Connection* 32 (2011) 78–88, 78–81.

12. J. Washington and N. J. Evans, "Becoming an Ally," in *Beyond Tolerance: Gays, Lesbians, and Bisexuals on Campus*, ed. N. J. Evans and V. A. Wall (Washington, D.C.: American College Personnel Association) 195. Also see, for example, Sandra L. Neumann, "The 'Why's' and 'How's' of Being a Social Justice Ally," in *Getting Culture: Incorporating Diversity across the Curriculum*, ed. Regan A. R. Gurung and Loreto R. Prieto (Sterling, VA: Stylus, 2009) 65.

ment of privilege, acting on the influence exerted by intimacy with others who have personal experience with oppression.[13]

When it comes to the question of doing the work of a social justice ally, there is broad agreement among scholars and among these activists themselves that the first consideration involves ownership of one's identity as a racial being, a step that is seen as nonnegotiable for whites and one that is perhaps the biggest obstacle inhibiting broader white participation in social justice work.[14] In interviews these activists insist that someone must admit to their own racism and privilege before becoming an antiracist activist and that "without that essential piece, you are living in denial" and without real hope that any authentic change can occur.[15] As with alcoholism, "the first step to recovery is admitting you have a problem.... [R]ecognition of white privilege [is] absolutely essential for white antiracism and... some form of self-work on racism [is] needed" in order to make a beginning.[16] This step is foundational because of the way that whiteness is invisible in our racialized society, which allows whites who do not have a critical consciousness to assume the universality of whiteness as the standard of human experience, something denied to people of color who are assumed to have narrow perspectives constrained by race or ethnicity.[17]

Second, and akin to the recognition of white racial identity as the precursor to antiracism work, is theory that explores the psychological, intellectual, moral,

---

13. Neumann, "The 'Why's' and 'How's' of Being a Social Justice Ally," 65. This last motivation, personal experience with oppression, may be significant since anecdotal evidence suggests that lesbians and Jews are overrepresented in antiracism work (Jennifer L. Eichstedt, "Problematic White Identities and a Search for Racial Justice," *Sociological Forum* 16 [2001] 449–50).

14. See, for instance, Neumann, "The 'Why's' and 'How's' of Being a Social Justice Ally," 68; Linda Martín Alcoff, "What Should White People Do?" *Hypatia* 13.3 (Summer 1998) 21; A. E. Lewis, "'What Group?': Studying Whites and Whiteness in the Era of 'Colorblindness,'" *Sociological Theory* 22 (2004) 623–46; C. Titone, "Educating the White Teacher as Ally," in *White Reign: Deploying Whiteness in America*, ed. J. L. Kincheloe, et al. (New York: St. Martin's Griffin, 1998) 159–76; Eichstedt, "Problematic White Identities," 445–70; and R. D. Reason and N. J. Evans ("The Complicated Realities of Whiteness: From Color Blind to Racially Cognizant," *New Directions for Student Services* 120 [Winter 2007] 67–76), who write of a racially cognizant self "that encompasses an understanding of guilt, power, and privilege yet avoids the paralysis and victim perspectives that some Whites assume" (p. 71). Similarly Kim Case finds that understanding the concept of white privilege is a precursor of white antiracist activism ("Discovering the Privilege of Whiteness," 79).

15. Case, "Discovering the Privilege of Whiteness," 84.

16. Ibid.

17. Robin DiAngelo, "White Fragility," *International Journal of Critical Pedagogy* 3.3 (2011) 54–70, 60. DiAngelo also exposes the similar operation of "individualism" as a strategy by which whites deny complicity in racist structures and the implications for wealth and access to resources, etc. I frequently encounter versions of these universalist ("We're all in the image of God") and individualist perspectives ("Each person must be accountable to God") when I teach about race and racism in theological education. These two perspectives thus become a Christian version of the secular defensiveness as manifest in such comments as "My family never did anything racist; therefore I don't have responsibility for racism."

and material costs to whites of racism.[18] Maintenance of racialized inequality means that whites must be psychologically conditioned for their place in the social order by adopting the ideology and rationalizations that reinforces thinking and behavior that perpetuates injustice and diminishes all humans.[19] Thus whiteness exacts psychological costs even if they are not equivalent to those that people of color experience. Accordingly, disorientation from a new experience of "feeling white" when combined with a desire to repudiate white privilege can disable whites' positive self-image and connection to community and history.[20] Thus, while it is important that we never forget that these effects are not comparable to those faced by people of color, the psychological effects are nevertheless real, even if they in no way constitute "oppression."[21] As Paulo Freire succinctly put it, "[a]s oppressors dehumanize others and violate their rights, they themselves also become dehumanized."[22] "Dehumanization, which marks not only those whose humanity has been stolen, but also (though in a different way) those who have stolen it, is a distortion of becoming more fully human."[23]

Diane Goodman's description of the psychological, social, moral/spiritual, intellectual, and material/physical costs of whiteness are thus helpful for situating this accounting of the negative effects of whiteness and can contribute to the cultivation of a critical white identity.[24] The psychological costs of whiteness involve diminished emotional and empathetic capacity and compromised mental health as whites are socialized to conform to certain rigid standards of behavior constrained by gender and class. For instance, white women may be constrained by stereotypes that lock them into infantile, subordinate, and diminished agency, just as white men

---

18. For more on this topic see the series of psychological studies that develop an instrument to measure the psychosocial costs of racism to whites: Lisa B. Spanierman, Nathan R. Todd, and Carolyn J. Anderson, "Psychosocial Costs of Racism to Whites: Understanding Patterns among University Students," *Journal of Counseling Psychology* 56 (2009) 239–52; Amy Sifford, Kok-Mun Ng, and Chuang Wang, "Further Validation of the Psychosocial Costs of Racism to Whites Scale on a Sample of University Students in the Southeastern United States," *Journal of Counseling Psychology* 56 (2009) 585–89. Also see Lisa B. Spanierman, et al., "Psychosocial Costs of Racism to Whites: Exploring Patterns through Cluster Analysis," *Journal of Counseling Psychology* 53 (2006) 434–41; and V. Paul Poteat and Lisa B. Spanierman, "Further Validation of the Psychosocial Costs of Racism to Whites Scale among Employed Adults," *The Counseling Psychologist* 36 (2008) 871–94.

19. Ruth Frankenberg, *White Women, Race Matters: The Social Construction of Whiteness* (Minneapolis: University of Minnesota Press, 1993) 121.

20. Alcoff, "What Should White People Do?" 7.

21. Diane Goodman, *Promoting Diversity and Social Justice: Educating People from Privileged Groups* (Thousand Oaks, CA: Sage, 2001) 103–24, 103–4.

22. Paulo Freire, *Pedagogy of the Oppressed* (New York: Herder & Herder, 1970) 42.

23. Ibid., 28.

24. Unless otherwise noted, information in this paragraph comes from Goodman, *Promoting Diversity*, 105–9.

may be imprisoned by expectations of aggressive, competitive, success-at-any-cost behaviors.[25] Students in my own classes that deal with race also report negative costs from being stereotyped as racists in encounters with some people of color. Studies show other negative health implications from pressure to achieve and maintain the success that is stereotypical of white status in a competitive environment. Areas with high income disparity also correlate with higher death rates for both rich and poor. Whites are inhibited by unconscious or conscious and sometimes debilitating fears of the other, of racial discomfort, of losing privileges and entitlements, and of retaliation; there may also be fears for the well-being of intimate friends and family in dominated groups. "People from dominant groups tend to develop unhealthy psychological mechanisms (such as denial, false justification, projection, disassociation, and transference of blame) to deal with their fears of minorities or people from oppressed groups."[26] They can become "soft" with an inability to deal with discomfort, pain, or challenge.[27]

To these psychological costs we could also add the social costs of isolation from being stereotyped by people of color as racist, rapists, elitist snobs, paternalistic, callous to human suffering, selfish, biased, spoiled, entitled, and untrustworthy.[28] Whites sometimes face ostracism within their own group for their antiracist postures or actions in confrontations with family, friends, or coworkers. The moral and spiritual costs of whiteness also include loss of integrity and feelings of guilt and shame. Embarrassed and guilty about having more than others, whites sometimes resort to "blaming the victim" as a response or else retreat into defensiveness. Christians especially can experience an integrity compromise when they experience difficulty in doing the right thing and risking the disapproval of friends or family or neighbors, or succumb to social pressure in decision making. There is pain from knowing that one participates in falling so far short of God's will. Intellectual costs to whites emerge from the fact that whites often are ignorant of their own ethnic culture, heritage, and the wisdom from their ethnic history and have a distorted or limited view of other cultures and their contributions to humanity, thus becoming out of touch with reality with an impoverished worldview and constrained expo-

---

25. See Amanda M. Durik et al., "Ethnicity and Gender Stereotypes of Emotion," *Sex Roles* 54 (2006) 430–31, and the scholarship cited there. Also see Patricia Hill Collins, *Black Sexual Politics: African Americans, Gender, and the New Racism* (New York: Routledge, 2004) 58; Bell Hooks, "Reflections on Race and Sex," in her *Yearning: Race, Gender, and Cultural Politics* (Boston: South End, 1990) 57–64.

26. Also see J. Fernandez, "The Impact of Racism on Whites in Corporate America," in *The Impacts of Racism on White Americans*, ed. B. Bowser and R. Hunt, 2nd ed. (Thousand Oaks, CA: Sage, 1996), cited in Goodman, *Promoting Diversity*, 109.

27. DiAngelo, "White Fragility," 54.

28. Material in this paragraph comes from Goodman, *Promoting Diversity*, 109–19.

sure to other ways of living. Again, these disadvantages are not comparable to the sometimes-lethal physical and material costs of racism to people of color like Native Americans, blacks, and some Latino/as. Yet there are indeed direct and indirect material and physical costs of racism for whites in addition to the aforementioned psychological, social, and intellectual damages. Whites experience the indirect and direct costs of social unrest from protests about injustice, poverty, and disenfranchisement from societal benefits. Whites can become virtual prisoners in gated communities with stunted social networks because of fears about safety, having to spend time, money, and energy trying to protect themselves and their belongings.

Third in importance in antiracist activist development is gaining knowledge about oppression through formal and informal educational experiences and interpersonal relationships with other activists and people of color. It may be that growth in this area is spiral in nature in that one may not be able to take even the first step of understanding one's white social location in development as an activist without having had prior exposure to the facts of ethnoracial oppression. Yet a related theme in activist literature and scholarship is the idea that antiracist whites must be careful to avoid communicating an expectation that people of color have the responsibility to educate whites about oppression, a posture which compounds and extends the paternalism of racial hierarchies.[29]

Activists report that maintaining one's commitment in the face of questions about credibility and lack of support from other white peers and significant others, including supervisors, friends, and family, is one of the most difficult aspects of antiracist work.[30] Robin DiAngelo's work suggests that this dilemma may emerge at least partially from what he calls "white fragility." According to DiAngelo racial privilege builds expectations for racial comfort among whites and lowers their ability to tolerate racial stress.[31] White fragility is defined as a state in which even a minimum amount of such stress triggers a range of defensive behaviors that function to reinstate a tolerable white racial equilibrium—behaviors including argumentation, silence, flight, and emotional outbursts of anger, fear, and guilt.[32] This fragility may be manifest in response to a number of challenges.[33]

---

29. Neumann, "The 'Why's' and 'How's' of Being a Social Justice Ally," 68; also Broido, "The Development of Social Justice Allies," 4. For a popular discussion of the dynamics of self-education for allies see Jamie Utt, "So You Call Yourself an Ally: 10 Things All 'Allies' Need to Know," *Everyday Feminism*, November 8, 2013, http://everydayfeminism.com/2013/11/things-allies-need-to-know/.

30. Neumann, "The 'Why's' and 'How's' of Being a Social Justice Ally," 72.

31. DiAngelo, "White Fragility," 55.

32. Ibid., 54–55.

33. Ibid., 61–65.

1. The challenge to white objectivity happens if someone suggests that a white person's viewpoint comes from a racialized perspective.

2. The challenge to white racial comfort occurs when people of color express perspectives on race in ways that do not protect white sensibilities by couching ideas in polite and subdued terms and without any show of emotional upset. When whites respond in ways that position themselves as victimized, blamed, attacked, or treated unfairly, and demand that attention be directed away from people of color and back onto white comfort, they become responsible for associating a lack of comfort in an explicit discussion of race with lack of safety in a way that plays into racist tropes of people of color as aggressive and dangerous.

3. The challenge to white solidarity takes place when a fellow white person refuses to concur with another white person's perspective.[34]

4. The challenge to meritocracy exists when whites refuse to countenance the idea that there is unequal access to resources.

5. The challenge to white authority may explain much of the virulent opposition to Obamacare on the right, especially since the policy is nothing more than a national adaptation of a Republican governor's health care solution. This happens in cases where whites encounter a person of color in a position of leadership.

6. The challenge to white liberalism can occur when whites who think they understand racism receive the feedback that their behavior or words had a racist impact.

Overcoming fragility and maintaining one's commitment in the face of social isolation may be aided by contact with others who have similar perspectives in white affinity groups.[35] Such a group provides a safe space to explore such issues as white guilt, sustaining antiracist activism, and the positive construction of white identity.[36] It is a place wherein whites process information about racism without hindering people of color in multiethnic conversations who are further along the trajectory of antiracist activism by virtue of their experience.[37] Thus, whites can practice talking about race with transparency, asking possibly ignorant questions, challenge themselves to do better, and examine and reflect on privilege more critically.[38] On

---

34. Compare this idea to the "advantaged-to-advantaged horizontal oppression" described in Patel, "Allyship for Racial Justice," 83–85.

35. Broido, "The Development of Social Justice Allies," 4. Also see especially Ali Michael et al., "Becoming an Anti-Racist White Ally: How a White Affinity Group Can Help," *Perspectives on Urban Education* (Spring 2009) 56–60. This article describes a group of white students at the University of Pennsylvania in a group called White Students Confronting Racism.

36. Michael et al., "Becoming an Anti-Racist White Ally: White Affinity Group," 56.

37. Ibid., 57.

38. Ibid., 57–58.

the other hand, a white affinity group can be critiqued because "whites may fail to detect much of the racism that people of color could easily pinpoint. White antiracists struggling to deconstruct racism face the possibility that they lack the skills necessary to even properly identify racism."[39] Still, such groups are valuable as public declarations of white antiracism and more importantly, offer a space where whites may educate themselves in a way that does not place undue burdens on people of color.

Fourth, it is important that allies take action in their own communities, and especially under the leadership of people of color when possible, resisting the impulse to jump in and take control.[40] This certainly includes participating in public demonstrations (i.e. attending marches and rallies, writing editorials, etc.), but more commonly involves interrupting the racist comments of family, friends, and coworkers, teaching about racism in classrooms and presentations, and advocating for diversity in everyday settings, by hiring, advocating for, or mentoring people of color in the workplace.[41] Taking action also means rejecting "covert racism" such as tacitly supporting the activities of power holders who discourage connections with people of color or who are disapproving when others bring attention to matters of race in all-white settings.[42] Other "white distancing" techniques must also be rejected and/or confronted, including active resistance or defensiveness (i.e., "I'm not racist"), nonverbal signals of disapproval such as the silent treatment, accusations of oversensitivity, attempts to end discussions of race, and flight.[43] Above all, it is important to realize that in this area of discourse, candid, constructive reflection on one's position and privilege as a white person is an important responsibility and form of action.[44]

Finally humility is essential in development as an ally. One article suggests that white allies can be an obstacle in social justice movements because of a perhaps unconscious belief in their own superiority and tendency to dominate the agenda.[45] Humility can be cultivated through self-reflection and perspective-taking, by learning the perspectives of the other and imagining oneself in those circumstances.[46] Some may find it counterintuitive to learn that self-confidence is as important as

39. Case, "Discovering the Privilege of Whiteness," 91.

40. Michael et al., "Becoming an Anti-Racist White Ally: White Affinity Group," 58.

41. Case, "Discovering the Privilege of Whiteness," 87; Broido, "The Development of Social Justice Allies," 2000.

42. Case, "Discovering the Privilege of Whiteness," 89.

43. Ibid., 90.

44. Michael et al., "Becoming an Anti-Racist White Ally: White Affinity Group," 58.

45. Ibid., 59–60.

46. Broido, "The Development of Social Justice Allies," 4.

humility in the process of internalizing the idea that whites are the beneficiaries of privilege. One study found that "[w]ithout confidence in themselves . . . participants were unwilling or unable to consider that their success was due in part to their dominant status in society, and the privilege they thereby incurred."[47] Thus, there is a need to balance humility and self-confident self-understanding, much like what we see in Jesus's model in John 13:3–5 (cf. Phil 2:6–8).

While the idea of constructing an identity around being a social justice ally is potentially appealing for white Christians and others, there is a lively debate about the very notion of "allyship" among activists and people of color. For example, Beverly Daniel Tatum's widely read book *Why Are All the Black Kids Sitting Together in the Cafeteria?* briefly touches on the notion of white identity development by describing how whites respond to racism in one of four ways: they may become overtly racist, colorblind, guilty, or develop as white antiracist allies.[48] According to Linda Martín Alcoff, whites who come to see their own whiteness while learning about the dynamics of race experience disorientation from "feeling white," which when combined with a desire to repudiate white privilege, can result in a negative self-image and a fractured connection to community and history.[49] For these whites, Tatum's "white anti-racist identity" becomes the only recourse.[50]

But there are problems embedded in this construction of identity. If a negative construction of whiteness as a result of a racialized society makes it difficult to have a positive white identity, this outcome represents the wages that all pay in living in a racialized society, one that affects people of color with far more serious consequences. The problem is that the effort to apply the language of fluid, fractured, and multiple identities to whites in a way that leaves room for agency while recognizing the structural aspects of identity may be viewed rightly or wrongly as an attempt to sidestep responsibility for ending racial oppression. Cynics could see in this attempt another instance of the trope of the fragile white victim who shifts attention away from the oppression experienced by people of color and onto the lesser problems surrounding white identity.[51] Another difficulty is that in combination with rampant individualism among whites, an amorphous white antiracist identity might allow

---

47. Ibid., 7, 10–13. Contrast this emphasis on humility with Julie Greenberg's struggle to accept the leadership of people of color in "Beyond Allyship: Multiracial Work to End Racism," *Tikkun* 29 (2014) 11–18.

48. Beverly Daniels Tatum, *Why Are All the Black Kids Sitting Together in the Cafeteria: And Other Conversations About Race*, 5th Anniversary Rev. ed. (New York: Basic, 2003).

49. Alcoff, "What Should White People Do?" 7.

50. Also see Richard Delgado and Jean Stefancic, eds., *Critical White Studies: Looking Behind the Mirror* (Philadelphia: Temple University, 1997).

51. Eichstedt, "Problematic White Identities," 448.

whites to distance themselves from the actions of their racial group and demand to be granted the benefit of the doubt in all cases. Thus, a corollary to such an amorphous and thus unracialized antiracist identity is the white person who recognizes whiteness as real, but as the individual problem of other "bad" white people.[52] Moreover, white antiracist identity discourse about allyship can be critiqued for the way that it leaves aside the nuance that coalitions against racism require by accounting for the particular ways that many communities of color experience racism and overlooking the need for collaborative alliances with and among different communities of color.[53] More importantly, some activists think that it is dangerous to talk about allyship as a status or identity that exists independent of ongoing acts of solidarity.[54] The status vs. process perspective can become troublesome, for instance, when a white activist responds to correction about a problematic racist comment or action by dismissing the correction on the basis of their past efforts—in effect invoking the "I marched with Martin Luther King Jr." defense. According to these activists, one should not proclaim one's identity as an ally; one should be claimed as such by those one is seeking to support.

These reservations are important and need to circumscribe the contours and nature of allyship as practiced by whites. However, I think it is unwise to withhold the possibility of positive identity construction for anyone suffering from the trauma of being racialized; to do so would be akin to the way that conservatives unfairly critiqued the "Black is Beautiful" movement in the 1960s. This is not to say that whites' need for a positive way of being white is as urgent as the need experienced by blacks and other oppressed groups. Rather, this is to say that in keeping with the love ethic in Matt 5:43–48, a Christian should not withhold a good from an enemy because of the chance for abuse. If praying for enemies represents the minimum in this ethic (5:44), the other verses show the boundlessness of Jesus's intention (5:45, 48). Thus, wisdom and love dictate that there should be possibilities for whites to craft an identity characterized by trust, humility, unceasing antiracist action, and solidarity with people of color. Further, we should create an analogous conversation about how communities of color can become allies in broader antiracist coalitions. In the next section we will look at depictions of enemies in Matthew's Gospel for help in fleshing out the shape of Christian love for the other.

---

52. DiAngelo, "White Fragility," 59.

53. Patel, "Allyship for Racial Justice," 78–81. Similarly Hak Joon Lee, *The Great World House: Martin Luther King, Jr., and Global Ethics* (Cleveland, Ohio: Pilgrim, 2011); and also Jeffrey Scott Mio, "Asians on the Edge: The Reciprocity of Allied Behavior," *Cultural Diversity and Ethnic Minority Psychology* 10 (2004) 90–94.

54. Utt, "So You Call Yourself an Ally."

Matthew and the Nations

Much like the tensions in the OT with respect to ancient Israelite ethnocentrism on the one hand and a welcome of outsiders through conversion on the other hand, Matthew, sometimes called the most "Jewish" Gospel, displays ambiguity that also expresses these tendencies.[55] Nothing could scream ethnicity more than Matthew's addition of a Jewish genealogy to the Marcan account of Jesus's ministry and passion. The genealogy traces Jesus's descent from Abraham, the Israelite patriarch, and from David, the people's ideal king, yet also has ambiguity as it mentions Jesus's Canaanite and non-Jewish forbearers—all depicted as women. Thus the genealogy in 1:1–18 that functions to identify Jesus as a Davidic messiah and which includes four Gentile women, captures Matthew's blend of universalism and particularism.[56]

In addition, the final scene in the Gospel contains the distinctive Great Commission that commands the small band of devoted disciples to embrace a global mission (28:19; cf. 24:14).[57] One would have to agree that this scene with its emphasis on a worldwide Gentile mission at the end of the narrative absolves this text of any charge of active racism or narrow ethnocentrism. Yet we should note that the Great Commission also contains an embedded promotion of Jewish particularity.[58] What else could one conclude from the exhortation about "teaching [the nations] to obey everything that I commanded" in 28:20, when "everything" would surely include

---

55. On Matthew's Jewishness, see for instance, John Nolland, *The Gospel of Matthew: A Commentary on the Greek Text*, NIGTC (Grand Rapids: Eerdmans, 2005) 17. On Matthew's ambiguity regarding Gentiles, cf. George B. Caird's statement: "The question of Jesus' approach to the Gentiles is yet another acute problem for the historical theologian." (*New Testament Theology*, ed. L. D. Hurst [Oxford: Clarendon, 1994] 393). Caird was speaking about the historical question concerning the continuity between the historical Jesus and the phenomenon of Gentile mission in the early Christian movement. For more on this question, see e.g., E. P. Sanders, *Jesus and Judaism: Practice and Belief, 63 BCE – 66 CE* (London: SCM, 1992). Michael Bird notes that this tension between inclusivism and exclusivism can sometimes appear side-by-side in Scripture and Second Temple literature: Isa 66:15–21; Pss. Sol. 17:22–25, 30–31; 2 Bar. 72:2–6; t. Sanh. 13:2. See his "Who Comes from the East and West? Luke 13.28-29/Matt 8.11–12 and the Historical Jesus," *NTS* 52 [2006] 450).

56. See John C. Hutchison's discussion of the common approaches to understanding Matthew's inclusion of references to Tamar, Rahab, Ruth, and Bathsheba in Matt 1:1–18 ("Women, Gentiles, and the Messianic Mission in Matthew's Genealogy," *BibSac* 158.630 [April–June 2001] 152–64). Also see Craig S. Keener, *A Commentary on the Gospel of Matthew* (Grand Rapids: Eerdmans, 1999) 78–81.

57. Theodore W. Jennings, Jr., and Tat-Siong Benny Liew ("Mistaken Identities but Model Faith: Rereading the Centurion, the Chap, and the Christ in Matthew 8:5–13," *JBL* 123 [2004] 467–94, 481) appeal to Matt 23:15 to point out that "there is little apprehension in Matthew's narrative world about the interaction between ethnic Jews and ethnic Gentiles," but perhaps go a bit further than the text when they insist that Matthew's Jesus "has no trouble associating with Gentiles" in light of 15:23–26.

58. Most scholars agree that Matthew was ethnically Jewish (e.g., Keener, *Gospel of Matthew*, 40), and Matthew's emphasis on Jewish practice has even lead some scholars to suggest that Matthew himself was not only Jewish, but also a Pharisee (Philip L. Culbertson, "Reclaiming the Matthean Vineyard Parables," *Encounter* 49 [1988] 257–58).

Jesus's teaching about doing Torah in 5:19? Such thinking prompts other scholars to see in the Great Commission less of an embrace of outsiders than an imperialistic program of conquest and domination, fodder for the later colonization of Africa and North America baptized with a thinly veiled pretext of religiosity.[59]

Indeed, Matthew abounds with positive images of Gentile outsiders. He narrates the arrival of the Magi who seek to worship the new king of Israel in a scene that many read as proleptic of the Gentile mission (2:1–12).[60] Along with the passages that commend the faith of a Roman centurion and a Canaanite woman (8:5–13; 15:21–28),[61] scholars note a positive posture towards Gentiles in the mention of a global eschatological banquet (8:11) and the exorcism of the two Gadarene demoniacs (8:28–34, though see below). Matthew also contains two citations of universalistic themes from Isaiah: from Isa 42, "He shall proclaim justice to the Gentiles," and the allusion to Isa 9 in the description of Jesus's ministry in "Galilee of the Gentiles" (12:18–19; 4:15–16). Some see hints of a Gentile mission in the kingdom parables of 21:28—22:14, especially in the reference in 21:43 to giving the vineyard, that is, the people of Israel, to an *ethnos* that produces the fruit of the kingdom.[62] Finally, there is the confession of the Roman soldiers in 27:54 ("Truly this was the son of God") and the command to love one's enemies (5:44), written virtually in the shadow of

---

59. Musa W. Dube Shomanah, *Postcolonial Feminist Interpretation of the Bible* (St. Louis: Chalice, 2000).

60. See Eugene A. La Verdiere and William G. Thompson, "New Testament Communities in Transition: A Study of Matthew and Luke," *Theological Studies* 37 (1976) 567–97; Warren Carter, "Matthew and the Gentiles: Individual Conversion and/or Systemic Transformation?" *JSNT* 263 (2004) 259–82; David C. Sims, "The Gospel of Matthew and the Gentiles," *JSNT* 57 (1995) 19–21; idem, *The Gospel of Matthew and Christian Judaism* (Edinburgh: T. & T. Clark, 1998); Schuyler Brown, "The Matthean Community and the Gentile Mission," *NovT* 22 (1980) 193–221; Donald Senior, "Between Two Worlds: Gentiles and Jewish Christians in Matthew's Gospel," *CBQ* 61 (1999) 1–23; Craig S. Keener, "Matthew's Missiology: Making Disciples of the Nations (Matthew 28:19–20)," *Asian Journal of Pentecostal Studies* 12 (2009) 3–20; Bird, "Who Comes from the East and West?" 445.

61. A number of scholars point out the interesting similarities between these two passages. Both appear to involve long-distance healings, both involve Gentiles who implore Jesus on behalf of a same-sex weaker member of their households, and both potentially underscore Jesus's hesitation about involving himself in ministry outside of the "lost sheep of the house of Israel" (10:5–6). The discussion below will explore the similarities and differences between these passages in more detail.

62. Some see evidence of a *tertius genus* motif in which Jews and Gentiles combine to form a new third race in 21:43 (Donald A. Hagner, *Matthew*; WBC [Dallas: Word, 1995] 2:623). Though the third race motif does occur in the NT (e.g., 1 Cor 10:32; Eph 2:11–15; 1 Pet 2:9), the common imagery of vineyard as a metaphor in Jewish thought and the larger context of Matthew favors an understanding that the vineyard itself is not being replaced in this parable, but only the *vinegrowers* who tend the vineyard. Thus, the parable does not anticipate a new and differently constructed people of God, but a new set of leaders for the people of God. In 21:43, *ethnos* refers to a small differentiated caste or group—here a group of leaders—as it sometimes does in other Greek literature of the period. For more on uses of *ethnos* in the period and the third race motif in Paul, see Love L. Sechrest, *A Former Jew: Paul and the Dialectics of Race* (London: T. & T. Clark, 2009). For more on vineyard imagery as a Jewish metaphor, see Culbertson, "Reclaiming the Matthean Vineyard Parables," 257–83.

devastating war and functioning as the pinnacle of altruism and the apex of Jesus's radical program of inclusiveness over the entire NT.[63]

Nevertheless, the Gospel does contain evidence of stereotypical portraits of Gentiles that combine to create more ambiguity than is often acknowledged.[64] Gentiles are ethnocentric, that is, hostile to outsiders (5:47), and they heap up empty words in prayers that vainly seek the attention of remote and distant gods (6:7).[65] Gentiles strive to accumulate empty material things (6:32), and they are known as brutal and arrogant tyrants (20:25). The saying at 7:6 about giving holy things to dogs and casting pearls to swine may possibly be a derogatory reference to Gentiles, and the command to "go nowhere among the Gentiles" in the missionary discourse explicitly excludes Gentiles from the disciples' ministry, a sentiment also reiterated in the passage about Jesus's encounter with the Canaanite woman (10:5-6; cf. 15:26).[66] Finally, in 18:17, we learn that Gentiles are stubborn, hard-hearted outsiders who refuse to bow to the will of the community. Even the context of the love command in 5:44, which towers as a pinnacle of Christian ethics promoting love of enemies and prayerful concern for one's persecutors, contains ambiguity about Gentiles by suggesting that Gentiles function as a negative foil for the Jewish righteousness commanded in it: "For if you love those who love you, what reward do you have? . . . And if you greet only your brothers and sisters, what more are you doing than others? Do not even the Gentiles do the same? (Matt 5:46-47)." While some would point to the separation of Sheep and Goats (25:31-46) as an example of an ethic of concern

---

63. Thomas E. Philips's survey of the contours of explicit love commands in the NT suggests that Matt 5:43-48 and the parable of the Good Samaritan in Luke 10:25-37 represent the clearest and least parochial statements of love for others in the NT, finding that commands to love in Revelation, the epistles, and the other Gospels are strikingly inwardly focused. My own work on the parable of the Good Samaritan suggests that it falls more into this latter category than the former, leaving Matt 5:43-48 as perhaps the lone explicit command of this type in the NT. I am grateful to Professor Phillips for allowing me to have a copy of his paper "Loving Neighbor, Loving One Another, and Loving Enemies: Three New Testament Ethics of Love," which was presented in the SBL "Ethics, Love, and the Other" Consultation in Atlanta in November 2010.

64. While many of these passages are dismissed as strange holdovers from the tradition that do not reflect Matthew's pro-Gentile viewpoint, it is true, as David C. Sims shows, that both retention of source material *and* deletion, additions, and modifications all communicate the editor's viewpoint ("Gospel of Matthew and the Gentiles," 29-30). Sims's conclusion that the Gospel of Matthew is flat out *anti-Gentile* have not proven persuasive to most Matthew scholars, foundering mainly on his inability to account for 28:19 (see Donald Senior's thorough critique in "Between Two Worlds," 1-23). His observations nevertheless do provide firm support for the fact that there is real ambiguity in the Gospel's portrait of Gentiles (cf. Schuyler Brown, "Matthean Community and the Gentile Mission"). Also see Jennings and Liew, "Mistaken Identities," 480, esp. n. 37.

65. Nolland, *Gospel of Matthew*, 284, esp. n. 307.

66. It is interesting that Schuyler Brown thinks that the context of 10:5-6 nevertheless indicates the existence of a separate or parallel (yet concurrent) Gentile mission, since 10:18 indicates that the persecution of the missionaries will be a testimony to Jews and Gentiles ("Mission to Israel in Matthew's Central Section (Matt 9:35-11:1)," ZNW 69 [1978] 73-90).

for the poor and marginalized of the world, others insist that it merely develops an inwardly focused ethic wherein Matthew holds the nations accountable for how they have treated "the little ones" in his movement.⁶⁷ What is commonly known as the "Gentile feeding narrative" in Mark 8:1–10, which symbolizes Jesus's abundant provision of salvation for the Gentiles, seems to have been moved back into Jewish territory in Matt 15:32–39.⁶⁸ Further, Jesus's encounter with the Canaanite woman in Matt 15:21–28 triggers a firestorm of protest about sexism and hierarchy and ethnic discourse.⁶⁹ Interpreters recoil at the evangelist's portrait of a woman who seems to participate in her own denigration, while other readers resent the subtle anti-Semitism that emerges when critics label Jesus's behavior as racist and then suggest that it was somehow typical of Jewish thought of the time.⁷⁰

Is the Gospel of Matthew "anti-Gentile" or "racist" in today's terms? If we find it impossible to read a passage like the Canaanite woman episode today without thinking about racism and sexism in light of hierarchical relations between groups in modern society, a judgment about the character of Matthew's Gospel would also have to account for the numerous positive and inclusive tendencies in the Gospel as well. In fact, it would be a mistake to identify Matthew as racist without carefully considering the historical and literary contexts of the Gospel of Matthew that gave rise to the ambivalence towards the outsider that we are discussing.

First consider the kinds of pressures in Matthew's historical milieu that would give rise to the negative polemics in the context. Written in the aftermath of the fall of Jerusalem in the Jewish War with Rome, Matthew participates in the ensuing debates within Judaism about the future of the people in terms of their worship, society, and leadership. Matthew's conflict with the emerging rabbinic movement in the aftermath of the war is clear in his critique of Pharisees, as they became the dominant force in the fragmented remnants of Jewish society (cf. 5:20; 21:43–45; 23:1–36).⁷¹ Since this Gospel was likely written in Syrian Antioch, the evidence sug-

---

67. Lamar Cope, "Matthew XXV:31–46 'The Sheep and the Goats' Reinterpreted," *NovT* 11 (1969) 32–44.

68. In Mark 7 Jesus invalidates food laws just prior to his encounter with the Syrophoenician woman, and in Mark 8, the second miraculous feeding of Gentiles abuts the encounter with the woman and becomes a narrative that symbolizes subsequent Gentile participation in a messianic banquet. Yet Matthew's changes to the Gentile feeding narrative in Mark 8 have so blurred the identities of the attending crowds that it is unlikely that Matthew envisioned this as a Gentile group, making it more likely that the scene functions as a climax in the mission to Israel. See J. R. C. Cousland, "The Feeding of the Four Thousand Gentiles in Matthew? Matthew 15:29–39 as a Test Case," *NovT* 41 (1999) 1–23.

69. E.g., Leticia A. Guardiola-Sáenz, "Borderless Women and Borderless Texts: A Cultural Reading of Matthew 15:21–28," *Semeia* 78 (1997) 69–81; Amy-Jill Levine, "Matthew's Advice to a Divided Readership," in *The Gospel of Matthew in Current Study* (Grand Rapids: Eerdmans, 2001) 22–41.

70. Levine "Matthew's Advice to a Divided Readership," 25.

71. W. D. Davies and Dale C. Allison, Jr., *A Critical and Exegetical Commentary on the Gospel*

gests that Matthew's community faced persecution and rejection on a second front.⁷² In the post-war period the Gentiles of that city initiated violent anti-Jewish mob action, which was followed by repeated petitions to Rome that Jews be stripped of all the civil rights that had been previously guaranteed by the Romans.⁷³

But settled in an area where the Jesus movement was already pursuing a Gentile mission, Matthew's community possibly also faced a positive pressure towards inclusivism from within the Christian movement. The book of Acts documents Syrian Antioch as the center of an energetic mission to Gentiles from dedicated missionaries who wanted the community to welcome these Gentile converts and others beside them.⁷⁴ Such associations might have increased the likelihood of opposition from the Pharisees, who might ridicule the Matthean community for being less observant and thereby prompt Matthew's stress on meticulous law observance, especially if any missionaries in the region were promoting a mission similar to the apostle Paul's, who was well known for active work among Gentiles in Antioch.⁷⁵ Thus, any Gentile mission in Matthew's community would only be able to proceed on strictly Jewish terms (5:17–20; 7:15, 22; perhaps 24:11).⁷⁶ A Matthean Gentile mission would be a

---

According to Saint Matthew, 3 vols., ICC (Edinburgh: T. & T. Clark, 1988–97) 3:692–704. According to Daniel J. Harrington, Matthew is one of three responses to the fall of Jerusalem post 70: apocalyptic Judaism (4 Ezra, 2 Baruch), Rabbinic Judaism, and Jewish Christianity (see "Polemical Parables in Matthew 24–25," *USQR* 44 [1991] 288–90).

72. Though complete certainty is impossible at this historical distance, many think that Antioch-on-the-Orontes fits the hints about provenance that emerge from the text and from other early Christian sources. Antioch was an urban center with a sizable Jewish population, and the location in Syria comports with Matthew's emphasis on locations in that region. As a known center of the mission to Gentiles in Paul's day, it would have had a population of Gentile converts. It might also be a likely place for the preservation of traditions about Peter in Matthew, given evidence that Peter was a frequent visitor there (e.g., Gal 2:11–12). Finally, some of the earliest references to the Gospel appear in the letters of Ignatius of Antioch, which, with the links between the Gospel and the *Didache*, also connect Matthew to that city. Though some are more guarded, there is wide agreement about this city as the likely location for Matthew's community. See Craig Keener, *Gospel of Matthew*, 41–42, and the scholars cited there; cf. Donald Hagner (*Matthew 1–13*, LXXV), who is a bit more cautious.

73. For a more detailed reconstruction of the situation in Syrian Antioch, see David Sims, *The Gospel of Matthew and Christian Judaism* (Edinburgh: T. & T. Clark, 1998) 166–86; and Wayne A. Meeks and Robert L. Wilken, *Jews and Christians in Antioch in the First Four Centuries of the Common Era* (Missoula, MT: Scholars, 1978) 1–54, esp. 4–5, 18. In "Matthew and Gentiles," 30–38, Sims sees evidence of this conflict with Gentiles in Matt 10:17–22; 24:4–14, and especially 24:9 ("hated by *all* nations"). Sims maintains that all but two of the prophecies in 24:4–14 contain descriptions that pertain to the community's present. Also see Warren Carter's discussion of the complicity of the Jewish leaders with the Romans and the Gospel's anti-Roman polemic in "Matthew and the Gentiles," 261–64, 271. Similarly, Warren Carter, "Resisting and Imitating the Empire: Imperial Paradigms in Two Matthean Parables," *Interp* 56 (2002) 260–72.

74. Sims, *Matthew and Christian Judaism*, 188–213.

75. Ibid.

76. Note that I discuss the *terms* of a Matthean mission and not a Matthean *antipathy* to a Gentile mission as some have suggested on the basis of 10:5–6, e.g., John P. Meier, *A Marginal Jew: Rethinking*

Torah-observant mission in its teaching and practice. Matthew's ambiguity towards Gentiles may emerge from the fact that his group faced pressure on three fronts: they faced active Gentile persecution in Antioch, hostility from Pharisees in the aftermath of the Jewish War,[77] and pressure within the Christian movement to accept local Jesus-believing Gentiles. In such a context it is no wonder that we see ambivalence in his posture towards outsiders, insisting on both Jewish priority and higher righteousness (10:5–6; 5:17–20), while at the same time embarking on a Gentile mission—but only so long as that mission is commensurate with "all that Jesus commanded" with regard to piety and practice (28:19–20).[78]

I contend that when read in light of the historical forces underlying the universalistic/ particularistic dialectic in Matthew, the love command and emphasis on forgiveness is nothing short of stunning. If Matthew's milieu was such that he and his readers were the oppressed in post-war late first-century Palestine, having been thoroughly defeated by Romans in the homeland and humiliated by Syrians in Antioch, this writer and these readers and hearers would completely understand the difficulty of enemy-love from the underside. In view of the questions with which we began, I suggest that when we imagine the fraught nature of love for one's conquerors when considering Matthew's Gospel, we also need to pose questions about what Matthew might have had in mind when he wrote about enemies. We will examine this question by looking at the rhetoric about and encounters with enemies in several passages in Matthew. Below we will briefly look at (1) animal metaphors for Gentile enemies in 7:6; (2) Jesus's encounter with the Gadarene demoniacs in 8:28–34; and (3) the healings of the centurion's boy and the Canaanite's daughter in 8:5–13 and 15:21–28. What we will see is that the depiction of Jesus's enemies in these passages

---

the Historical Jesus (New York: Doubleday, 1991) 3:544; cf. Richard Bauckham, "Forward" to James LaGrand, *The Earliest Christian Mission to "All Nations" in the Light of Matthew's Gospel* (Grand Rapids: Eerdmans, 1999).

77. The source of the persecution and hostility is debated. For instance, Schuyler Brown ("Matthean Community and the Gentile Mission," 216–17) suggests that the persecution emerged from the Jewish community and reads 10:5–6 as a concession to members of the Matthean community who were not in favor of a Gentile mission (218). Alternately, David Sims focuses on Gentile persecution in *Matthew and Christian Judaism*, 188–213.

78. Similarly, see Senior: "What I am suggesting here is that Matthew . . . was attempting to bridge more than one divide at once. First of all, he was fending off attacks about his community's essential Jewish character from other factions within the Jewish community, but with equal conviction he wanted to communicate that heritage to a new generation of Christians, Jewish and Gentile" ("Between Two Worlds," 21; cf. 18). Somewhat similar is Schuyler Brown's conclusion: "The difficulty in finding a satisfactory theological explanation for the contradiction between Jesus' restriction of the mission to 'the lost sheep of the house of Israel' (Matt 10:6) and his extension of the mission to 'all nations' (28:19) suggests that the gentile mission may have been an object of current controversy within the evangelist's community." Schuyler Brown, "Matthean Community and the Gentile Mission," 193.

functions analogously to a modern discussion of the nature of allyship, allowing us to do Christian reflection on what it means to be a loving enemy.

Gentiles, Pigs, and Dogs (7:6; 8:28–34)

Literally, the logion in Matt 7:6 advises discretion when it comes to interaction with dogs and pigs, particularly when it comes to offering them what is precious, in this case "holy things" and "pearls": "Don't give holy things to dogs, and don't throw your pearls in front of pigs. They will stomp on the pearls, then turn around and attack you" (CEB).

The verse clearly uses figurative language since it is hard to imagine scenarios in which pearls are literally offered to barnyard animals, but there is some debate about how to understand the language. Is Matthew using ethnic epithets wherein the dogs and pigs in this verse represent Gentiles? For some, the unambiguous reference to non-Jewish outsiders as dogs in Jesus's encounter with a Canaanite in 15:26–27 is decisive on this question (cf. 2 Pet 2:22), so that on this reading 7:6 contains the use of dehumanizing imagery about Gentiles.[79]

Yet it may help to proceed from surer ground to the less rocky terrain by starting with an examination of the figurative use of "pearl" since the word appears elsewhere in Matthew. In 13:44–51 three parables appear in which the center parable uses "pearl" figuratively for the kingdom of heaven (13:45, 46). If these three parables should be interpreted as a set as with other triads in Matthew, then the first two describe people who understand that the kingdom is unexpected, treasured, and costly, but the third adds that the kingdom will gather the common and unworthy alongside the joyful and discerning, until a final sorting of the evil from the righteous at the end of the age. Thus the treasure-finder of 13:44, the pearl-merchant of 13:45, and the evil and righteous of 13:49 represent people with different attitudes vis-à-vis the kingdom. If 7:6 is analogous, then we would say that the pearls in this saying represent the treasures of the kingdom and the pigs represent people with a certain negative disposition regarding the kingdom. Thus, the giving of holy things, which are parallel to the pearls in 7:6, is a way of speaking of evangelism and discipleship through the proclamation of the kingdom.[80] Didache, a well-regarded early

---

79. For a discussion about evidence that "dog" was a polemical reference to Gentiles see Vincent Taylor, *The Gospel According to St. Mark: The Greek Text with Introduction, Notes, and Indexes* (London: Macmillan, 1952) 350; contra Nolland, *Gospel of Matthew*, 634; Levine, "Matthew's Advice to a Divided Readership," 32.

80. The adjective "holy" is in the neuter in the Greek text at Matt 7:6, translated literally as "holy things." Aside from its somewhat ambiguous use in this verse, the adjective "holy" is applied to several other entities in Matthew: the Holy Spirit (neuter: 1:18, 20; 3:11; 12:32; 28:19); the holy city (feminine: 4:5; 27:53); the temple (e.g. "the holy place" [masculine]: 24:15); and holy people (masculine:

Christian text, possibly confirms this conclusion with its allusion to Matt 7:6, which would suggest that the earliest interpreters of Matt 7:6 thought that dogs and pigs in the verse referred to those outside of the Christian movement (i.e., the unbaptized): "But let no one eat or drink of your Thanksgiving (Eucharist), but they who have been baptized into the name of the Lord; for concerning this also the Lord hath said, 'Give not that which is holy to the dogs'" (Did. 9:5).

In Jewish literature pigs often function to mark that which is distinctively "un-Jewish," representing the basal measure of what is unclean. Pigs are described as unclean in the Torah (Deut 14:8; Lev 11:7) and thereby figure in narratives where abstinence from touching or eating swine is a distinctive marker of Jewish religion (Isa 65:4; cf. Isa 66:3; *Ant.* 12.253; *Ag. Ap.* 2.141; 2 Macc 6:18—7:42).[81] Given that their unclean status banned domesticated pigs from Jewish regions, swine (especially wild boars as in 2 Sam 17:8 LXX) also thus come to be associated with Gentiles, as in Matt 8:30–32.[82] First and second-century Jewish Christian texts also make explicit this association between unclean swine and those who do not worship God according to Torah:[83]

> Testament of Asher 2:8–10: Another commits adultery and fornication, and *abstains from meats*, and when he fasts he does evil, and by the power of his wealth he overwhelms many; and notwithstanding his excessive wickedness

---

27:52). Thus the grammar supports the idea that in this verse the "holy things" are those things that pertain to the Holy Spirit of God. In Matthew the Holy Spirit gives life (1:18, 20), animates ministry by anointing and affirming (3:11, 16), directs (4:1), inspires (10:20; 12:1; 22:43), and exorcises evil (8:16; 10:1; 12:28). Since the Holy Spirit is God-given, it is more likely that the giving of holy things mentioned in Matt 7:6 is a way of speaking of evangelism and discipleship through the proclamation of the kingdom.

81. Josephus, *Ant.* 12:253: "And when the king had built an idol altar upon God's altar, he slew swine upon it, and so offered a sacrifice neither according to the Law, nor the Jewish religious worship in that country. He also compelled them to forsake the worship which they paid their own God ... and made them ... raise idol altars ... and offer swine upon them every day." Josephus, *Ag. Ap.* 2:141: "For the histories say that two things were originally committed to their care by their kings' injunctions.... Accordingly, these priests are all circumcised, and abstain from swine's flesh; nor does anyone of the other Egyptians assist them in slaying those sacrifices they offer to the gods."

82. Matthew 8:30–32 (parallels in Mark 5:11–16; Luke 8:32–33): "Now a large herd of swine was feeding at some distance from them. The demons begged him, 'If you cast us out, send us into the herd of swine.' And he said to them, 'Go!' So they came out and entered the swine; and suddenly, the whole herd rushed down the steep bank into the sea and perished in the water." A similar dynamic appears at Luke 15:15–16, where a Jew's proximity to swine also adds a note of reproach and humiliation.

83. The dating and authorship of the *Testaments of the Twelve Patriarchs* is uncertain. Scholars debate whether this is a Jewish collection with Christian interpolations originally written in the first or second century BC or an essentially Christian document written sometime in the second century AD. While the larger part of the *Testament of Asher* appears to reflect Second Temple thought, some might see a Christian redaction in 7:2–3. Likewise, the Epistle of Barnabas is most likely written between the first and second Jewish Wars with Rome and is thoroughly Christian in outlook and possibly anti-Jewish at points (e.g., 4:7).

he does the commandments: this, too, has a twofold aspect, but the whole is evil. *Such men are wild pigs, hares; because they are half-clean,* but in truth they are unclean. For God in the tablets of heaven has so declared (emphasis added).

Barnabas 10:1, 3, 9–10: ¹Now, wherefore did Moses say, "Thou shalt not eat the swine, nor the eagle, nor the hawk, nor the raven, nor any fish which is not possessed of scales?" . . . Moses spoke with a spiritual reference. ³For this reason he named the swine, as much as to say, "*Thou shalt not join thyself to men who resemble swine.*" For when they live in pleasure, they forget their Lord; but when they come to want, they acknowledge the Lord. And [in like manner] the swine, when it has eaten, does not recognize its master; but when hungry it cries out, and on receiving food is quiet again. . . . ⁹Moses then issued three doctrines concerning meats with a spiritual significance; but they received them according to fleshly desire, as if he had merely spoken of meats. ¹⁰David, however, comprehends the knowledge of the three doctrines, and speaks in like manner: "Blessed is the man who hath not walked in the counsel of the ungodly . . . *and hath not stood in the way of sinners,*" even as those who *profess to fear the Lord, but go astray like swine* (emphasis added).

With respect to dog imagery, the first-century Jewish philosopher Philo describes dogs as wild animals that are vicious and ravenous (*On Giants* 1.35; *On the Decalogue* 1.114).[84] This description may make them suitable symbols of outsiders in *On the Contemplative* Life 1:40, where those who hold the Sabbath as "one of perfect holiness" (1:36) are contrasted with "others" who have raucous and rude drunken banquets:

. . . for others, when they drink strong wine . . . or even the most formidable thing which can be imagined for driving a man out of his natural reason, rage about and tear things to pieces like so many ferocious dogs, and rise up and attack one another, biting and gnawing each other's noses, and ears, and fingers, and other parts of their body, so as to give an accurate representation

---

84. *On Giants* 1.35: "Let not then our appetites rush eagerly in pursuit of all the things that are pleasant to the flesh, for the pleasures are often untameable, when like dogs they fawn upon us, and all of a sudden, change and bite us, inflicting incurable sounds. So that by cleaving to frugality, which is a friend to virtue, in preference to the pleasures akin to the body, we shall defeat the numerous and infinite multitude of irreconcilable enemies. And if any occasion should seek to compel us to take more than what is moderate or sufficient, let us not yield; for the scripture saith, 'He shall come near to him to uncover his nakedness.'" (In this case wildness is associated with the figurative enemy of immoderate cravings). *On the Decalogue* 1.114: ". . . but in this case I shall be constrained to use an entirely opposite language. You who are men, are imitators of some wild beasts. Even the beasts have learnt and know how to requite with service those who have done them service. Dogs who keep the house will defend their masters, and encounter death for their sakes when any danger suddenly overtakes them. And they say that the dogs employed among flocks of sheep will fight on behalf of the flocks, and endure till they either obtain the victory or meet with death, for the sake of protecting the shepherds themselves from injury."

of the story related about the Cyclops and the companions of Ulysses, who ate, as the poet says, fragments of human flesh.[85]

It is possible that the same thing may be going on in Ps 22:16 where the parallelism suggests that the psalmist is describing the "company of evildoers" that is encircling him like a pack of dogs (cf. Ps 59:6, 14). Moreover, sections of the second-century BC Jewish apocalyptic work 1 Enoch also exhibit this motif in the Book of Dream Visions, an animal allegorical retelling of conflicts in Israelite history where sheep represent Israelites and pigs and dogs represent Edomites and Philistines, respectively:

> And the dogs began to devour the sheep and the boars . . . until the Lord of the sheep raised up one ram from the sheep. [43] And this ram began to gore and pursue with the horns, and it charged into . . . the boars; and it destroyed many boars, and after them it injured the dogs. . . . [46] And he proceeded to it and he spoke to it alone in secret, and he raised him up into a ram and into a leader and into a leading one of the sheep; and the dogs on the basis of all these things were troubling the sheep. [47] And the first ram pursued the second ram, and he fled from his presence; then next I was observing the first ram until he fell in front of the dogs. . . . [49] And the sheep grew and were multiplied; and all the dogs . . . fled from him and were becoming frightened of him. (1 Enoch 89:42–49)

In this text both dogs and wild boars represent those who have a tendency to "trample" or to "turn and maul," and this suggests that 7:6 is not so much about dehumanizing the other as it is about issuing a warning about the danger inherent in making peace with enemies—Romans and perhaps Syrians in Matthew's case. In 7:1–5 Matthew counsels caution in making hasty judgments out of self-deception, while 7:6 warns against taking this counsel about caution in making judgments too far. Taken together, 7:1–6 instructs believers to exercise discernment when it comes to sharing the holy things of the kingdom with those who either lack the ability to discern the value of such precious treasure, or from whom one has reason to fear violence. If we have approximately described the competing tensions in Matthew's context, which reminds us that Jesus represents an oppressed, marginalized, and defeated people, it may be that this warning could also be intended as counsel for those engaged in the Gentile mission in another note of ambivalence.[86] The text

85. Similarly *Good Person* 1.90: ". . . others again having converted their barbarous frenzy into another kind of wickedness, practicing an ineffable degree of savageness, talking with the people quietly, but through the hypocrisy of a more gentle voice, betraying the ferocity of their real disposition, fawning upon their victims like treacherous dogs, and becoming the causes of irremediable miseries to them, have left in all their cities monuments of their impiety, and hatred of all mankind, in the never to be forgotten miseries endured by those whom they oppressed."

86. Similarly see Robert A. Guelich, *The Sermon on the Mount: A Foundation for Understanding*

describes a way of approaching potential friends who are or have been enemies. One must approach judiciously and carefully, lest one gets trampled and mauled, with a compassion that grows out of a rejection of self-deception (7:1–5), and with the dignity that may withhold what is precious in order to avoid further harm.

It may be that Matt 8:28–34 offers a live illustration of 7:6 in Jesus's encounter with the Gadarene demoniacs. The story represents one of Jesus's few incursions into Gentile territory in Matthew and thus is relevant to our discussion about the nature of the Christian's engagement with the other. The story describes an encounter with Gentiles and is placed virtually on the heels of Jesus's successful engagement with a Roman centurion discussed below. Instead of being greeted with faithful deference, he is confronted with demon-possessed men who live in the midst of concentrated Gentile impurity—both corpse impurity given that they live among tombs, and food impurity given that they live close to where swine are herded. The men are agitated and fiercely violent, presumably so much so that they cannot live in community (8:28). The violence of the demons that possess these men becomes apparent in the aftermath of Jesus's exorcism when the demons are transferred from the men to the herd and the animals immediately rush to their death in the sea, apparently driven to suicide by the demons.

The passage thus depicts these Gentiles as impure, unfit for community, and highly dangerous. Jesus's exorcism exposes the dangers inherent in association with Gentiles, which are alluded to in 7:6. More interesting for our purposes, the passage also raises questions about the demeanor of the Gentile community that receives Jesus's gift of healing.[87] Instead of eliciting faith, service, or gratitude (cf. 8:9–10, 13–15), this exorcism only prompts rejection in a way that shows the wisdom of the discretion counseled in 7:6. The whole town, the entire community, who have just received their own back from living among the dead, would rather reject Jesus than deal with the person who brings gifts of deliverance. What was it about Jesus that prompted such a seemingly incomprehensible response from the townspeople? There is no direct evidence in the passage that they objected to his message. Could they have focused simply on rejecting his person, in spite of the gifts that he brings? Was Jesus "not their kind" in some way, and if not, what was it about his person that

---

(Waco, TX: Word, 1982) 353; R. T. France, *Matthew*, Tyndale New Testament Commentaries (Grand Rapids: Eerdmans, 1985) 144; and Hagner (Matthew 1:171–72) who while noting the possibility that the logion prohibits the Gentile mission concludes that the caution applies to both Jewish and Gentile evangelism, where my interpretation emphasizes that this logion cautions those involved in the Gentile mission.

87. Nolland (*Gospel of Matthew*, 374) likewise suggests that the story's emphasis is on the response of the townspeople: "Matthew is not interested in the experience of the demoniacs (only in Jesus' act and the reaction of the townsfolk)."

was so objectionable? Though Jews could not be reliably differentiated from Gentiles by physical appearance, it might be that Jesus was demonstrably Jewish in his dress.[88] I suggest that there is an undertone of ethnic conflict in the story, especially as it appeared in Matthew's source in Mark with the less than subtle references to Roman legions (Mark 5:9, 10, 15, and perhaps 17a). I propose that Matthew's abbreviated version has retained these elements, though in a more attenuated and nuanced way that reveals his potentially more welcoming posture to Romans.

The story is likely an adaptation of what appears to be the parallel account in Mark 5:1–20 and may reflect Matthew's interest in communicating that one must be very careful when it comes to engaging with Gentiles. Does the single demon-possessed man of Mark that has become a pair of men in Matthew subtly insinuate that one is more likely to encounter Gentiles like these violent and possessed men than the respectful and humble individual Gentiles in 8:5–13 and 15:21–28?[89] In the final analysis it may be that Matthew wants to be clear in saying that Gentiles do not all approach Jesus with the respect and deference that characterize these two, and that the wise evangelist will do well to keep that in mind when taking the gospel to the nations.

The Centurion and the Canaanite (8:5–13; 15:21–28)

Jesus's encounters with two other Gentiles will provide additional insight on the theme of encountering enemies. There are four stories in Matthew where a parent or guardian seeks healing for a son or daughter, and in addition to the main characters there are other similarities among them (8:5–13; 9:18–26; 15:21–28; 17:14–21). For instance, the healings of the synagogue leader's daughter and the centurion's boy-child potentially involve Jesus's travel to the patient (cf. 8:7; 9:19), and the epileptic's father and the Canaanite mother both plead for mercy (cf. 17:15; 15:22). Further, there are similarities between each of them and other healing narratives in the Gospel. The centurion's child suffers paralysis as does the patient of 9:2 (cf. 8:6), and Peter's kinswoman and the leader's daughter both rise at Jesus's touch (cf. 8:15; 9:25). To my eye no two of these accounts have more in common than the healings of the centurion's boy-child (8:5–13) and the Canaanite's daughter (15:21–28).

As in the other healing narratives, both the centurion and the Canaanite ask for healing for a dependent who is not present, he for a boy-child and she for her

---

88. Jennings and Liew, "Mistaken Identities," 491 n. 59.

89. Similarly, Nolland (*Gospel of Matthew*, 375) notes that the doubling of the demon possessed characters here against Mark 5:1–20 "probably represent nothing more than an insistence that the incidents were not 'one-offs' but part of a larger pattern."

daughter.⁹⁰ Both exhibit urgency about their need for Jesus's intervention on behalf of their dependents. She repeatedly asks for help, overcoming repeated rebuffs from the disciples who want nothing but that she cease her petitions. The urgency in the centurion's speech is seen in his attitude of pleading that is accompanied by a vivid description of the boy-child's torment. What is especially striking about these two stories is that both of the supplicants are Gentile and, unlike the Gadarenes in Matt 8, they are the only Gentiles in the Gospel who have dialogue with Jesus.⁹¹ Though the epileptic's father addresses Jesus as "Lord," the fact that these two Gentiles acknowledge his Lordship and accord him dignity and authority is much more surprising (8:6; 15: 22).⁹² In fact, the particular identities of the Roman and the Canaanite raise the stakes on confessing the superiority of this wandering rabbi. The Roman represents the oppressive military force that has within living memory of the community receiving this Gospel devastated the Jewish people, temple, and

90. There is a great deal of ambiguity in the use of the word παῖς in 8:5–13. In favor of the translation "son": (1) Matthew uses *doulos* in 8:9 when the centurion describes his authority over others; (2) *pais* refers to children vs. servants in the three other times it is used in Matthew outside of the OT quotation in 12:18 (where it is "servant"): child/children (21:15); male children (2:16); son (17:18, note *huios* is used as a synonym for this person in an earlier verse). Some suggest that Matthew uses the more ambiguous term because of the possibility that the child was illegitimate due to the ban on marriage for Roman soldiers during the empire (see Jennings and Liew, "Mistaken Identities," 470–71), but this ban did not apply to officers like the centurion (D. B. Saddington, "The Centurion in Matthew 8:5–13: Consideration of the Proposal of Theodore W. Jennings, Jr., and Tat-Siong Benny Liew," *JBL* 125 [2006] 140-42, 141). Perhaps influenced by the parallel account in Luke 7:1–10, others adduce that *pais* refers to a servant (Alfred Plummer, *An Exegetical Commentary on the Gospel according to St. Matthew* [New York: Charles Scribner; London: Elliot Stock, 1909] 196), though others wonder about the "deep emotional attachment" for a slave (J. Duncan M. Derrett, "Law in the New Testament: The Syro-Phoenician Woman and the Centurion of Capernaum," *NovT* 15 [1973] 161-77, 174). Appealing to Roman military culture and a well-known use of *pais* to designate the passive partner in a same-sex relationship, Jennings and Liew suggest that the *pais* is the centurion's youthful "boy-love" in a pederastic relationship. However, D. B. Saddington questions the relevance of the authors' heavy appeal to a "love triangle" in *Tibullus* 1.1.53–58, while also pointing out that the passages they cite regarding homosexuality among centurions actually refer to rape instead of the kind of emotional intimacy proposed (Jennings and Liew, "Mistaken Identities," 467–94; Saddington, "Consideration of the Proposal of Jennings and Liew," 140–42). It is probably best to render the word "boy" in a way that captures the ambiguity as I have here and recognizes those who think that either term is possible: Derrett ("Law in the New Testament: Syro-Phoenician and Centurion," 174) says it is deliberately ambiguous; similarly R. Bultmann, *History of the Synoptic Tradition* (Oxford: Blackwell, 1968); H. F. D. Sparks, "The Centurion's παῖς," *JTS* 42 (1941) 179–80; A. J. Levine, *The Social and Ethnic Dimensions of Matthean Social History: "Go Nowhere Among the Gentiles . . ." (Matt. 10:5b)* (Lewiston: Edwin Mellen, 1988), 108, 119; Ulrich Luz, *Matthew 8–20: A Commentary*, trans. James E. Crouch (Minneapolis: Fortress, 2001) 8, 10 n. 17.

91. However, neither episode represents a Gentile mission per se, especially in view of 10:5–6. In my judgment these episodes help prepare the terms of the Gentile mission that Jesus calls for in 28:18–20 by helping the earliest disciples identify those Gentiles who will be likely to respond to the gospel.

92. Jack Dean Kingsbury, "Observations of the Miracle Chapters of Matthew 8–9," *CBQ* 40 (1978) 559–73 (566).

capital city, inflicting horrific losses that threatened to crush the very heart of the people. The Canaanite represents a different kind of enemy but one no less potent, embodying deep-rooted, longstanding, and entrenched hostility that is intertwined with a peculiar kind of intimacy that is anchored in shared life, shared land, and even shared ancestry.[93]

No doubt, this aspect of their interactions with him contributes somewhat to Jesus's commendation of them for their faith, but both go even further.[94] Even as the centurion manifests a healthy sense of his own agency, he also exhibits belief in Jesus's ability to do what he himself cannot (8:8). For her part the Canaanite exhibits extraordinary agency and persistence in the face of the disciples' overt obstructionism and Jesus's more passive distancing silence and active rebuff (15:3–5).[95] Some think that Jesus's obvious reluctance in the encounter with the Canaanite is also manifest with the centurion. Though Jesus's reluctance to engage the centurion in 8:5–13 is debated, it emerges most surely in those interpretations that understand 8:7 as a question versus a statement,[96] as seen in the difference between "Shall I come

---

93. The Canaanite addresses Jesus as Lord, as does the centurion and the epileptic's father, but she adds to her confession the idea that she sees him as "Son of David." On her lips the phrase seems to be a particularly *Israelite* appellation that alludes to the opening genealogy of Matthew, which includes a reference to another Canaanite woman (1:5). For more on the connection between the Canaanite women of the genealogy and the Canaanite woman of Matt 15:21–28, see Hutchison, "Women, Gentiles, and the Messianic Mission in Matthew's Genealogy," 152–64. See especially Levine, "Matthew's Advice to a Divided Readership," 26, 36–37. Further, we should reflect on the fact that Jesus's Canaanite ancestry problematizes the racial purity aspect of the ethnocentric message in Matt 10:5–6. Just like the findings of modern genetics that renders the idea of pure races dubious, Matthew's genealogy suggests that the icon of Judaism, the Davidic Messiah-King Jesus, is himself "mixed race."

94. Kingsbury's observation ("Observations of the Miracle Chapters," 571 n.56) that Jesus's response in these miracle stories sometimes closely parallels the language of the original request seems to hold up in this case (cf. Matt 8:8 and 13), and according to Kingsbury, helps identify these people as models of faith. It is also interesting that while the Canaanite and the centurion are both commended for their faith, the faith of the leader's father in 9:18 who believes that Jesus can restore his dead daughter to life goes unremarked. This narrative detail may give further confidence to the idea that Matthew intends a more deliberate contrast between the centurion and Canaanite stories.

95. For more on the woman's agency see Guardiola-Sáenz, "Borderless Women."

96. Almost all of the more than 160 questions in Matthew contain some word or syntactical construction that indicates the presence of a question. Of the relatively few that do not contain a marker of this kind, most are clearly questions based on the surrounding context. For instance, only nine verses without a clear word or phrase in the context result in different translations among seven major English versions: NRSV, CEB, NASB, NET, NIV, NJB, and NLT. Only in 8:7 is there a significantly different meaning in the resulting translations. Though it is more likely that 8:7 is a statement than a question (see Jennings and Liew, "Mistaken Identities," 478–80), one may, however, still detect a level of reluctance in this verse on other grounds. If 8:7 is not a question, then as Levine argues there must still be something in the verse that invites the centurion's response about not needing Jesus to actually travel to the patient in 8:8–9 ("Matthew's Advice to a Divided Readership," 30). The need to connect Jesus's statement in 8:7 with the centurion's response in 8:9 is satisfied by translating the former with a fairly common interpretation of the adverbial participle in 8:7a (*egō elthōn*) as a conditional: "If I come, I will heal him." For more on the conditional adverbial participle see Daniel B. Wallace, *Greek*

and heal him?" (NIV) and "I will come and heal him" (NRSV and many others).[97] Others see a reluctance in the use of the emphatic pronoun in 8:8 ("Shall I myself [*egō elthōn*] come . . ."), which might signal Jesus's aversion for entering Gentile territory (cf. 8:28–34) or a Gentile's domicile (cf. Acts 10:28). In any case, the Canaanite and the centurion are both enemies who reach out to Jesus for grace across the lines of profound enmity. They demonstrate their desire to be connected to Jesus and to receive his grace and mercy, overcoming understandable resistance from him in light of the past that they share with him. They are humble, respectful, and deferential. They believe Jesus, trust him, and have confidence in his ability to meet the presenting needs.

Yet there are interesting differences between these two stories, some of which will prove helpful for our consideration of Jesus's encounters with those who are enemies of the Jews. The most salient difference involves that of gender, which likely also has implications on interpretations of these scenes. The centurion is among the most powerful males in the given social context, while the Canaanite is presented as an isolated, utterly abject and helpless female, and the ways that the gender of the dependent aligns with the gender of the protector only amplifies this difference. Modern readers may be especially troubled by these differences, especially if they are correlated with the differing postures that Jesus takes vis-à-vis the man and the woman. For even if some interpreters see reluctance in Jesus's interaction with the centurion, nothing in his interaction with the centurion approaches what contemporary readers can only see as an outright scandalous exchange in his dialogue with the woman.[98] In 15:24–26 Jesus expresses his unwillingness to violate his exclusive mission to Israel in a metaphor that likens the woman and her sick child to dogs. Some interpreters try to dismiss or soften the scandal by describing the dog as a

---

Grammar Beyond the Basics: An Exegetical Syntax of the New Testament (Grand Rapids: Zondervan, 1996) 632.

97. For a defense of understanding 8:7 as a question see Amy-Jill Levine ("Matthew's Advice to a Divided Readership," 30), who says that the question "foreshadows the conversation with the Canaanite" in 15:21–28 and also offers a basis for the centurion's counterproposal in 8:8–9. Jennings and Liew ("Mistaken Identities," 482 n. 40), on the other hand, think that it is a mistake to let parallels with 15:21–28 drive the exegesis of 8:7 and ask "Why is it not equally valid to argue that Jesus' response to the centurion must parallel his . . . [receptivity] to the paralytic's friends in 9:1–7 because both sufferers are paralyzed?" My own position is that the parallels with 15:21–28 are absolutely appropriate in light of the numerous indications about Matthew's ambivalence about Gentiles as described above, so that the narrative thus invites comparisons between these two actual encounters with Gentiles and which share more similarities than any of the other healing stories considered.

98. For an extended consideration of how this text might function in a biblical approach to race and racism, see Love L. Sechrest, "The Gospel of Matthew as Anti-Racist Literature," in *Race Relations and the New Testament* (Eerdmans, forthcoming).

puppy,[99] the situation as a test of the woman's faith,[100] or teasing and/or humor in a spectacularly unfunny moment.[101] The most sensitive interpreters will agree that none of these attempts prove fully satisfactory in the end.[102]

Though we are not able to explore the many interesting issues for race relations in the episode with the Canaanite, the angle that is most salient for our purposes is the woman's response to what appears to many to be analogous to a racialized stereotype.[103] In 15:26 Jesus's characterization of Israelites as children and outsiders as dogs corresponds to the deployment of the images of swine and dogs in Matt 7:6 discussed above, and hence amounts to the construction of Gentiles as ferocious, ravening beasts like those Jesus met in 8:28–34.[104] Yet rather than trying to resist the categorization, the woman accepts the image and channels it in a way that advances her plea.[105] If it is possible to characterize this acceptance as something akin to internalized racism, a more generous understanding is that she recognizes that the label is a part of the cost of seeking a relationship with a long-time enemy. She understands that she lives in a world that she did not construct and which does not facilitate entering into the relationship she seeks. Her only way forward is to trust that Jesus's love can transform the terms of this encounter.

That a relationship is established between Jesus and these former enemies is even clearer in the episode with the centurion, who as a Roman male in the period might be viewed as one who knew himself to be entering into a patron-client

---

99. Derrett, "Law in the New Testament: Syro-Phoenician and Centurion," 163; but compare Levine, "Matthew's Advice to a Divided Readership," 32: "As feminists frequently remark, being called 'little bitch' is no improvement to being called 'bitch.'" Also note Roy A. Harrisville ("The Woman of Canaan: A Chapter in the History of Exegesis," *Interp* 20 (1966) 283), who finds no justification for reading "dog" as a house pet, since rabbinic materials see dogs as despised wild beasts.

100. E.g., Derrett, "Law in the New Testament: Syro-Phoenician and Centurion," 162.

101. Robert H. Mounce, *Matthew*, A Good News Commentary (San Francisco: Harper & Row, 1985) 153; A. H. McNeile, *The Gospel According to St. Matthew* (London: Macmillan, 1915) 31; France, *Matthew*, 247; critiqued by M. Eugene Boring, *The Gospel of Matthew*, vol. 8 of *The New Interpreter's Bible* (Nashville: Abingdon, 1994), 336 n. 343.

102. See John Nolland, *Gospel of Matthew*, 633–35, for a thoughtful discussion of the problems in this text.

103. For more on this passage and the woman's apparent internalization of a negative stereotype see Sechrest, "Gospel of Matthew as Anti-Racist Literature."

104. Note that while the available data does not support a conclusion that "dog" was a common stereotype for Gentiles in the period, this construction does appear valid within the narrative world of Matthew; cf. Nolland, who notes that dogs function as a negative metaphor for Gentiles in later rabbinic materials, rightly disputing the idea that the imagery is a common one for Gentiles in that period (*Gospel of Matthew*, 634). This same tactic is implicit in my discussion about the imagery, though Nolland neglects to reckon with how the imagery functions in Matthew (e.g., in considering 7:6; 8:28–34; and 15:21–28 together) as I do here.

105. On the way that the woman uses trickery to accomplish her goal, see Guardiola-Sáenz, "Borderless Women."

relationship on the basis of the request for healing.[106] If patronage is what happens in Roman culture when people seek extraordinary resources from individuals who possess them or control access to them, then the centurion's decision to approach a leader from a despised religious sect is remarkable from the soldier's viewpoint as well as the Lord's perspective.[107] There is no explicit mention or detail that would suggest that the centurion saw himself as Jesus's social equal, and on the contrary, his use of the word "Lord" constitutes an acknowledgement of Jesus's superior power as a patron. When the centurion calls attention to the ways in which he and Jesus both command power, it demonstrates his understanding of the honor owed to a superior, even as he begs for grace as a client on behalf of someone for whom he has both responsibility and affection.[108]

Perhaps the most important difference between the two episodes for our purposes is the difference in the kind of enemies the two represent. He is a more recent enemy, and though he clearly has associations with the then-recent violence with Rome, she is from a people with a longstanding record of hostility and strife. If there are any differences in the level of tension with which Jesus greets the two supplicants, it may be connected to the fact that it is sometimes easier to reconcile with a new enemy than to make peace with one with whom one shares a centuries-long fraught and complicated history of aggression. Perhaps that is why there is also a slight difference in the commendations that they receive from Jesus: his is a faith that was not seen elsewhere in Israel, but her faith and humility are great and exemplary of those who are called greatest in the kingdom of heaven (15:28; cf. 18:1–4).

Loving the Other: Neighbors, Allies, Foes, and "Frenemies"

As we seek a synthesis between our consideration of the interaction between Jesus and his enemies in Matthew and our earlier review of the concept of allyship, we have seen the importance of Jesus's framework of love for enemies established in 5:43–48, as well as his caution regarding the approach to enemies in 7:6. We are attempting to imagine ourselves in the posture of those who began as enemies toward Jesus in the Gospel of Matthew, either through their own circumstances or through the intrusion of the history of nations, a history that can and often does transform

---

106. Jennings and Liew, 483, though I do not side with them regarding the implications they draw about the centurion's fears that Jesus would expect sexual favors from the *pais* (484; see Saddington's rebuttal). However, they rightly conclude that the Gospel has ample evidence that Jesus himself had no interest in such a power arrangement (486–88).

107. David A. DeSilva, *Honor, Patronage, Kinship, and Purity: Unlocking New Testament Culture* (Downers Grove, IL: InterVarsity, 2000) 96.

108. Ibid., 95–119.

one-on-one interactions into intergroup tension. Accordingly, in trying to take our cues about enemy-love from the depiction of these characters in the Gospel, we find that the Gadarenes, the centurion, and the Canaanite represent various possible ways of entering into a discussion of allyship. Of course, these stories are first and foremost about how these outsiders encountered and demonstrated faith in the Son of the God of Israel. Still, in remembering that Jesus was a Jew and thus from a people who had experienced oppression from some and conflict with others, we can also model our approach in the modern world on analogy with theirs when it comes to approaching those in our communities who have previously experienced violence and oppression.

The centurion and the Canaanite illustrate what it might look like to be loving enemies or allies, while the episode with the Gadarenes demonstrates the importance of discernment in undertaking this work. In seeking to find and be allies, it is important to remember that, stereotypes notwithstanding, individual members from groups with whom there is or has been conflict will vary in terms of their willingness and capacity for relationship. Some like the centurion and the Canaanite will have the character and awareness of their own history and identity so as to inhabit humility and demonstrate love, while others like the Gadarenes will be resistant, inhospitable, and callous. In this vein we can take note of the fact that in the two healing stories the faith of the boy and girl who need healing was irrelevant and that it was the faith of those who acted on their behalf who provided the crucial link, which is yet another way of recognizing the important contributions and limitations of individual agency and group identity.[109] The humility of these allies stands out, and though their unusual deference to Jesus was first and foremost rooted in their recognition of his status as the Messiah of Israel and theirs as outsiders, it is not too much of a stretch to imagine that their understanding of their social history also played a part in their demeanor. The narrative world of the Gospel of Matthew makes this possibility more likely given the clarity of Jesus's mission to Israel (15:24; 10:5–6). Here we get hints of some of the same issues that drive the literature on allyship. Allies start with the recognition of one's own identity and social location, they adopt a posture of humility by acknowledgement of one's own shortcomings (8:8a), they exercise agency by foregrounding urgent and necessary action (15:22–27), and they return to work among their own people as a key ingredient in forming relationships with the other. Above all, these exemplary allies exhibited full confidence in Jesus's ability to do what was needed because they knew who he was. Analogously, Christians need to recognize that communities of color are endowed by their Creator with all the resources of agency and co-regency in creation when it comes to

---

109. Derrett, "Law in the New Testament: Syro-Phoenician and Centurion," 183.

leading work that participates with Christ in bringing justice and healing to earth as it is in heaven. Good allies will trust in these God-given talents instead of succumbing to narratives of imputed inferiority and stereotypes.

Our discussion of these texts also examined the differences in the depictions of these enemies, and these distinctions will also be fruitful for our construction of the nature of Christian allies. We have already noted that Matthew reveals that we can expect some with deference and honor will invite the creation of community, while others will prove dangerous and prejudiced. We have also noted differences in engaging enemies that are directly related to the intensity and proximity of the opposition. Romans are intense but recent enemies to Jews, and Canaanites are longstanding, bitter enemies from the past, while Gadarenes might represent the local active hostilities that Matthew's community might have faced in Syrian Antioch. Accordingly, it is possible to see in each of these narratives a different way of being a biblically shaped ally. We will discuss "neighbors," "allies," "foes," and "frenemies" in light of these and other texts.

We see in the Roman the "neighbor" who represents allyship among communities of color, an area that we saw was underdeveloped in the literature on allies. The centurion exhibits a respectful demeanor when he engages Jesus, and one exposition of the centurion's situation can help us to see how we may envision this as a posture that helps communities of color ally with others who are oppressed. According to Robert Bertram the centurion's situation involves a problem with autonomy, unworthiness, and co-enslavement, and each of these circumstances adheres when neighbors enter into allyship with other people of color.[110] Like other disadvantaged communities, neighbors experience diminished capacity with respect to their autonomy because of the effects of racism and other forms of discrimination. Just as the centurion experienced the limits of his autonomy when he was unable to relieve the boy's pain and was driven to seek help, so too must people of color learn to develop alliances with others who understand something of the pain of disenfranchisement and constraint. The literature on allyship is by and large focused on white antiracist identity construction and abounds with an emphasis that whites who wish to be allies to blacks and other people of color must first overcome the invisibility of whiteness and grow an awareness of how their identities have been racialized as white. Here we emphasize that something analogous is also necessary for the Christian "neighbor" who as a person of color also needs to learn about the nature and processes of racialization experienced by other oppressed communities. Like whites and as exemplified by the centurion of Matt 8, neighbors must acknowledge

---

110. Robert W. Bertram, "The Complete Centurion," *Concordia Theological Monthly* 39.5 (1968) 311–27.

their "unworthiness" regarding the experiences of others, by learning through research and interpersonal contact about their particular experiences of oppression. As neighbors who relate in line with the demeanor of Matthew's centurion, they too will take their agency in hand and act in a manner that befits the urgency to relieve the suffering of those with whom they are co-enslaved. Like all allies, however, they will be characterized by epistemic humility. When it comes to issues that directly affect the communities with whom they want to ally, they will acknowledge the superior knowledge in these communities and follow their lead, doing unto others just as they would want others to act towards themselves.

The Canaanite represents the white "ally" who is the subject of most of the scholarship on white antiracist identity development. The Canaanite is the perennial enemy of the Jewish people just as whites occupy that position vis-à-vis people of color and especially blacks. In light of the wider narrative in Matthew, the Canaanite helps establish the truth found in contemporary race relations that it is virtually impossible to live in isolation and that one's enemy always constrains one's life in some way or another. Indeed, the author of the Gospel did not or could not even describe Jesus's ancestry without having to talk about Canaanites. It is quite possible that the protracted and entangled history of conflict between Canaanites and Jews bears on the woman's portrait in the Gospel.[111] My guess is that her submissiveness and respectfulness is even more pronounced than the centurion's because issues of trust come to the forefront, and similar considerations will complicate interactions between white antiracist activists and especially African Americans. The woman's position of profound humility and lowliness out of the spotlight is an acknowledgment that the world is not structured in a way that typically makes room for her needs and desires. She knows that her reception by Jesus is bound up in the history of conflict

---

111. Matthew's changes to the earlier, milder version of the episode in Mark 7:24–30 remove several features that in Mark communicate a greater welcome to Gentiles. Matthew eliminates Mark's mention that Jesus actually enters a Gentile home and possibly eats there by placing the meeting outside, after she has come out to him to make her request (cf. Mark 7:19; Matt 15:17–20). Just prior to the passage in Mark 7, Jesus invalidates food laws, and afterwards the miraculous feeding of Gentiles in Mark becomes a narrative that symbolizes Gentile participation in a messianic banquet. Yet Matthew's version of this feeding narrative from Mark 8 has blurred the identities of the attending crowds so that it is unlikely that Matthew envisioned this as a Gentile group. Matthew also deletes the phrase from Mark 7:27 "Let the children be satisfied first," removing the implication from the Marcan account that Gentiles will eventually receive the benefits of Jesus's mission. Matthew changes Mark's identification of this woman from "Syro-Phoenician" to "Canaanite," which identifies her as an archenemy of the ancient Israelites. The woman's response in Matthew is more submissive, with her references to the "master's table" (Matt 15:27; cf. Mark 7:28), and her explicit confession that Jesus is Lord (Matt 15:22; cf. Mark 7:26). In Matthew, Jesus initially refuses even to acknowledge her request and possibly even her presence. When finally consenting to respond to her in 15:26, Jesus implies that the woman and all such Gentiles are dogs who should not receive the blessings reserved for the house of Israel.

between their peoples. Likewise, white antiracists must learn what it means to be imprisoned by stereotypes of white bigotry that, while damaging, represent only the merest fraction of the material, emotional, and spiritual harm endured by those wounded by institutional racism. White allies like the Canaanite must squarely face the lack of trust and conflict bequeathed on them by history, but must nonetheless dare to imagine the new creation that Jesus represents. This work demands the cultivation of a character that imitates their Lord, where they do "not wrangle or cry aloud, nor will anyone hear [their] voice in the streets" (Matt 12:19–20). They listen and learn, and like the Canaanite, they engage deeply with what the oppressed say, even when it hurts. "When criticized or called out, allies listen, apologize, act accountably, and act differently going forward."[112] In solidarity with those who have no respite from racism and prejudice, allies are endlessly persistent and refuse to back down, take breaks, or retreat back into privilege.[113]

In Matthew's version of the conflict at Gadara the exorcized men and the townspeople represent "foes" in the work of social justice. Though it is clear that Jesus loves these people as he has loved any in the narrative, sharing the mercy of God with them in freeing them from their oppression, these people prove by their own actions that they are not as yet ready for community. The exorcism of the demon-possessed Gentiles in Gadara serves as an illustration of the warning against offering holy things and pearls to those with volatile tempers or destructive tendencies in 7:6. The demons leave the men, enter a herd of pigs, and drive the herd to their deaths, which powerfully reveal the forces that may be unleashed when attempting to establish relationships with former enemies in the arena of race relations. I think that this is especially true of our context in which racism can well be compared to a spiritual power of evil that exercises control beyond the ken of a single individual as it inhabits institutions and cultures, blanketing our society like smog.[114] When Jesus breaks off contact with this inhospitable and isolationist community, it is a decision that they ultimately bring on themselves.

We cannot end this consideration of Jesus's enemies in Matthew without an abbreviated look at the Pharisees, the group with whom he has the most intense conflict of all. However, the Pharisees are better described as "frenemies," enemies that one finds right in one's own household, rather than those typifying encounters with the ethnic other.[115] Though it is beyond the scope of this paper to examine the

112. Utt, "So You Call Yourself an Ally."

113. Ibid.

114. Beverly Tatum Daniels (*Black Kids in the Cafeteria*) describes racism as a smog that affects everyone in a racialized society.

115. For more information on the nature of the sibling-rivalry-like conflict between Jesus and the Pharisees see E. P. Sanders's *Judaism: Practice and Belief.*

numerous interactions between the Pharisees and Jesus in Matthew, we will keep with the theme of animal metaphors and touch on the three passages where Jesus calls the Pharisees "snakes" and a "brood of vipers" (3:7-12; 12:34; 23:33).

In biblical and postbiblical literature, snakes and other serpents function to signal sin (Gen 3:1-15), deception (4 Macc 18:8), and death by virtue of being poisonous. In the Testament of Abraham, the true, frightening appearance of death uses vivid viper and other snake imagery, while other texts combine these motifs.[116] For instance, Sirach 21:2 combines poisonousness with sin ("Flee from sin as from a snake; for if you approach sin, it will bite you . . . and can destroy human lives"). In Ps 58:3-4 the venom of the snake is a metaphor for the lies of wicked sinners (cf. Ps 140:3). Thus when Matthew introduces the Pharisees in 3:7-12 by calling them a brood of vipers, he is describing them as conveyors of the poison of deception, sin, and death, a characterization that shares some of the characteristics of the Gadarenes. They are told that they must produce fruit of repentance in word and deed (3:8; 12:34), exhortations that echo the emphasis on reflection and action in the literature on building alliances. Matthew's Pharisees are hypocrites who teach one thing but do another (23:3) and seem to care only about status and the accoutrements of religious status: fringes, phylacteries, good seats, and fancy titles (23:2-3, 5-12). Possibly they are puffed up and puff themselves up, forgetting that we are all brothers and sisters under God (23:5-12). Instead of a clear-eyed vision of their posture vis-à-vis the emerging Christian movement, the Pharisees rely on their ancestry and completely miss the opportunity present in the historical moment (3:9; cf. 23:30-33). The Pharisees are the "frenemies" represented by the vast majority of white Christians who remain in blissful ignorance about the suffering and oppression experienced by their brothers and sisters of color in Christ. Rather than build a problematic analogy between contemporary white bigotry and the ancient Pharisaic precursors of modern Rabbinic Judaism, I would rather reflect on the way that Jesus and the Pharisees were bound together in deeply engaged debate about issues that mattered. Would that the debate about race relations in the church mimicked Jesus and the Pharisees, where they could not escape the other in real life, and where

---

116. *T. Ab.* 17.12-14: "Then Death put off all his comeliness and beauty, and all his glory and the form like the sun with which he was clothed, and put upon himself a tyrant's robe, and made his appearance gloomy and fiercer than all kinds of wild beasts, and more unclean than all uncleanness. And he showed to Abraham seven fiery heads of serpents and fourteen faces, (one) of flaming fire and of great fierceness, and a face of darkness, and a most gloomy face of a viper, and a face of a most terrible precipice, and a face fiercer than an asp, and a face of a terrible lion, and a face mixed and snake-like." Cf. *T. Ab.* 19.14-15: "I showed you also the poisonous wild beasts, asps and basilisks, leopards and lions and lions' whelps, bears and vipers, and in short the face of every wild beast I showed thee, most righteous one, because many men are destroyed by wild beasts, and others by poisonous snakes, serpents and asps and cerastes and basilisks and vipers, breathe out their life and die."

each is constantly testing the ideas of the other, desperately fixated on understanding God's will for the whole community.

Conclusion

In this consideration of Matthew's depiction of enemies, we began with a tentative reconstruction of Matthew's social location in order that we might properly contextualize the depictions of those who were Jesus's enemies. By using the most common associations regarding the probable setting for Matthew's composition in post-war Syrian Antioch, we were able to identify at least three social pressures operating at that time of the Gospel's composition: Gentile persecution from Romans and Syrians, both remembered and locally active; hostility from Pharisees in the aftermath of the Jewish War; and internal pressure to welcome local Jesus-believing Gentiles. We imagined that these pressures might well have given rise to Matthew's ambivalence about Gentiles, sometimes describing them positively and leaning in to the idea of a Gentile mission, and sometimes describing them in negative terms, likening them to vicious animals and exhorting a more careful and distant posture. We then examined the postures of various enemies depicted in Matthew. We saw the blinded and recalcitrant Pharisees as "frenemies" within the household of faith, and the violent Gadarenes who are forever frozen in our minds as demon-possessed, violent, unpredictable, and inhospitable "foes" of social justice. We considered the thoughtful centurion, who actively engages with Jesus on behalf of a valued friend as a "neighbor" to other oppressed communities, and we described the strategic Canaanite who as an "ally" acknowledges that the world is not structured in a way that makes room for her needs and desires, but who nonetheless dares to imagine the new creation that Jesus represents.

The goal of allyship is not for people in privileged groups to be shamed, punished, or retaliated against but to eliminate the conditions that dehumanize us all, to restrain evil in our midst, and to seek our common good.[117] Each and every one of us needs to be able to see what and who have been previously invisible as we cautiously move towards inhabiting the kinds of relationships that give honor to the gospel, risking pain but persisting in our desire to build the beloved community. Regarding movements towards justice, it has been said that the powerful will not willingly lay down their power, but this reticence should not be true of those who follow the crucified Savior.[118]

---

117. Goodman, *Promoting Diversity*, 123.

118. Reinhold Niebuhr, *Moral Man and Immoral Society: A Study in Ethics and Politics* (New York: Scribner, 1960) 34; Martin Luther King Jr., *The Papers of Martin Luther King, Jr.*, ed. Clayborne Carson et al., (Berkeley: University of California Press, 1992) 4:127.

RESPONSE TO SECHREST

Rebecca Gonzalez

What I heard as I perused Love Sechrest's paper on loving the other was an invitation. It was not the first time I have received this invitation—I have perceived it, acknowledged it, and accepted it many times before. The first time I received this invitation I was sitting in a pew, and the response appeared as a taste-test of juice and bread. I came to realize the invitation was a sacrament, a time of worship to remember the sacrifice Christ bore for my sins. As an adult I realized my impressions as a child and a young adult were not at all wrong but were merely the start in coming to understand the depth of the invitation that originated when Jesus instituted the Last Supper, the invitation in Matt 26:17–30.

This invitation was not just to partake of the Lord's Supper; it was to come, sit, and partake of the communion table. To engage, to contribute, to enjoy, to listen, to hear, to feel, to see, to taste, to grow, to bless, to be enlightened, to love, to forgive, to honor, to serve, to receive, and through it all be reconciled and be part of community—Communion, reconciliation, community. At the Communion table there is communication of a promise or need, there is confession of shortcomings or unwavering grace and mercy, and there is a conversion of the heart or the soul. Communication, confession, and conversion are what Sechrest's manuscript affirms as the elements that must take place in order for one to be able to fulfill God's commandment of loving your enemy, as depicted in Matt 5:44.

We see these three components in the healing of the Canaanite's daughter and the servant of the centurion. As Sechrest indicates, these two Gentiles were the only "two to dialogue with Jesus"—here we see communication. Both reached out to "Jesus for grace across the lines of profound enmity" and "show their desire to be connected to him," thus confession. Then we witness conversion: "they are humbled, respectful and deferential"; "they trust Jesus," "have confidence in his ability to meet the presenting needs," and were healed.

An additional component I would like to highlight in these two Gentiles is their disposition and the manner in which they choose to exercise their will. To respond to the invitation, to exercise communion, to commit to community and to love our enemies is dependent on our will, posture, inclination, and resolve. It is our choice; it starts with me.

Though Communion at church in the company of believers is sacred and has its own unique purpose, can we challenge our paradigms to believe that this act of worship, reflection, sanctification, transformation, and reconciliation can also be embodied each time we accept the invitation to engage with others—to love others, exercise "enemy-love," enter into community, and love mercy and do justice"?

When Sechrest shares the steps "for doing the work of social justice allies" or engaging in "antiracist activist development," she is really inviting us to exercise Communion within our everyday context. Many of her expressions are elements that permeate this sacred act of worship: "ownership of one's identity as a racial being," "theory that explores the psychological, intellectual, moral, and material costs to whites of racism," "gaining knowledge about oppression through formal and informal educational experiences and interpersonal relationships," "take action in their own communities," and "humility." Or, is it that God, our faith, and our beliefs begin to permeate who we are and our everyday life, and being an ally is not just about doing but also about being?

I must admit that because of my culture and heritage I have witnessed and experienced racism first hand from individuals in the white community, but I have also experienced discrimination among people of ethnic communities, and at times even my own race, culture, and family. The dynamics of Communion and the invitation to be allies must be applied wherever power and privilege have allowed for "the other" to be dehumanized and injustice has dominated relations.

As depicted in Sechrest's essay, whether allies, neighbors, foes, or frenemies, this invitation is for you. This invitation is for all of us. We chose to be here. Actually, I can confidently state that just by being here we have already accepted the invitation. We have come to the table of Communion, we have come to be reconciled, and we have come to enter into community. Let us abandon our post, our comfort zone, and our paradigms, and let us enter into communication with God and with each other. Let us confess our faults to God and to each other, and may we all be converted, transformed, and renewed in God's presence and in the presence of each other.

Let us as Sechrest stated, "squarely face the lack of trust and conflict bequeathed" and "dare to imagine the new creation that Jesus represents," the "beloved community."

THE LYNCHING OF THE SUFFERING SERVANT OF ISAIAH: DEATH AT THE HANDS OF PERSONS UNKNOWN

Bo H. Lim

Theological Interpretation, Race, and Reading Isaiah 53 as Christian Scripture

In this paper I provide a theological reading of Isa 52:13—53:12 (hereafter referred to simply as Isa 53). This well-known passage describes the ignominious affliction and death of an anonymous person deemed Yahweh's servant, and therefore this figure is often referred to as the suffering servant. Given that I describe his fate as a lynching, and lynching is obviously anachronistic for an ancient Israelite prophetic text, it behooves me first to provide an explanation for how such a reading is theological.

As a biblical scholar I identify with the movement known as the theological interpretation of Scripture that has gained much support in theological and biblical studies in the past two decades. This line of inquiry had just begun to blossom as a distinct field of study while I was in graduate school. I was schooled in theological interpretation, and I joined a biblical studies faculty where all of us are committed to this practice of reading Scripture.[1] Kevin Vanhoozer and Stephen Fowl, leading voices in this discipline, have been influential to me; Kevin as a professor and Stephen as a colleague, even while they share differing views on the subject.[2] Daniel Castelo and I have just published a commentary in a series devoted to the theological interpretation of the OT.[3]

Yet, even though I am a card-carrying member of theological interpretation, I continue to experience dissonance with this discipline. In addition to the theological interpretation group, at the annual Society of Biblical Literature meeting I will

---

1. See Robert W. Wall and David R. Nienhuis, eds., *A Compact Guide to the Whole Bible: Learning to Read the Scripture's Story* (Grand Rapids: Baker Academic, 2015).

2. See D. Christopher Spinks, *The Bible and the Crisis of Meaning: Debates on the Theological Interpretation of Scripture* (New York: T. & T. Clark, 2007).

3. Bo H. Lim and Daniel Castelo, *Hosea*, Two Horizons Old Testament Commentary (Grand Rapids: Eerdmans, 2015).

typically attend sessions on Asian-American interpretation, the formation of Isaiah, the exile and forced migration, and minoritized criticism. Many scholars within these study groups are openly opposed to theological interpretation as a discipline. At times I find myself wondering what distinguishes papers in the theological interpretation sessions from presentations in other study groups. I have asked myself what qualifies an interpretation of the Bible as theological and what disqualifies it from this designation? I have often wondered what distinguishes theological interpretation from "contextual" readings of the Bible, another field of study that has grown tremendously in recent years.[4] Once I gave a homily on what I considered an Asian-American Reading of Isaiah and my colleague's comment, "That was deeply theological," took me by surprise since in my mind I was engaging in "contextual" interpretation rather than theological interpretation.

I also find the range of topics engaged by practitioners of theological interpretation narrow in scope and at times disconnected from my intellectual and pastoral concerns. Not a single article in the *Journal of Theological Interpretation* is devoted to race or racism, and the *Dictionary for the Theological Interpretation of the Bible* contains a rather thin two-page entry on racism.[5] Currently, if one is interested in the question of how the Bible addresses race and racism, one does not look to theological interpreters for resources. This phenomenon is unsurprising when I am repeatedly one of the few nonwhite males at sessions on theological interpretation at SBL. I suspect some skeptics view theological interpretation as a cipher for white, conservative, male, Christian interpretation. One of the tenets of theological interpretation is to read Scripture with and for the church. Suspicions are warranted when this line of inquiry translates into readings resourced solely by white influences and intended for a white audience, even though the church past and present is far more diverse. While I do not reduce the task of interpretation to the above mentioned factors, I do think it is important to acknowledge that biblical scholars are embodied persons who operate in particular social contexts driven by economic interests. Their work inevitably fails to address the needs and concerns of those who do not inhabit the same social contexts.

The differences in nomenclature demonstrate that the crux of the matter lies in how one defines theology and the task of interpretation. I intend to outline why reading Isa 53 as the lynching of the suffering servant is theological. I am certainly not claiming my reading ought not be classified as a "contextual" interpretation or

---

4. By "contextual" I refer to a multiplicity of hermeneutical approaches that take into consideration the social, economic, and political forces at work in the interpretation of the Bible among varied audiences.

5. Hugo Magallanes, "Racism," *Dictionary for Theological Interpretation of the Bible*, Kevin J. Vanhoozer, ed. (Grand Rapids: Baker Academic, 2005) 657–58.

another designation. Reading Isa 53 in this manner is not novel; many have proposed reading Isa 53 in light of varying social contexts, although they may not have claimed to be doing theological interpretation. My intention in doing so is to expand the scope of theological interpretation among its current practitioners by reading the text according to their assumptions.

In my reading of Isa 53 as the lynching of the suffering servant I make the following theological and hermeneutical assumptions. First, the normative reading is not the historical reading but rather the literary and canonical reading since that horizon is understood by the people of God to be revelatory and authoritative. Second, Scripture's function is understood within its role within the divine economy. In the divine economy, Scripture mediates Trinitarian relationships, informs the identity and mission of Jesus, and mediates God's presence to the people.[6] Third, because Christ is central and fundamental to the divine economy, Scripture must be interpreted in light of Christ's person and work of salvation. Biblical scholars typically eschew such assumptions since they are often viewed as constraints to their research because they predetermine interpretation and minimize the contribution of biblical criticism. Such seemingly overly-determined readings diminish the contribution of biblical scholars, since it is they who specialize in unearthing the literal or plain sense of the text. Yet I would argue that theological interpretation need not and ought not eviscerate the importance of the plain sense. The plain sense of Scripture, while not functioning as the sole meaning of Scripture, does provide a norm that regulates its reception by Christian communities throughout the ages.[7] Theological readings are extensions of the plain sense as Moberly describes, "Development is characteristically expressed in terms of *realizing the implications* of the original, or *determining what is compatible* with it."[8] My task then is to demonstrate that reading Isa 53 as a lynching is compatible with the plain sense of the text, and that it attends to the three dimensions of theological interpretation that I have outlined.

The Theological Meaning of Lynching

Theological interpretation involves reading Scripture in light of the work of Christ's salvation, and therefore this reading of Isa 53 finds its foundation in the crucifixion of Christ. For many Americans the lynching tree provides the means to understand

---

6. Telford Work, *Living and Active: Scripture in the Divine Economy of Salvation* (Grand Rapids: Eerdmans, 2001); Brevard S. Childs, *Isaiah*, OTL (Louisville, KY: Westminster John Knox, 2001) 423; Murray Rae, "Texts in Context: Scripture and the Divine Economy," *JTI* 1 (2007) 23–45.

7. See John Barton, *The Nature of Biblical Criticism* (Louisville, KY: Westminster John Knox, 2007).

8. R. W. L. Moberly, *Old Testament Theology: Reading the Hebrew Bible as Christian Scripture* (Grand Rapids: Baker Academic, 2013) 161, author's emphasis.

more profoundly the significance of the cross. Philip Dray observes, "To antilynching reformers, Jesus was the 'first lynchee,' the prototypical victim of mob violence born to his fate by a cruel and uncomprehending society."[9] This understanding of Christ is found in Countee Cullen's "The Black Christ," which equates the cross with the lynching tree:

> Somewhere the Southland rears a tree,
>
> (And many others there may be
>
> Like unto it, that are unknown,
>
> Whereon as costly fruit has grown).
>
> It stands before a hut of wood
>
> In which the Christ himself once stood -
>
> And those who pass it by may see
>
> Nought growing there except a tree,
>
> But there are two to testify
>
> Who hung on it . . . we saw Him die.
>
> Its roots were fed with priceless blood.
>
> It is the Cross; it is the Rood.[10]

Du Bois' short story, "The Son of God," ends with the lynching of Joshua, the Black Christ figure, and his mother Mary exclaiming, "Behold the Sign of Salvation—a noosed rope."[11] In this story Mary also quotes from Isa 53:3 to describe her son, "He is despised and rejected of men, A man of sorrows and acquainted with grief."[12] James Cone argues that the lynching tree ought to be central to an American theology of the cross: "The lynching tree—so strikingly similar to the cross on Golgotha—should have a prominent place in American images of Jesus' death. But it does not. In fact, the lynching tree has no place in American theological reflections about Jesus' cross or in the proclamation of Christian churches about his Passion."[13]

For Cone, any failure to associate lynching with the cross reflects a defective theology rather than any dissimilarity between the analogues. Within the historical

---

9. Philip Dray, *At the Hands of Persons Unknown: The Lynching of Black America* (New York: Random House, 2002) 80.

10. Countee Cullen, *The Black Christ & Other Poems* (New York: Harper & Brothers, 1929) 110.

11. W. E. B. Du Bois, "The Son of God," *Crisis* 40 (1933) 277.

12. Ibid.

13. James H. Cone, *The Cross and the Lynching Tree* (Maryknoll: Orbis, 2011) 30. Cone critiques Reinhold Niebuhr, who was known for his realism, for his failure to make this connection: "Niebuhr was a Christian theologian of the cross who knew all about Jesus' solidarity with the poor and the consequences he suffered for that from the Roman Empire. . . . How could Niebuhr make the tragedy of the cross the central theme in his theology while ignoring the obvious tragedies of slavery, segregation, and lynching in the United States?" (63).

context of the United States, the lynching tree provides the means for Americans to grasp more fully the theology of the cross.

The vital connection between Isa 53 and Jesus's crucifixion is well established within Christianity. Isaiah 53 is the single text most often quoted or alluded to by NT authors and the reading the Common Lectionary assigns for Good Friday. Hermeneutically, Isa 53 and lynching both provide a means of interpreting the events of Christ's passion and death. In this case, both lynching and Isa 53 are anachronistic with Jesus's crucifixion; Christ's followers made these associations post-Easter so one need not establish authorial intent to legitimize this interpretation.[14] Privileging the Christ event fulfills one of the criteria of theological interpretation—Christ serves as the hermeneutical lens from which to read texts. The suffering servant and lynching need not be equated, but each finds correlation with the passion and death of Jesus. Their connection to Christ allows for descriptions of lynching and the suffering servant to gloss each other to produce a theological interpretation of Isa 53. It is this triangulation of Christ, Isa 53, and lynching that informs my reading of Isa 53. Do Isa 53 and lynching possess equal authority in interpreting the person and work of Christ? No, Scripture is elected in the divine economy to serve a special role. Yet to the extent that lynching finds correlation with the plain and canonical sense of Isaiah, it can serve as a theological extension of their meaning.

Reading Isaiah 53 as a Lynching

Harlem Renaissance figures like DuBois, Cullen, and Hughes are well known for their ambivalence or rejection of Christianity, so I recognize that some might object to my appropriation of their poetry for a theological reading of Scripture. Yet I would argue that exact analogues are not required for typologies in theological interpretations of Scripture. For example, while Isa 53 repeatedly describes the servant as possessing physical infirmities, the repeated NT references to this passage never describe Christ in this manner but rather identify him as the healer of infirmities.[15] Many victims of lynchings were culpable of some form of transgression,[16] whereas

14. Whether or not Jesus understood his vocation in terms of Isa 53 continues to be a matter of debate. See William H. Bellinger and William R. Farmer, eds., *Jesus and the Suffering Servant: Isaiah 53 and Christian Origins* (Harrisburg: Trinity Press International, 1998); and Bernd Janowski and Peter Stuhlmacher, eds., *The Suffering Servant: Isaiah 53 in Jewish and Christian Sources* (Grand Rapids: Eerdmans, 2004).

15. See Jeremy Schipper, *Disability and Isaiah's Suffering Servant* (Oxford: Oxford University Press, 2011) 72–73.

16. I am well aware that many lynching victims were not entirely innocent of the charges brought against them. It was primarily blacks who resisted white domination who were the victims of lynching. See Kidada E. Williams, "Resolving the Paradox of Our Lynching Fixation: Reconsidering Racialized Violence in the American South after Slavery," in *Lynching Reconsidered: New Perspectives in the*

Isaiah's servant is described as entirely innocent of any crime. So there exists both similarity and dissimilarity between the analogues, yet the typology can still remain intact. What follows is a selective appropriation of the text that contributes to a theological reading that triangulates Isa 53, the crucifixion of Christ, and lynching. I acknowledge that reading Isa 53 in this manner will result in other interpretations, some of them even deleterious, which cannot be covered in this paper. I assume that theological interpretation requires a community of wise practitioners committed to reading the Bible oriented to the knowledge of the Triune God.[17]

Langston Hughes' original version of "On Christ in Alabama" provides a helpful entrée into some of the literary complexities of Isa 53. The first and last stanzas of the poem equate Christ with an African American lynching victim:

> Christ is a Nigger,
> Beaten and black—
> *O, bare your back.*
> Most holy bastard
> Of the bleeding mouth:
> *Nigger Christ*
> *On the Cross of the South.*[18]

Both Hughes and the author of Isa 53 describe their victims in anonymous terms, in both holy and profane concepts, in great detail regarding their physical affliction, and from the vantage point of varying unidentified voices. The italics suggest direct quotations originating either from white racists speaking contemptuously of black persons, or it may reflect the sentiments of blacks encouraging other African Americans to act with a Christ-like submission. Karen Ford comments on the rhetorical effect of this ambiguity and writes, "The first two stanzas of the earlier version confuse the fact of oppression with the glorification of suffering that can result from it, especially in Christianity. The speaker here is both commentator and

---

Study of Mob Violence, ed. W. D. Carrigan; (London: Routledge, 2008) 102–3.

17. Castelo writes, "What we are proposing is a form of reading in which all participants bring to the table of deliberative interpretation their experience, hardships, and joys as vital features of the hermeneutical process.... Readers must be united in this single task by both the commitment to Scripture as Holy and the desire to see how it intersects with the variety of situations and circumstances in which we find ourselves. Readers must become a group of disciples, attuned to God's presence and the work of healing and repair. The goal here is not to apply Scripture in some instrumentalized and accommodating way; rather, the aim is to see, patiently and imaginatively, how Scripture and lived life can inflect and condition one another within the practice of Christian discipleship" (Lim and Castelo, *Hosea*, 236).

18. "Christ in Alabama," *Contempo* 1 (1931) front page; reprinted in *Scottsboro Limited: Four Poems and a Play in Verse* (New York: Golden Stair, 1932). A second edition was published in *The Panther and the Lash* (New York: Vintage, 1967) 37, from which Hughes removed the italics.

chorus, preacher and parishioner, whose voice blends in disturbing ways with the oppressor's."[19] Hughes's poem contains a tangled narrative since several undefined different voices inhabit the poem.

A similar literary phenomenon occurs in Isa 53, which contains at least two different narrative perspectives. A divine address begins the passage in 52:13–15 and concludes the poem in 53:11c–12. In these sections, the address is given in the first person and the servant is referred to as "my servant" (52:13; 53:11). In between these passages lie the "we" address (53:1–11b) in which an unidentified group describes the unjust persecution of the servant who suffers because of the sins of this community. Notable in the poem are the many unidentified pronouns: "I," "we," "he," "they"[20] and the references to "the many." Theories abound as to the historical identities of the people to whom reference is made. While one may speculate on their historical referents, the final form of the text does not clearly identify these persons, and therefore their significance lies at the literary level. Their identities are bound in their relation to one another, and these relationships can be understood as a series of concentric circles. At the outer edge are "many nations" (52:15) whose salvation is dependent upon the servant of Yahweh and whose destiny is bound up in the redemption of Israel (cf. 42:1, 6; 49:6). In the next layer are the "many" who also can be equated with the "they" in 53:9 who are culpable of making a grave for the servant among the wicked. This "they" can be associated with the nation of Israel. The "we" are to be distinguished within the circle of Israel as, in the observation of Hermisson, "a limited group who speak representatively in the name of the many for all Israel."[21] The servant is an individual originating from within Israel (41:8–9) who can stand apart from Israel in order to restore it (49:5–6). Therefore he can fulfill the unique role of suffering as representative of the "we" group and Israel, and in turn make many righteous, including the nations.

Just as the anonymous characters of Isa 53 are representative of larger communities, so lynched individuals were representative of a larger constituency. As to the identities of the perpetrators, Dray writes, "The coroner's inevitable verdict,

---

19. Karen Jackson Ford, "Making Poetry Pay: The Commodification of Langston Hughes," in *Marketing Modernisms: Self-Promotion, Canonization, Rereading*, ed. K. J. J. Dettmar and S. Watt (Ann Arbor: University of Michigan Press, 1996) 281.

20. See David J. A. Clines, *I, He, We, and They: A Literary Approach to Isaiah 53* (JSOTSup 1; JSOT, 1976). A second person reference occurs in both the MT and LXX versions of 52:14, "Just as many were appalled at you" as well as 53:10, "When you make his life an offering for sin" (NRSV). In the first instance other versions instead contain the third person pronoun and for the latter the verb may be interpreted as a third feminine singular rather than a second masculine singular. In the LXX the "you" references are more pronounced in both 52:14 and 53:13 and clearly emphasize a second person reading.

21. Hans-Jürgen Hermisson, "The Fourth Servant Song in the Context of Second Isaiah," in *The Suffering Servant: Isaiah 53 In Jewish and Christian Sources*, 34.

'Death at the hands of persons unknown,' affirmed the public's tacit complicity: no *persons* had committed a crime, because the lynching had been an expression of the community's will."[22] The resonances with the corporate nature of the servant's unjust persecution in Isa 53 is striking: "By a perversion of justice he was taken away. Who could have imagined his future? For he was cut off from the land of the living, stricken for the transgression of my people. They made his grave with the wicked and his tomb with the rich, although he had done no violence, and there was no deceit in his mouth" (Isa 53:8–9).

Given the coroner's verdict one would assume lynchings were carried out in the secrecy of night, but such was not the case. The recent report by the Equal Justice Initiative recalculates the number of lynchings between 1877 and 1950 to 3959 and describes them in the following manner: "Terror lynchings were horrific acts of violence whose perpetrators were never held accountable. Indeed some 'public spectacle lynchings' were attended by the entire white community and conducted as celebratory acts of racial control and subordination."[23] As a public act of terror, a lynching was not merely punishment directed toward an individual, but rather the lynchee served as a representative of the entire black community. Like the suffering servant, the lynchee represented the community, and any black individual lynched was a message to every African American man or woman that they dare not threaten the dominant order of white citizenship or conception of white chivalry.[24]

It is difficult to determine to what degree Isa 53 literally describes the physical affliction of the servant figure. Similarities abound between the description of the servant's suffering and that of other poetic and prophetic texts (e.g. Psa 22; Jer 11). Earlier in Isa 38:9–20 Hezekiah's speech of his deliverance from the gates of Sheol refers not to a resurrection from the dead but rather his healing from sickness. Is the language describing the servant's suffering, death, and exaltation to be taken literally or metaphorically? Commentators typically interpret the descriptions as metaphorical and tradition-bound so that no *Sitz im Leben* or biographical information can be determined.[25] Yet one wonders if such analyses minimize the performative

---

22. Dray, *At the Hands of Persons Unknown*, ix, author's italics.

23. Equal Justice Initiative, *Lynching in America: Confronting the Legacy of Racial Terror* (Montgomery: Equal Justice Initiative, 2015) 5.

24. Dray (*At the Hands of Persons Unknown*, 18) observes that by 1905 lynching had come almost exclusively to be associated with the execution of Southern black men. Yet it is important to note that women, both black and white, were lynched and even children. Anyone who was even perceived to threaten the Southern caste system, based on the oppressive economic model of sharecropping and an anti-miscegenation boundary for sexual relations, was vulnerable to lynching. See Jacquelyn Dowd Hall, *Revolt Against Chivalry: Jessie Daniel Ames and the Women's Campaign Against Lynching* (New York: Columbia University Press, 1993).

25. See Henning Graf Reventlow, "Basic Issues in the Interpretation of Isaiah 53," in *Jesus and the*

force of the text. Because of their obsession with precision, for modern critics the ambiguities of the text may result in interpretations suspended within their own semiotic webs. Premodern readers such as the NT authors were able to draw deep connections between the text and actual individuals or communities.

Recently Jeremy Schipper has argued that the servant suffered from an undefined physical disability that served as the motivation for his persecutors. He revives and modifies Duhm's thesis that the servant died not at the hands of others but due to leprosy.[26] He argues that the servant experiences the same skin anomaly that plagued Uzziah since the word "stricken" (*ngʿ* 53:4, 8) describes both their experiences (see 2 Chr 26:20). Isaiah 53 repeatedly describes the servant as experiencing "infirmities" (*ḥly*, 53:3, 4; *ḥlh*, 53:10), and Schipper observes that this term suggests a disability rather than a physical injury caused by humans.[27] It is important to note that Schipper does not hold to a medical or social definition of disability but rather to a cultural model where disability is the social experience of persons with impairments.

Why do I bring up disability when addressing the topic of race? I in no way wish to suggest that African Americans as a people are physically impaired in any way. I bring up Schipper's study because he highlights how the servant was persecuted because of the social and cultural ideologies his persecutors associated with his physical condition, and this observation is important to reading the text against the backdrop of lynching. The poem clearly states that the purported "marred form" and "appearance" of the servant is the cause of his rejection and suffering: "Just as there were many who were astonished at him—so marred was his appearance, beyond human semblance, and his form beyond that of mortals [Isa 52:14] . . . . For he grew up before him like a young plant, and like a root out of dry ground; he had no form or majesty that we should look at him, nothing in his appearance that we should desire him" (Isa 53:2).

Like the suffering servant, because of mythical stigmas attached to their physical appearance, blacks were deemed subhuman and subordinate to whites. A bestselling book published in 1900 entitled *The Negro a Beast* asserted that the Negro is not human and part of the "Adamic family" but rather of the lowest rank in the beast kingdom.[28] The significance of the physical characteristics of the servant and their repercussions ought not to be minimized due to the poetic dimensions of the text.

Suffering Servant: Isaiah 53 and Christian Origins, 27–29 and Hermisson, "The Fourth Servant Song," 46.

26. Bernhard Duhm, *Das Buch Jesaia*, HKAT (Göttingen: Vandenhoeck & Ruprecht, 1892) 368.
27. Schipper, *Disability and Isaiah's Suffering Servant*, 43.
28. Dray, *At the Hands of Persons Unknown*, 101.

Just like the servant is persecuted because of his marred form and appearance, so too African American men and women were lynched because they were black.

Central to a Christian understanding of Isa 53 is the understanding that the servant suffers vicariously on behalf of the people.[29] Isaiah 53:4–6 emphasizes this point: "Surely he has borne our infirmities and carried our diseases; yet we accounted him stricken, struck down by God, and afflicted. But he was wounded for our transgressions, crushed for our iniquities; upon him was the punishment that made us whole, and by his bruises we are healed. All we like sheep have gone astray; we have all turned to our own way, and the LORD has laid on him the iniquity of us all."

Verse 11 goes on to assert that the servant, as God's righteous one, makes many righteous by his suffering, and v. 10 states that he is made a sin offering (*'šm*). One need not necessarily associate the word *'šm* with the cult, nor does the passage insist God requires violence to atone for the sins of the people. The word refers to a restitution or indemnity (cf. Gen 26:10; Num 5:7–8; 1 Sam 6:3–4, 8, 17) because of a situation arising from guilt. Janowski goes on to summarize the message of 53:10, "Israel, which is in no position to take over the obligation arising from its guilt, must be released from this obligation in order to have any future. This liberation comes from an innocent one who surrenders his life."[30]

Lynchings were public spectacles that possessed a ritualistic quality to them. Orlando Patterson argues that for whites the lynching of black bodies served to atone for all that Southern Whites had lost in the Civil War and Reconstruction. He writes:

> After the trauma of Appomattox, the Southern community had to be restored in the most extreme compact of blood, and its God propitiated in the most extreme form of sacrifice known to man. . . . It takes little imagination, and almost no feeling for the workings of the religious mind, to understand how, as the flames devoured the flesh and soul of each Afro-American victim, every participant in these heinous rituals of human sacrifice must have felt the deepest and most gratifying sense of expiation and atonement.[31]

Yet as evidenced in the poems by Hughes and Cullen mentioned earlier, African American writers and activists depicted lynching as a Christian offering made to atone for the sins of a white society. Amy Wood writes, "By imagining lynching

---

29. See Antti Laato, *Who Is the Servant of the Lord? Jewish and Christian Interpretations on Isaiah 53 From Antiquity to the Middle Ages* (Turku: Åbo Akademi University, 2012); and Bellinger and Farmer, *Jesus and the Suffering Servant*; and Janowski and Stuhlmacher, *The Suffering Servant*.

30. Bernd Janowski, "He Bore Our Sins: Isaiah 53 and the Drama of Taking Another's Place," in *The Suffering Servant: Isaiah 53 in Jewish and Christian Sources*, 69.

31. Orlando Patterson, *Rituals of Blood: Consequences of Slavery in Two American Centuries* (Washington DC: Civitas Counterpoint, 1998) 215.

as a Crucifixion and its victims as Christian martyrs, black Protestants could claim African Americans as the true inheritors of Christian salvation and redemption and their white oppressors as unholy savages."[32] Both blacks and whites associated lynching with atonement, yet interpreted the significance of the act in differing ways. According to African American writers and artists, "The black man became a potential savior not only for the oppressed community but also for his persecutors, southern whites."[33] In both lynching and Jesus's crucifixion, the perpetrators of murder find their redemption in the mutilated body of their victims.

In the case of Isa 53 and the matter of lynching, one's salvation is dependent upon properly interpreting the suffering of the victims. Isaiah 53 describes the "we" group narration of the suffering and death of God's servant as past events in 53:1–11b. Yet in the opening and concluding verses of the poem, the author writes from an eschatological perspective where the servant who was once humiliated is exalted. The "we" group has come to realize that the one who was despised and rejected is the very one through whom their infirmities and iniquities are healed, and based upon this insight they can number themselves among the many who are made righteous. According to Hermisson, "The Servant will have success when Israel finally comes to understand the suffering and death of this miserable figure; when it grasps, agrees, believes: for Yahweh has exalted precisely this suffering one, who by his vicarious suffering bore the sin—that is, the unbelief—of the 'many.'"[34] The "we" group has perceived a double insight; through the realization of the servant's innocence they recognize their own culpability in his death. Janowski observes that their redemption is predicated upon this realization and writes, "Israel turns back to Yahweh only because it has 'understood' the meaning of this death and thereby its own situation."[35]

If the suffering servant of Isa 53 is a lynchee, then Americans are confronted with the task of recognizing the innocence of the lynching victims, and in so doing acknowledging their own guilt in these acts of terror.[36] Such acts of interpretation are not merely intellectual exercises but instead are deeply ethical and spiritual matters since one's salvation is at stake. There is no place for a disinterested interpreter since in this case the very act of reading calls for an identification with the "we" group

---

32. Amy Louise Wood, *Lynching and Spectacle: Witnessing Racial Violence in America, 1890–1940* (Chapel Hill, NC: University of North Carolina Press, 2009) 48.

33. Edward J. Blum and Paul Harvey, *The Color of Christ: The Son of God and the Saga of Race in America* (Chapel Hill, NC: University of North Carolina, 2013) 195.

34. Hermisson, "The Fourth Servant Song," 41.

35. Janowski, "He Bore Our Sins," 70.

36. It seems that Black poets also wrote with this goal in mind. Cullen's "The Black Christ" begins with the following introduction, "(Hopefully dedicated to White America)," signaling that the poem was intended to help white Americans realize their guilt in America's racist past.

for whom the servant suffered and died. Since the beginning and conclusion of the poem describe the exalted status of the servant, the proper response to Isa 53 is worship and obedience. If, as Cone has argued, the lynching tree is fundamental to a United States theology of the cross, then every American Christian must be asked the question, "Who do you see hanging on the lynching tree?" If the cross is the lynching tree, and the lynchee is the suffering servant, then salvation for Americans rests upon their acknowledgement of our racist past, most exemplified in the mass terror lynchings of African Americans. The inability to see Christ as the first lynchee results not merely from a lack of information but a lack of faith. Yet those who see that Christ was lynched on a tree can claim, "But he was wounded for our transgressions, crushed for our iniquities; upon him was the punishment that made us whole, and by his bruises we are healed" (Isa 53:6).

Conclusion

The genesis of this paper was a homily I delivered at last year's Good Friday Service at the university where I teach and serve as interim University Chaplain. Given the racial crisis facing our country, and in particular the killing of black people at the hands of law enforcement, the connection between the cross, the lynching tree, and Isa 53 came quite naturally. So although I have addressed the topic from an academic context, namely the discipline of theological interpretation, my initial and ongoing concerns are pastoral. The lynching of the suffering servant as revealed in Jesus Christ is not something merely to be written about for academic journals; it is something that is to be preached in pulpits across the United States. For the racial challenges we face are not merely intellectual but also spiritual. James Cone describes Reinhold Niebuhr's inability to draw the connection between his theology of the cross and racism, "Niebuhr had 'eyes to see' black suffering, but I believe he lacked the 'heart to feel' it as his own."[37] More than the reading of papers on this topic is required to move people's hearts to feel black suffering. Ending slavery by no means ended racism, and America's original sin simply took on other manifestations. If our congregations are able to see how the legacy of lynching continues to affect law enforcement and the judicial system, particularly in police violence directed toward black communities and state sponsored executions of black men, perhaps they might make steps toward possessing hearts to feel this problem as their own.

As I write this article, whether "Black Lives Matter," that is, whether people see black suffering, continues to be contested across the United States. Yet another story of a conspiracy that involves law enforcement, the judicial system, and politicians to

---

37. Cone, *The Cross and the Lynching Tree*, 41.

cover up the execution of a black man by police has surfaced in Chicago. Comparisons can be drawn between these killings and their ensuing cover-up to lynchings. If so, this paper has argued, receiving the gift of salvation extended through the suffering of the servant requires the ability to see not an anonymous "thug" lying dead in the street shot by police, but rather the Christ crucified.

RESPONSE TO LIM

Evelmyn Ivens

Isaiah 53 (52:13—53:12) is one of those passages which immediately makes us think of the crucifixion of Jesus Christ. As Lim states, Isa 53 is a passage frequently quoted by NT authors and is referenced in Matt 8:17; Acts 8:32–33; and 1 Pet 2:22–25. Taking into consideration the three dimensions of theological interpretation of Scripture, Lim then proposes reading the narrative of the suffering servant of Isaiah as an act of lynching with a theological meaning.

In addition to the three dimensions of theological interpretation, this paper does not leave out the plain sense of Scripture to develop the idea that lynching can be understood theologically. Lim seeks to demonstrate that by using both the conditions of theological interpretation and the plain sense of Scripture we can understand that the suffering servant experienced lynching. He introduces James Cone's argument that the lynching tree needs to be central in the American theology of the cross. I prefer to use the term "United States" instead of "American" because I believe that by saying "American theology" we are limiting ourselves to Western European influenced theology. This leaves other expressions like "Black," "Latina/Hispanic," "Asian American," "Native American," "Womanist," and "Mujerista" theologies on the margins. This alludes to the point made by James Cone that, if we do not include the association between the lynching tree and the cross, contextual interpretations are neglected, and for Cone this is a failure, something with which I fully agree.

I appreciated the comparison between the suffering servant and the African American lynching victim in the first and last stanzas of the poem "On Christ in Alabama." One of the interesting similarities is that in both the poem and the Isaiah text the victim does not have a name and, even though there are other voices present (they, we, he, many), these voices do not have a defined identity either. We know that the suffering servant was an individual in Israel (41:8–9), and he represented the whole community. His life served as a sacrifice for his own people. The lynching victim also represented his—and sometimes her—own community. However, it is important to mention that those victims of lynching in our history indeed had names, families, and personal stories.

Nonwhite theologians have the task, burden, and responsibility, depending on social location, to provide alternative interpretations and/or narratives to the church. I think this paper is an important contribution because it lets us explore a different perspective. As a nonwhite I find it very helpful to look for that theological meaning in the lynching of the suffering servant. Just as I identify myself with the *mestizo* Jesus proposed by theologian Virgilio Elizondo because of my cultural background, reading Isa 53 in this context of lynching makes much sense given the history of our country.

Community and corporate responsibility are two themes I want to highlight. It is very difficult to imagine how a person can decide to commit an act of violence such as lynching. It is more disturbing to think that people saw it as a way of justification. These awful acts of violence were committed by one community against another. The servant of Yahweh and the victim of lynching never knew what they were guilty of; nonetheless, they both became a symbol of martyrdom.

The oppressed community and the oppressor community continued to live side by side, even though they never became true neighbors. Unfortunately we still see this today; with violence against black lives one community continues to be oppressed. I recently visited Memphis, Tennessee, and as someone who is neither blank nor white I situated myself in the middle and observed and listened to conversations. What I can say is that racial dynamics are as messy as ever. In my view one community continues to be the punisher, and the other is still a victim. When I say "victim," it is not because the African American community is weak or does not have a voice of its own, but it is a victim because of the systemic injustices that persist. For women of color there is another layer added to this complex reality.

Regarding corporate responsibility, I believe that racism and discrimination are not individual expressions but rather a corporate response. Just as it is biblical to lament in community, in issues of injustice there is also a corporate or communal responsibility. As stated in the paper, lynchings in many instances were public spectacles and celebrations by the white community in the belief they were atoning for all that whites had lost in their defeat. Although they were acts committed by a few, those few were often not held accountable. Who was responsible? It was both the few who took action and the community that observed because they became accomplices. This exact issue is one that is still relevant when we talk about the history of slavery, racism, and lynching. Are we all responsible? We are responsible if we continue to avoid talking about slavery and pretending that it does not affect our present. We are responsible if we are not humble enough to join in the painful journey of understanding the lives of those who are discriminated against. We are responsible if we see the immigrant as a statistic instead of a human. We are responsible if we keep objectifying women, instead of giving them the value that they deserve. We are responsible if we continue to sacrifice the lives of many at the hands of violence.

I want to end by raising the following questions: How do we translate the connection between the Isaiah narrative, the cross, and the lynching tree to the ordinary individual? How does it relate to the immigrant who recently arrived because she had to flee violence in her home country? How does it relate to the person with no high school diploma and who lives in an under-resourced community? My concern is to make our theologizing practical in the lives of people.

WHAT'S MISSING? THEOLOGICAL MUSINGS ON A HERMENEUTICS OF ABSENCE

Néstor Medina

> The reading of the Bible is a meeting of histories and traditions: a reading of our past, of the history of our forbears.[1]
>
> People believe that as they read the Bible the Holy Spirit unlocks new meanings; reading is therefore not just a mental/cognitive exercise. I suggest the focus on the Holy Spirit in hermeneutics is one of the reasons why the historical critical method [did not succeed]. No proper hermeneutics can take place until the divine pneumatological hermeneutics mediates an understanding.[2]

I am not the first person to ask: How are we to read a book that has as its primary goal to read us? Speaking from my Latina/o ethnocultural background, I argue that no one tradition or cultural/ethnoracial group has a monopoly on the interpretation of the Bible. I am not promoting absolute hermeneutical relativity; I am suggesting that the interpretive process occurs at the complex intersection of multiple factors such as religious traditions, faithful devotion, and social location and concerns. There are at least three levels to this complexity of intersecting factors.

In the first level the Bible is interpreted in the context of community. The questions, concerns, and challenges a community faces in their day-to-day reality shape the kinds of questions they will ask from the biblical text and the kinds of answers they will find. The topic is race and racism, but given the fact that we know that the existence of "races" is a sociocultural construction designed to organize peoples around superior and inferior groups, I will instead speak of the racialization of culture. It is this negative experience of racialization of entire communities that directly impacts people's reading of the Bible.

In the second level the Bible narrative, what we could call the "world of the Bible," also reflects the social-cultural and ethnoracial context of its time. The Bible

---

1. Silvia Regina De Lima, "Rereading the Bible as a Latin American Black Woman," in *Women's Perspectives: Articulating the Liberating Power of the Gospel* (Geneva: World Council of Churches, 1996) 23–27, 26.

2. Néstor Medina, "Orality and Context in a Hermeneutical Key: Toward a Latina/o Canadian Pentecostal Life-Narrative Hermeneutics," *PentecoStudies* 14 (2015) 97–123, 118.

does not present to us a sanitized story of salvation. It should not be a scandal to say that the biblical text is not neutral in terms of racialization; racialized difference and racism are found among groups in the pages of both the Hebrew Bible and the NT. If we take seriously that the Hebrew Bible is first the collective memory of the people of Israel, we should not be surprised to find a strong Israelite ethnocentrism within it. There is no point at romanticizing some passages where there are obvious attitudes of xenophobia, and we should not resort to spiritualizing specific pericopes that seem to offer us critical social relevance. We should also be able to agree that the NT embodies the collective memory of the earliest Christians. Because they were part of their immediate social, cultural, political, and economic context, the way they went about making sense of their newfound faith included elements from their Jewish, Roman, and Greek cultural and religious world.

The affirmation of the context of the early Christians leads to the third level, by which I seek to acknowledge the church as a community and collective of believers who often reflect the social, political, and economic tensions one finds in the larger culture. Racialization and racism are alive and well inside the church, and such phenomena impact how we live the Christian faith and interpret the Bible.

These few remarks help me make explicit the radical changes that biblical interpretation has to undergo, and in some ways has already been undergoing, in order to speak to contemporary issues of racism and racialization of culture. What hermeneutics is today is not what it used to be! It is crucial to retrace the long path hermeneutics has gone and also show how it is shifting today by incorporating ethnoracial and cultural backgrounds as key hermeneutical elements.

With that in mind, I divide this paper into three brief "moments." In the first section I focus on the emergence of hermeneutics within the Western European intellectual tradition. I mark how both philosophical and biblical hermeneutics contributed to building a sophisticated network of ideas and approaches that dominated hermeneutics up until about the middle of the twentieth century. In the second section I briefly mention the recent (from the middle of the twentieth century to today) emergence of multiple currents that have brought about the reconfiguration of hermeneutics and provoked a rethinking of the interpretive task. In the third section I provide some practical examples of how those new currents help us elucidate aspects in the biblical text that have often gone unnoticed. I want to show how recent approaches reclaim elements often missing from pervasive readings of the biblical narrative. More specifically, I propose what I call a "hermeneutics of absence," by which I mean two things: one, the interpretive stance that dares to ask about the possible reasons, social circumstances, or authorial intentions for which specific elements were not included in the text; and two, the critical posture that inquires about the context, social location, cultural background, or prejudicial attitudes that might shape the way people interpret the text. My hope is to invite you to dare to imagine the biblical interpretive process from the multiple vantage points of the vanquished, those that are missing in traditional interpretive approaches.

Retracing the Steps: A Brief Sketch on Philosophical and Biblical Hermeneutics

Gone are the days when biblical interpretation was dominated by German scholars, and when philosophical approaches understood hermeneutics as an "objective" scientific endeavor.[3] In both philosophical and biblical hermeneutics few can dispute the importance of Friedrich Schleiermacher. In the eighteenth century Schleiermacher was raising important questions concerning the interpretive dynamics. He was persuaded that hermeneutics could be exploited to explain the meaning of every author and was applicable beyond written texts.[4] In order to interpret a written text, readers needed to go beyond the linguistic meaning and into the historical situation of the author. He thought that the use of linguistic, literary, and aesthetic forms of criticism coupled with divination of the author's process of composition would lead to a heightened understanding of the text. He acknowledged the distance between the written discourse and its understanding by those who read it. If only grammatical elements are used, the results would be superficial. However, by reconstructing the text and with it the intention of the author (divining), the discourse and the understanding by the readers would be brought closer together. The reader would understand the author better than they understood themselves.[5]

Drawing on Hegel's transcendental *Geist* ("spirit") and Scheleiermacher's attention to the linguistic, Wilhelm Dilthey later emphasized hermeneutics as an attempt at understanding the expression of human inwardness as it finds its "complete, exhaustive and objectively comprehensible expression" in literature.[6] His goal was to gain "objectivity" in hermeneutics by basing it on the "inner nature of the science" (that aspect of existence to which the natural sciences cannot gain access). Herme-

---

3. The term "hermeneutics" goes as far back as Aristotle's work *Hermeneia*. See Aristotle, *On Interpretation*, E. M. Edghill, http://www.bocc.ubi.pt/pag/Aristotle-interpretation.pdf (accessed June 30, 2015).

4. Friedrich Schleiermacher, "The Academy Addresses of 1829: On the Concept of Hermeneutics, with Reference to F. A. Wolf's Instructions and Ast's Textbook," in *Hermeneutical Inquiry: The Interpretation of Religion* 43, ed. David E. Klemm, American Academy of Religion Studies in Religion (Atlanta: Scholars, 1986) 63.

5. Ibid., 72.

6. Wilhelm Dilthey, "The Development of Hermeneutics (1900)," in *Hermeneutical Inquiry: The Interpretation of Religion*, 95.

neutics was to be the epistemology of the "sciences of the spirit" (*Geisteswissenschaften*), which included the grammatical, historical, and psychological aspects to interpretation. He proposed an "objective" method by which "readers" would come to a better understanding of a work as a whole from its linguistic constitution and from the mentality of its author.[7]

Understanding a text, Dilthey claimed, entailed tracing the linguistic expressions forward to clarify the contexts of meaningfulness that determine its meaning and backwards to the historical experiences that produced the text as an intention.[8] This cycle was repeated in the relation from the individual work (grammar) to the mentality (psychology) and development (history) of its author and recurred again in the relation of such an individual work to its literary genre. The dynamic allowed one to get at the intentional act of writing (what Schleiermacher called divining) as developed within its "proper cultural and linguistic context."[9] While Dilthey regurgitated Schleiermacher's hermeneutical maxim of understanding "authors better than they understood themselves," he needed to create a hermeneutical framework that included the grammatical and psychological interpretations in order to get at the meaning of a text.[10]

Two of the most influential contemporary hermeneuts are Hans-Georg Gadamer and Paul Ricoeur. They are known for being critical of modern linguistics and scientific, positivist claims to interpretation, which operated under the assumption that there is one single authoritative meaning and interpretation from written texts, as exemplified by Schleiermacher and Dilthey. By contrast, they sought to expand the ways we can understand the intersection between text and interpretation by paying greater attention to the dynamics involved in speech-discourse, the act of writing a text, the actual content of a written text, and the actual readers.

Among the many things that can be said about the work of Hans-Georg Gadamer, in terms of hermeneutics, he explored how a text stands in relation to language and the nature of communication between two speakers.[11] Gadamer proposed a dialogical approach by which language plays a crucial role, but it does not set limits to what can be communicated. Language, he says, provides us the limits with which we can make sense of reality, but because humans are finite language can

---

7. Ibid., 104.

8. David E. Klemm, "Introduction to Dilthey's 'The Development of Hermeneutics,'" in *Hermeneutical Inquiry: The Interpretation of Religion*, 90.

9. Dilthey, "The Development of Hermeneutics," 91.

10. Ibid., 104.

11. Hans-Georg Gadamer, "Text and Interpretation," trans. Dennis J. Smidt and Richard Palmer, in *Dialogue and Deconstruction: The Gadamer-Derrida Encounter*, ed. Diane P Michelfelder and Richard E. Palmer (New York: SUNY, 1989) 27.

never communicate meaning inexhaustibly. There is always something else that can be said because existence and the experience of meaning cannot be reduced to a set of specific concepts.[12]

With regard to written texts Gadamer insists interpretation is much more than the application of techniques for interpreting. He viewed language as mediating access to the world. Language is a midworld between thinking and speaking, a bridge between them but also an obstacle because language can never exhaust reality in its attempt to explain it. Because language never fully completes the mediation, interpretation becomes necessary. As he wrote, "Only in the light of interpretation does something become a fact, and only within processes of interpretation is an observation expressible."[13]

As Gadamer saw it, the text must be understood as a hermeneutical concept because it is self-contained. The text is not regarded from the perspective of grammar and linguistics and divorced from any context (by which he means its internal theme) that it might have. Only when a text cannot be understood are questions asked about the linguistic composition and character of the text. For the hermeneutical point or from the standpoint of the reader, the text is a mere product, "a phase in the event of understanding." The assumption is that the act of writing presupposes the act of reading-interpretation. Gadamer argued the very act of writing creates a "virtual horizon" of interpretation and understanding to be filled out by the reader; thus, the cycle of interpretation is complete.[14]

Of no less importance in written texts is the function of the interpreter. As Gadamer explains, whatever is alienating in a text, whatever makes it unintelligible, is to be overcome and cancelled out by the interpreter. "The interpreter steps in and speaks only when the text (the discourse) is not able to do what is supposed to do, namely be heard and understood on its own."[15] But, he adds, the interpreter disappears completely when the full harmony in understanding is achieved; the interpreter "has entered into the text." When the interpreter steps in and helps readers to an understanding of the text, his/her own stepping back is not a disappearance in any negative sense. It is an entering into the dialogical communication with text in such a way that the tension between the horizon of the text and the horizon of the reader is dissolved, creating a "fusion of horizons." The process of understanding a text tends to captivate and take the reader into what the text says and into its textual world. In this fusion the text also drops, but not as if we leave it behind or as if forget-

12. Ibid., 24–25.
13. Ibid., 30.
14. Ibid., 35.
15. Ibid., 41.

ting it. Instead, we allow ourselves to enter into it. As a result, the original distance between the text and the reader is closed.

Nevertheless, for Gadamer not all texts are created equal. He tells us that there are all kinds of "texts" that really are ill-conceived because of their inability to convey meaning: antitexts, pseudotexts, and countertexts. He insisted that the highest expression of texts are "literary texts" because these do not disappear in our act of understanding them. But what makes literary texts so different, according to Gadamer? For him literary texts have a kind of quality for which they must be listened to and not only read. The dynamic in the interpretation process should be one of reading these texts out loud. In literary texts the words are laden with meaning in such a way that their very sound shines forth full meaning.[16] Although it remains unclear what criteria Gadamer applied to determine what qualifies as literature and what does not, it is worth noting that for him, literary texts did not just render oral discourse into a fixed form but possessed their own authenticity. In other words, interpretation is interconnected to the very act of reading those texts out loud, even if only to hear them by the inner ear.[17]

The practical implication is that these texts cannot be mastered nor their interpretation prescribed. Literary texts have an inherent power in the face of which readers/listeners can only take a passive role in discovering their multiple meanings. Reading and listening to those texts must be understood as part of the hermeneutical experience of the dialogical nature between the text and the reader. But understanding is always temporal as it needs to be reenacted by every present moment when the text is encountered again.

By contrast, Paul Ricoeur began his proposal on hermeneutics at the level of linguistic analysis. He argued that linguistics needed to move beyond the study of the word as the lexical sign and focus on the sentence as the basic unit of meaning.[18] Ricoeur adopted and modified Saussure's division of language as *langue* (language, word, symbol) and *parole* (speech), which he viewed as only a large composition of semantic units.[19] His position derived from the view that words in themselves are polysemic—they have a plurality of meaning; they do not yet refer to something specifically. A word does not communicate something (is not yet discourse) unless it is placed within the confines of a semantic structure, i.e., until it is placed

16. Ibid., 43.
17. Ibid., 44.
18. Mario J. Valdés, "Introduction: Paul Ricoeur's Post-Structuralist Hermeneutics," in *A Ricoeur Reader*, ed. Mario J. Valdés (London: Harvester Wheatsheaf, 1991) 4.
19. Paul Ricoeur, "Structure, Word, Event," trans. Robert Sweeney, in *The Conflict of Interpretations: Essays in Hermeneutics*, ed. Don Ihde, Northwestern University Studies in Phenomenology and Existential Philosophy (Evanston, IL: Northwestern University Press, 1974) 85.

in a sentence.[20] When that happens, the word becomes a discourse, and language becomes an event; something is being said and communicated. This communicative move, Ricoeur insisted, marks the moment when language (words and signs) goes beyond itself and its polysemic character and becomes limited to a specific message. Its plurivocity is reduced according to its semantic context.[21] It is from this complementing dialectic between word and sentence, language and discourse, and semiotics and semantics that Ricoeur opposes the structuralist focus on words as semantic units independent of their functional context and without a proper analysis of the sentence as something more than a set of words and signs put together.

An offshoot of Ricoeur's linguistic analysis is his treatment of the dynamics between discourse and writing. For him, writing is the moment at which discourse (the event of language as message) becomes fixed, not discourse in the immediate moment of transcribing something previously stated but discourse that could have been said but is written precisely because it is not said. Writing takes the place of speech in the sense that the text is the "full manifestation of something that is in virtual state, something nascent and inchoate, in living speech."[22] But in the act of writing, a rupture takes place between the original intent of the author and the verbal meaning of the text, between what the author meant and what it means now. In writing, the original language-event (discourse) becomes separated from the event itself.[23] As a result, the text gains autonomy from its author; it becomes itself a "reservoir of meaning" opened to multiple possible readings.[24] Still, for Ricoeur no writing is complete without a reader. While the text is an important source of meaning, the function of the reader is to interpret (decode) the meaning and message inscribed in it.[25]

Reading, Ricoeur proposed, is only the first step toward interpreting a text. To read a text on the way to interpretation includes two important aspects: explanation and understanding in a dialectical relation. Explanation makes the text appropriately clear on its way to understanding. It brings out the internal structural relations of dependence within the text.[26] The initial aspect of explanation goes beyond finding

20. Ibid., 92–95.

21. Paul Ricoeur, *Interpretation Theory, Discourse and the Surplus of Meaning* (Forth Worth: Texas Christian University Press, 1976) 17.

22. Paul Ricoeur, *Hermeneutics and the Human Sciences: Essays on Language, Action and Interpretation*, trans. John B. Thompson (Cambridge: Cambridge University Press, 1981) 146.

23. Ricoeur, *Interpretation Theory*, 25–29.

24. See Ricoeur, *Interpretation Theory*, 31, 93. See also, Paul Ricoeur, *From Text to Action: Essays in Hermeneutics*, ed. James M. Edie, trans. Katheen Blamey and John Thompson (Evanston, IL: Northwestern University Press, 1991) 2:83–84.

25. Valdés, "Introduction: Paul Ricoeur's Post-Structuralist Hermeneutics," 7.

26. Ricoeur, *Interpretation Theory*, 60–64.

the intention of the author (or redactor) and the meaning of the text as perceived by its originally intended audience. Explanation goes beyond an analysis of the text as systematically arranged, i.e., beyond a focus on the text by itself without consideration of the human element. Understanding is more than cognitive apprehension and more than just repeating the speech event. It is the creation of an altogether new event of discourse. Understanding grows out of the active immersion of the reader in the world of the text. It is the moment in which the dialectic between distanciation[27] and appropriation is finally resolved.

It must be made clear that for Ricoeur appropriation is a moment of "letting go" a "divestiture." It means to allow oneself to be carried off towards the horizon of the text and not merely taking as our own the alien experience or the distant intention of the author. Rather, it means owning the horizon of the world towards which a work directs itself independently from the author. This world of the text is not something that lies behind the text but is found in front of the text. "It is not a question of imposing upon the text our finite capacity for understanding, but for exposing ourselves to the text and receiving from it an enlarged self."[28]

Interpretation was for Ricoeur the actualization of the meaning of the text for the present reader. It allows for the participation of the reader in the production of new meaning. Proper interpretation involves placing oneself en route towards the orientation of the text, towards the meaning that the text itself supports.[29] Ricoeur would be the first to reject the idea that there is only one correct meaning hidden behind the text and that the job of interpretation is to find it. For him texts can be subject to various and quite different readings; conflict of interpretations is inevitable.

Reflecting on the Bible, Ricoeur argued that what distinguishes reading the Bible from reading any other text is the fact that it departs from a vantage point of faith. The Bible is a discourse of the faith of a people; its inherent literary forms are inseparable from this "confession of faith" in God.[30] By "faith" he did not mean an uncritical posture but a type of a post-critical "second faith," the kind of faith that emerges after one has engaged the processes of explanation and understanding.

27. For Ricoeur distanciation refers to the gap that exists between the written work and our world. It is also the separation of the message from the speaker, from the initial situation, and its initially intended audience. But for Ricoeur this distanciation is not of a negative character. This *alienating* distanciation makes it possible for a condition of objectification so prevalent in the human sciences. This *productive* distanciation, as he calls it, offers the opportunity to approach the text without preconceived notions of authorial intent. But the text does not remain there, this so-called *distanciation* is effectively overcome through reading by which the meaning of the text is rescued from its estrangement and put into new proximity to the readers. See Ricoeur, *Interpretation Theory*, 43, 73; Ricoeur, *Hermeneutics and the Human Sciences*, 131.

28. Ricoeur, *From Text to Action*, 43.

29. Ricoeur, *Hermeneutics and the Human Sciences*, 150, 162.

30. Ricoeur, *From Text to Action*, 90.

Coupled with revelation, the act of reading the Bible is always an act of interpretation in search for what is unfolding before us. Revelation is a feature of the world proposed by the text, which is encountered by the readers as they enter the world of the text.

As we think about these philosophical approaches, we can see the diverse ways in which they conceived the task of hermeneutics. In the case of Schleiermacher the rational human capacity was the arbiter in the interpretation of texts, while in Dilthey we find the wedding of a rational capacity and scientific approach applied to what cannot be proven scientifically. Dilthey attempted to develop a scientific method and apply it to the human spirit in its attempt at communicating through written texts. By the same token Gadamer and Ricoeur emphasized the role of the text and its impact on the reader. With Gadamer the reader takes on a passive role and enters the world of the text which results in a fusion of horizons. In the case of Ricoeur there is indeed conflict of interpretations because of the multivalent character of written texts.

It goes without saying that I am not doing justice to the rich and long history of scholarly developments on philosophical hermeneutics. Despite their differences, however, these authors display the same confidence in the human rational capacity and multilevel application of the scientific method in order to draw meaning from written texts, including the Bible. For them the task of hermeneutics takes place within the confines of "objective" human rational engagement. Nevertheless, these scholars paid no attention to their own social location and cultural background. They also did not consider the Eurocentric character of the intellectual tradition within which they operated, the assumptions they made about reality, and the reliance on human rational capacity as the final arbiter of hermeneutics.

Recent Hermeneutical Currents: The Actual Author and the Actual Reader

Biblical hermeneutics has an equally long history of developments that cannot be engaged in this brief reflection. Generally Bible scholars have displayed the same confidence on reason and the universal, objective applicability of the scientific method in hermeneutics as the philosophers previously discussed. The search for the historical Jesus, as initially articulated by Albert Schweitzer, points to the tensions scholars found between the actual historical characters and their portrayal by biblical authors.[31] Since the early twentieth century the task of hermeneutics has

---

31. Albert Schweitzer, *The Quest of the Historical Jesus: A Critical Study of Its Progress from Reimarus to Wrede*, trans. W. Montgomery (London: Adam and Charles Black, 1910, repr., New York: Macmillan, 1964). Although not a biblical scholar himself, Schweitzer applied the scientific method in

been reconfigured multiple times. From Julius Wellhausen and his documentary hypothesis[32] to Rudolf Bultmann and his proposal of demythologization[33] to Robert Funk and the birth of the Jesus Seminar[34] to Willi Marxen's application of redaction criticism to the resurrection of Jesus,[35] biblical hermeneutics was reduced to critical analyses on specific pericopes, which resulted in the utter fragmentation of the biblical narrative. The shift can be traced as far back as the late eighteenth and early nineteenth centuries, and in the twentieth century resulted in what Hans Frei called the "eclipse of biblical narrative."[36] Of course, Frei's own Eurocentrism is revealed here as he did not include an analysis of the hermeneutical contributions outside of the Western European, North Atlantic hermeneutical tradition. Many of these changes in hermeneutics contributed to a radical change of perception of the Bible from a sacred document to a mere piece of great literature.

From a theological standpoint one of the problems with "reading" the Bible as any other piece of literature is that it is not just like any other book. Its authors intended to write stories about their people, and their immediate historical, economic, cultural, and religious contexts. They did not intend to write "scripture" per se, but sought to record in the Hebrew Bible the stories, dynamics, and life of characters that contributed to the formation of a people's identity, culture, historical imaginary and religion. Building on the Hebrew Bible, the NT contains the recorded stories about Jesus, the central figure of the Christian movement, and the initial developments of these religious communities. As communities of faith affirmed the content of the biblical text as telling the saga of divine love throughout the ages, it became equated with containing the divine message of good news; it became equated with Scripture.

Drawing on narrative criticism, Mark Allan Powell notes that the Gospels "are stories about Jesus, not compilations of miscellaneous data concerning him. They are intended to be read from beginning to end, not dissected and examined

---

terms of empirical and historical data to the Bible and concluded the Bible stories were more fictional than real. See also James M. Robinson, *A New Quest of the Historical Jesus*, SBT 25 (London: SCM, n.d.).

32. Julius Wellhausen, *Prolegomena to the History of Ancient Israel*, trans. J. Sutherland Black and Allan Menzies (Edinburgh: Adam and Charles Black, 1885; repr. Cleveland: Meridian, 1961).

33. Rudolf Bultmann, *Kerygma and Myth*, ed. Hans Werner Bartsch, trans. Reginald H. Fuller (New York: Harper and Row, 1953); Rudolf Bultmann and Karl Kundsin, *Form Criticism: Two Essays on New Testament Research*, trans. Frederck C. Grant (New York: Harper and Row, 1963).

34. Robert W. Funk, *Language, Hermeneutic, and Word of God: The Problem of Language in the New Testament and Contemporary Theology* (New York: Harper and Row, 1966).

35. Willi Marxen, *The Resurrection of Jesus of Nazareth*, trans. Margaret Kohl (Philadelphia: Fortress, 1970).

36. Hans W. Frei, *The Eclipse of Biblical Narrative: A Study in Eighteenth and Nineteenth Century Hermeneutics* (New Haven: Yale University Press, 1974).

to determine the relative value of individual passages."[37] The central concern should be the narrative in the text. To that extent narrative criticism deployed the idea of an "implied author" as the missing link in the interpretive process. The advantage of such an approach is that the interpretive dynamic remains focused on the text itself, without considering anything extrinsic to the narrative.[38] Narrative criticism created a useful framing by focusing on aspects left untouched by historical criticism and by using the concepts of an implied author and implied readers. A careful look at the proposal of narrative criticism, however, shows disconnect in terms of the interpretive dynamic. Hermeneutically, the actual author and the actual reader are placed outside of the scope of the text. As a result, the text becomes independent from the actual author (Ricoeur) and the readers are viewed as not adding anything of significance to the interpretive process (Gadamer).

From the middle of the twentieth century the bracketing out of the actual author and actual readers has been challenged in numerous ways. Within the Western European Anglo North Atlantic tradition, postmodernism brought three destabilizing critiques. One, it challenged notions of objectivity and the dependence on a scientific approach as the only form of or most reliable gateway to knowledge.[39] With this critique the "modernist dream of disinterested . . . distanced, abstract [universally applicable] truth" and objective interpretation of the Bible became impossibilities.[40] Second, it highlighted a wide range of other forms of knowledge largely left untouched by the scientific approach. For Jean François Lyotard the unequal relationship between "narrative knowledge" and "scientific knowledge" is the result of the "entire history of cultural imperialism from the dawn of Western civilization."[41] From a hermeneutical perspective this critique hinted at the colonial dynamics operating in traditional approaches. Indeed, "there is no innocent reading of the Bible."[42] Moreover, the emphasis in other forms of knowledge corresponds with the aversion of postmodernism to the notion of "metanarrative," thus rejecting the idea that a single strand of history or form of knowledge can claim to have universal applicability or pretend to speak for all of human experience. In the same way, it can be stated that there is no single correct reading of the biblical text; the text is always

---

37. Mark Allan Powell, *What is Narrative Criticism?* (Minneapolis: Fortress, 1990) 2.

38. Bultmann and Kundsin, *Form Criticism*, 5.

39. Jean-François Lyotard, *The Postmodern Condition: A Report on Knowledge*, trans. Geoff Bennington and Brian Massumi, Theory and History of Literature, vol. 10 (Minneapolis: University of Minnesota Press, 1984) 7.

40. George Aichele, et al., *The Postmodern Bible*, ed. Elizabeth A. Castelli, et al. (New Heaven, CT: Yale University Press, 1995) 14.

41. Lyotard, *The Postmodern Condition*, 27.

42. Aichele, et al., *The Postmodern Bible*, 4.

opened to other interpretations. And third, postmodernism highlighted the social location of knowledge and knowledge construction. In many ways postmodernism already signaled the socially constructed character of meaning. In terms of biblical interpretation, it helped us see the interconnectedness between individual readers and the impact of their larger social context.

From an entirely different vantage point poststructuralism also brought serious challenges to ideas concerning the neutrality of written discourse. Different from the postmodern concern that knowledge is produced to be consumed and purchased,[43] poststructuralism focused on the discursive role of power and knowledge. Particularly Michel Foucault noted that the production of knowledge had as its end the conditioning of human behavior,[44] which resulted in the control and legislation of members of society,[45] and the establishment of hegemonic forms of knowledge dominated by the "experts."[46] Fundamental to his proposal is that power relations permeate all social structures and are informed by discursive ideological underpinnings.[47] In light of this proposal we become increasingly aware of the social structures and dynamics of power relations in the biblical text and how these function to shape the narrated story.

As the Western European, Anglo, North Atlantic societies entered their own intellectual, cultural and religious crisis because of the two world wars, the twentieth century also witnessed the emergence of the cultural communities from the global South. Resisting the temptation of aligning with either one of the two reigning Western sociopolitical and economic alternatives (capitalism and communism), and invested in seeking for alternative solutions to their own social problems, these countries engaged in systematic anticolonial movements with profound political, economic, and cultural implications.[48] Part of this anticolonial posture in Africa, Asia, and Latin America was the reclaiming of their own traditions, customs, cultures, and at times religious traditions. In many places among Christian communities this reclaiming included the rejection of the Western European, Anglo, North

---

43. Lyotard, *The Postmodern Condition*, 4.

44. Michel Foucault, *Madness and Civilization: A History of Insanity in the Age of Reason*, trans. Richard Howard (New York: New York American Library, 1967); Michel Foucault, *An Introduction*, vol. 1 of *The History of Sexuality*, trans. Robert Hurley (New York: Random House, 1978).

45. Michel Foucault, *Discipline and Punish: The Birth of the Prison*, trans. Alan Sheridan (New York: Vintage, 1979).

46. Michel Foucault, *The Archaeology of Knowledge and the Discourse on Language*, trans. A. M. Sheridan Smith (New York: Pantheon, 1972).

47. Michel Foucault, *Power / Knowledge: Selected Interviews and Other Writings 1972–1977*, ed. Collin Gordon (New York: Pantheon, 1980).

48. Robert C. Young, "Postcolonialism: From Bandung to the Tricontinental," *Historein* 5 (2005) 11–21, http://www.nnet.gr/historein/historeinfiles/histvolumes/histo5/historein5-young.pdf.

American expressions of Christianity and the affirmation of their own culturally conditioned expressions and theologies.[49]

As a result, many of these communities in different places and times began the painstaking task of thinking theologically and interpreting the biblical text from their immediate sociocultural context. During this period, the Christian world saw a massive proliferation of approaches to theology and biblical hermeneutics.[50]

These numerous approaches were certainly different, and they were written from different vantage points. Latin American liberation theologies emphasized questions of class and the unique role of the Bible in critiquing social and economic structures of oppression. According to Lee Cormie liberation theology's approach created a revolution in hermeneutics in the reading of the Bible.[51] Juan Luis Segundo's hermeneutical circle provided important analytical tools for engaging the social context, for critiquing the ideological superstructures used to justify exploitation of the poor, and for appropriating the biblical message of liberation.[52] Hermeneutics became essential for dismantling pervasive economic structures of exploitation and class asymmetry. In the United States, black liberation theologians emphasized the need to take seriously the racialized content of traditional theological approaches. They insisted that racial identity and background played a central role in the way people do theology and read the biblical text.[53] For this reason one ought to be at-

---

49. Robert Schreiter, *Constructing Local Theologies* (Maryknoll, NY: Orbis, 1985) ch. 1.

50. While the voluminous nature of this enterprise impedes a proper treatment, a small sample deserves mentioning: Choan-seng Song, *Third-Eye Theology: Theology in Formation in Asian Settings* (Maryknoll, NY: Orbis, 1979); Choan-seng Song, *Theology from the Womb of Asia* (Maryknoll, NY: Orbis, 1993); R. S. Sugirtharajah, ed., *Asian Faces of Jesus* (Maryknoll, NY: Orbis, 1993); Bénézet Bujo, *African Theology in Its Social Context: Christian Leadership in Africa* (Maryknoll, NY: Orbis, 1992); Charles Villa-Vicencio, *A Theology of Reconstruction: Nation Building and Human Rights* (Cambridge: Cambridge University Press, 1992); Kosuke Koyama, *Water Buffalo Theology* (Maryknoll, NY: Orbis, 1999); Gustavo Gutiérrez, *A Theology of Liberation: History, Politics and Salvation*, ed. and trans. Sister Caridad Inda and John Eagleson (Maryknoll, NY: Orbis, 1973). In biblical hermeneutics the production was no less voluminous. See Itumeleng J. Mosala, *Biblical Hermeneutics and Biblical Theology in South Africa* (Grand Rapids: Eerdmans, 1989); José Severino Croatto, *Exodus: A Hermeneutics of Freedom*, trans. Salvator Attanasio (Maryknoll, NY: Orbis, 1978); José Severino Croatto, *Biblical Hermeneutics: Towards a Theory of Reading as the Production of Meaning*, trans. Robert Barr (Maryknoll, NY: Orbis, 1984); José Severino Croatto, "Biblical Hermeneutics in the Theologies of Liberation," trans. Robert Barr, in *Irruption of the Third World: Challenge to Theology*, ed. Virginia Fabella and Sergio Torres (Maryknoll, NY: Orbis, 1983) 140–68.

51. Lee Cormie, "Revolutions in Reading the Bible," in *The Bible and the Politics of Exegesis: Essays in Honor of Norman Gottwald on His Sixty-First Birthday*, ed. David Jobling, Peggy L. Day, and Gerald T. Sheppard (Cleveland: Pilgrim, 1991) 173–93.

52. Juan Luis Segundo, *Liberation of Theology*, trans. John Drury, (Maryknoll, NY: Orbis, 1979).

53. The resources available on black theology are vast, and there are differences and tensions among black theologians. For the purpose of this paper, those mentioned are merely a sampling of their rich and insightful contributions. James H. Cone, *Black Theology and Black Power* (Maryknoll, NY: Orbis, 1997); Simon S. Maimela, ed., *Culture, Religion and Liberation: Proceedings of the EATWOT*

tuned to the way racialized relations take place in the biblical narrative. Feminists, womanists, and women scholars of color insisted on a hermeneutics of suspicion, a rereading of the Bible in ways that challenged the androcentric character of the books of the Bible, rejected those passages that contributed in preserving ideological, social, and religious patriarchal structures, and highlighted the silencing-marginalization of women both in the Bible and society.[54] Latina/o theology and hermeneutics provided yet another current that highlighted the conditioning character of culture.[55] United States Latina/o theologians reminded us of the profound impact of culture when reading the Bible and doing theology.[56] Other developments include postcolonial expressions of theology and hermeneutics emerging from these cultural communities.[57] These many approaches uncover the wide range of issues that were left untouched and unaddressed by traditional approaches and which today we have the onerous task of teasing from the biblical text and engaging in theological reflection. Stated differently, we cannot merely allow ourselves to be confronted and absorbed by the world of the text or merge with the horizon of the text (á la Ricoeur or Gadamer respectively) without recognizing that our world impinges upon the

---

Pan African Theological Conference, Harare, Zimbabwe, January 6–11, 1991 (Praetoria, South Africa: Penrose, 1994); Jacquelyn Grant, *White Women's Christ and Black Women's Jesus* (Atlanta: Scholars, 1989); Delores S. Williams, *Sisters in the Wilderness: The Challenge of Womanist God-Talk* (Maryknoll, NY: Orbis, 1993).

54. There are many differences within these currents among women scholars, and many of them do not even ascribe to the label of "feminist." I use both labels conscious of the fact that there are many tensions and differences that deserve attention, but which go beyond the scope of this paper. For some examples see Chung Hyun-Kyung, "The Wisdom of Mothers Knows No Boundaries," in *Women's Perspectives: Articulating the Liberating Power of the Gospel* (Geneva: World Council of Churches, 1996) 28–35; Mercy Amba Oduyoye, "Gospel and Culture in Africa: Through Women's Eyes," in *Women's Perspectives*, 36–47; Ofelia Ortega, "Seeing the World Through Women's Eyes," in *Women's Perspectives*, 48–51; Letty M. Russell, *The Liberating Word: A Guide to Nonsexist Interpretation of the Bible* (Philadelphia: Westminster, 1976); Barbara E. Reid, *Taking up the Cross: New Testament Interpretations Through Latina and Feminist Eyes* (Minneapolis: Fortress, 2007); Rosemary Radford Ruether, *Sexism and God-Talk: Toward a Feminist Theology* (Boston: Beacon, 1993); María Pilar Aquino, Daisy L. Machado, and Jeanette Rodríguez, eds., *A Reader in Latina Feminist Theology: Religion and Justice* (Austin, Texas: University of Texas Press, 2002).

55. Néstor Medina, *Mestizaje: (Re)Mapping "Race, Culture, and Faith in Latina/o Catholicism* (Maryknoll, NY: Orbis, 2009); Orlando O. Espín, *Grace and Humanness: Theological Reflections Because of Culture* (Maryknoll, NY: Orbis, 2007); Justo L. González, *For the Healing of the Nations: The Book of Revelation in an Age of Cultural Conflict* (Maryknoll, NY: Orbis, 1999).

56. Justo L. González, *Santa Biblia: The Bible Through Hispanic Eyes* (Nashville: Abingdon, 1996); Justo L. González, *Mañana: Christian Theology from a Hispanic Perspective* (Nashville: Abingdon, 1990); and Medina, "Orality and Context in a Hermeneutical Key."

57. Some notable examples are Musa W. Dube Shomanah, *Postcolonial Feminist Interpretation of the Bible* (St. Louis: Chalice, 2002); Kwok Pui-lan, *Postcolonial Imagination and Feminist Theology* (Louisville: Westminster John Knox, 2005); R. S. Sugirtharajah, *The Bible and the Third World: Precolonial, Colonial and Postcolonial Encounters* (Cambridge: Cambridge University Press, 2001); Johnny Bernard Hill, *Prophetic Rage: A Postcolonial Theology of Liberation* (Grand Rapids: Eerdmans, 2013).

text a wide range of concerns and questions that until now have been absent from mainstream hermeneutics.

Despite their differences, these theological and hermeneutical currents coincide in crucial methodological points. They agree that theology cannot be done in the abstract and that the interpretation of the Bible cannot ignore the racioethnic, cultural, gender, and class differences in the narrative or in our present reality. Issues of class, ethnicity, gender and culture do not operate independently from each other; they are part of a complex web of power dynamics and key features of a more complex intellectual network inherited from imperial/colonial relations. Social context and location can provide an essential prism for biblical hermeneutics. These many and diverse approaches to reading the Bible help us in understanding that the written texts are not neutral, nor are they independent from the actual author as Ricoeur assumed. They also unmask the fallacy of the objective reader. As we engage the biblical narrative, we must dare to inquire how the author's own context finds concrete expression in the written text. We must also bring to bear the way the dynamic interaction between the actual reader and the text is impacted by the reader's biases, prejudices, questions, concerns, and interests. In other words, the identity of the actual readers in terms of gendered, racialized, and cultural background shapes the kinds of questions they ask of the Bible and the kinds of answers they get from the biblical text. In this sense we ought to approach the Bible with a deep sense of hermeneutical humility.[58]

Musings on Hermeneutics of Absence

As I have argued, liberation and post/decolonial[59] approaches to interpretation help us elucidate many of the dynamics and interactions we find among Bible characters. In suggesting a hermeneutics of absence I do not so much wish to propose an approach or method, a kind of formula that if applied will yield fruitful results. Rather, what I want to propose is more a "stance of inquiry" by which we ask the Bible the kinds of questions related to our contemporary issues. Having read the Bible many

---

58. I draw from the work of Otto Maduro as he reminds us that all forms of knowledge are always produced collectively and communally. For him there is no knowledge that is not involved in some power struggle. The genre or style has more impact than what is claimed as knowledge. See his "An(Other) Invitation to Epistemological Humility: Notes Toward a Self-Critical Approach to Counter-Knowledges," in *Decolonizing Epistemologies*, ed. Ada María Isasi-Díaz and Eduardo Mendieta (New York: Forham University Press, 2011) 87–103.

59. "Decolonial" stems from Latin American efforts to analyze colonial assumptions and develop options to challenge and separate from colonial forms of power and thinking. Such efforts unmask the complex web of colonial power relations in the establishment and production of "Western" knowledge and reclaim those forms of knowledge external to the colonial matrix.

times, I want to invite us to ask ourselves what is missing. What have we not yet asked the Bible? I want to invite us to allow the Bible to surprise us. In the same vein my intention is to problematize further the reading of the Bible and ask why our readings of the Bible are so sanitized. Why do our readings of the Bible not deal with the human struggle of racialized differences, the uncertainty and destructive power of human evil because of racism, how ethnoracial differences find themselves manifested in the text, and how those issues help us understand the God of the Bible. Stated in a positive light, how can we scrutinize the circumstances and conditions in the Hebrew Bible that provoked specific and even radical changes in the self-perception of the people of Israel that eventually led to the inclusion of others? It is worth asking about the ways in which Israel related to different neighboring communities and how their faith in God contributed to such relations. In the NT we can also ask about the shifts, changes, and conditions that allowed for reconceptualizing the divine covenant to include Gentiles. Those are questions of an ethnocultural and racialized nature that ought to be addressed diligently.

One could say that cultural criticism makes us aware of issues like honor and shame social dynamics and the subaltern role of women, but that does not help us in asking the fundamental questions of the absence of specific aspects in the narrative. For example, we are often aware that the names of many women do not appear in the stories. Feminist scholars have helped us notice that the absence of women's names unveils specific patriarchal prejudices in the author and the immediate cultural context. Similarly, we often speak of the events related to the Last Supper in light of those that we are told were there, but what if we consider the event from the perspective of those that are not mentioned in the story, those that are absent? We can safely assume that neither Jesus nor the disciples cooked the meal. There must have been servants and women involved in the preparations for the meal. So we must ask why the author did not think it necessary to mention them.

In other words, what are those missing links that need to be reconstructed and reimagined that will enable the interpretive process? What are the social structures, cultural conditions, and value systems that contribute to such dynamics of absence in the narrative? Asking why a story is structured in the way it is goes a long way in unveiling for us a wide range of social issues pertinent to the context of the narrative and that in some important ways can speak to our present context and enrich our vision of God. In this case the question I am asking is how racialized and ethnocultural issues are missing from mainstream interpretations. So in what follows I explore biblical passages to show that racialized ethnocultural identity impacted the stories in the Bible and the way the people of Israel understood the divine.

Processes of cultural, ethnic, and racialized identity formation are fluid and carry internal controversy and conflicts, and Israel is not the exception. Some of those processes are revealed by the story of Jephthah in Judges 12. Readers are introduced into an internal story depicting clans being divided by internal strife and discriminatory acts among them (ch. 13). Jephthah, the "champion" and defender of the people of Israel is threatened by his cousins as he struggles to hold power.[60] So what often is missing in prevailing interpretations is that the narrative unveils questions of identity formation. On one hand, the people of Gilead are described as "renegades from Ephraim and Manasseh" (12:4). The phrase questions the status of the Gileadites in terms of belonging and suggests their identity as outsiders or refugees, not "original" to the area.[61] These are issues of outright discrimination. As a result, the Gileadites felt insulted and decided to exact revenge on the Ephraimites by entering into battle with them (12:3–5). In order to guard their borders the Gileadites devised a clever, racialized culturally identifiable strategy to distinguish them from the Ephraimites. Here the regional dialect differences stand out. Since the Gileadites would not have been able to tell the differences between them and the Ephraimites by ways of physical features, they opt for the obvious linguistic differences instead and focus on the (mis)pronunciation of the *sh* sound in "shibboleth," which identifies the Ephraimites as foreigners.[62]

Now today "shibboleth" is used to point to specific customs, principles, or beliefs that distinguish a particular class or group of people, but in the narrative it refers more directly to the linguistic nuances, accents, and regional inflections by which people were distinguished and through which questions of identity get negotiated. In the case of the Ephraimites it was this distinct, racialized, culturally identifiable mark, this "simple" test word which forty-two thousand Ephraimites were unable to pronounce to ensure their survival.[63] This is not a religious story but a racialized cultural story of insider-outsider within the tribes of Israel and the actual human damage it caused. We know that notions of identity and the understanding of insider-outsider are fluid and in constant change. The multilevel ethnocultural boundaries are always actively negotiated-in flux, and tensions are momentarily "resolved" by way of clashes and sometimes bloody encounters. This particular incident shows an instance of internal negotiation between insiders and how the boundaries

---

60. Susan Niditch, *Judges: A Commentary* (Louisville, KY: Westminster, John Knox, 2008) 137.

61. Ibid.

62. For a fuller discussion on the role of language and its connection to foreigners see Niditch, *Judges*.

63. Ryan Roger, *Judges*, New Bible Commentary (Sheffield: Sheffield Phoenix, 2007) 94.

between insider and outsider were constituted as Israel's cultural and ethnic identity developed.

Shifting to Israel's relations with other ethnoracial and cultural groups, the book of Ruth provides useful insights. The entire account allows us to see how permeable the boundaries of identity are. I want to focus on the dynamics of the religious activity of "redemption" in terms of the way such a notion functions in establishing responsibilities between people of the same genealogical tree and in the ways Israelites related to foreigners.[64]

The story revolves around the Moabite "faceless" woman named Ruth;[65] missing in the story is a fuller description of her, which we can infer relates to her "lower" status for being a woman and a "foreigner." Nevertheless, we are told Ruth decided to accompany her Israelite ex-mother-in-law Naomi back to the land of her ancestors. As the narrative unravels, Ruth makes the heart-wrenching decision to leave behind the world she knew and accompany Naomi to Bethlehem. As a widow who does not have many resources, Naomi finds that she still has distant relatives. Two themes emerge in the story, although they are not explicitly stated: (1) the good treatment of foreigners as mandated by God in the Law (Exod 22:21; Lev 19:33; Deut 10:19), (2) the instruction to Israel not to exploit the poor (Lev 25:35; 27:19). The social apparatus that should protect these two women is already in place. The poor, the widow, and the foreigner are included together when instructions against injustice are given in the Law (Deut 27:19). There is something about the vulnerability of those who fall in these categories that God admonishes the Israelites to protect and care for them. Not to care for the poor, the widow and the foreigner then runs counter to the divine intent. Ruth and Naomi together represent these three groups as widows, poor women, and in the case of Ruth, as racially, culturally, and "nationally" a foreigner. The narrative reminds the readers of very important divine mandates with social, political, and racialized cultural implications to regulate the people of Israel, while leaving the reader expecting to see how this entire saga will unfold.

Boaz wished to marry Ruth and in turn provide offspring in memory of Elimelech and his sons (Deut 25:5), but he was also aware of a relative in the line of "redemption" prior to him (Ruth 3:12). He was obviously interested in Ruth, yet he wanted to follow the proper cultural-religiously established protocol. The tension between the divine duty and the observance of the culturally required public

64. For a brief discussion on the role of the redeemer in the OT see Vanthanh Nguyen, "Dismantling Cultural Boundaries: Missiological Implications of Acts 10:1–11:18," *Missiology: An International Review* 40 (2012) 455–66.

65. For a full discussion on Ruth's facelessness and its social implication in the Bible see Mishael Maswari and Rachel S. Havrelock, *Women in the Biblical Road: Ruth, Naomi, and the Female Journey* (Lanham, MD: University Press of America, 1996) 155–90.

formalization becomes evident. The nearest kinsman-redeemer agreed to buy the piece of property from Naomi and by extension from Ruth (4:4), but when he became aware that the land came attached with responsibility to Ruth and to provide offspring to Elimelech and preserve his name (4:5), the kinsman-redeemer backed out. It is unclear whether the perceived risk by the nearer kinsman-redeemer to his own state was related to the fact that Ruth was a foreigner. What is clear is that a public ceremony exposing his unwillingness for not "building up his brother's house" is carried out, which traditionally included the cultural gestures of removing his sandals—and henceforth being known as "the house of the unsandalled one"—and having Ruth spit in his face to shame and humiliate him (Deut 25:5-10).[66] Although the spitting is not recorded, we are told that the relative did remove his sandal (4:8). Consequently, Boaz married Ruth. Implicit in the story is that by marrying Ruth, Boaz fulfilled his divine duty not only to Elimelech by preserving his name but also to Ruth as a widow, a poor person, and a foreigner (4:9-13).

The intersection between the cultural and religious dimensions and identity cannot be overstated in the story of Ruth. The story reveals the dynamic and changing character of ethnocultural and racial boundaries and the porous nature of identity formation. It also shows how the divine mandate is particularly invested in protecting these vulnerable people, which to me signify the "others." By the end of the story, Ruth and Boaz are included in the ancestral line of David (4:22). By the time one gets to the NT, Ruth is celebrated as ancestress in the distinguished lineage of Jesus along with Rahab (Matt 1:5). Ruth embodies the fulfillment of Israel's duty toward the foreigner by welcoming them.

In the Hebrew Bible some of the most obvious examples concerning racialized prejudices and racialization of culture relate to questions of marriage. We have seen that in the case of Ruth the outcome can be interpreted as potentially liberative and welcoming for "foreigners."

In the case of Ezra-Nehemiah it can be (mis)construed as having xenophobic implications. One ought to be careful not to apply anachronistic views of racism. At the same time, the Ezra-Nehemiah incident on endogamy can serve modern readers as a cautionary tale of the potentially exclusionary perils of nationalist ethnoracial and cultural identity.

The books of Ezra (9-10) and Nehemiah (13:23) record the incident related to mixed marriages. The books record the painstaking process of rebuilding the city of Jerusalem by the Israelites who had returned from exile. There are enormous commonalities between both accounts: both include the challenge of mixed marriages,

---

66. Calum M. Carmichael, "A Ceremonial Crux: Removing a Man's Sandal as a Female Gesture of Contempt," *JBL* 96 (1977) 321-36.

both mention radical measures toward endogamy, and both connect mixed marriages to the larger concern of idolatry borrowed from other nations and the Israelite sin of unfaithfulness through marriage to foreign women. But there are some crucial differences as well. Mixed marriages in Ezra relate not necessarily to our contemporary notions of "racialized prejudices." Rather, it relates to the complex process of asserting differences in order to exert control over the region and establish and maintain the lines of ethnic boundaries.[67] Racialized differences were being created and religion played a central role in this negotiation. In Ezra, marriage with other groups is perceived not so much as a biological-racialized threat as involving irreconcilable cultural and religious differences. Since the racialized cultural and the religious are so intertwined, intermarriages could potentially signify the eventual undermining of the people's own ethnocultural traditions and religious understanding. Attitudes of cultural and racialized xenophobia expressed in the books expose the nexus between the desire to reclaim their sense of identity as people and the necessity to reject foreigners in order to protect their cultural traditions. The concern about miscegenation with neighboring groups relates to the perceived long-standing differences and the memory of the emotional trauma of historical exile embodied in those who returned and those who stayed.

In the case of Nehemiah it is unclear what will happen with those who marry foreign women, but the taboo against it is made clear. The prior rejection of intermarriage with their Ammonite and Moabite cousins (Gen 19:37–38) is connected to their centuries old unwelcoming attitude.[68] Remember, Ruth was a Moabite. As to the women from Ashdod, they may have been considered descendants of the earlier enemies of the Israelites, the Philistines.[69] In Nehemiah the responsibility for purity fell upon the Levites who are instructed to purify themselves "of everything foreign" (13:30). Curiously, Nehemiah centers on the intersection between the "holy" character of the people of Israel being "set apart," and implicit "other" cultural elements that threaten it. We are told that Nehemiah was enraged when he discovered that half of the children of the men of Judah "spoke the language of Ashdod or the language of one of the other peoples, and did not know how to speak the language of Judah" (13:24). In this passage a connection is made between religious affiliations and devotion, cultural elements, and ethnoracial identity. The linguistic-cultural element symbolizes, for Nehemiah, religious faith and extreme religious zeal.

67. Katherine E. Southwood, *Ethnicity and the Mixed Marriage Crisis in Ezra 9–10: An Anthropological Approach* (Oxford: Oxford University Press, 2012) 125.

68. ". . . because they had not met the Israelites with food and water but had hired Balaam to call a curse down on them" (Neh 13:2).

69. R. J. Coggins, *The Books of Ezra and Nehemiah: A Commentary* (Cambridge: Cambridge University Press, 1976) 143.

In both instances intrinsic to the decision of the priestly class to separate themselves from their foreign wives was the conscious awareness of their own identity as "holy people." Nasili Vaka'uta reminds us that there are several ways in which notions of uncleanness and impurity operate in this passage. For him there are at least three ways in which these can be interpreted: the people of the land as untouchables (potentially racialized), ceremonial impurity (ritual or sexual-ethical), and geographical uncleanness. These three meanings have been loaded by the "chiefs" "on to the phrase 'peoples of the land,' providing . . . a strong basis for their objection to inter-marriage" between the men among the returned exiles and the women of the people of the land.[70] The allusion to Solomon in Neh 13:26 confirms the fears of idolatry. But as Katherine Southwood explains, the theological language of the "elected" status of Israel operates as the "motivation for avoiding intermarriage (Deut 7:3–4) or any alliances with other nations."[71] The implication is that by turning away and serving the "other gods" of the nations, "Israel would compromise its 'holy' status (Deut 7:4–5)."[72] So it seems, she claims, that Ezra conflated these notions of holiness and applied them to all of Israel; they ought to regulate the people's personal lives in the fashion that was only required from the priests. In the Ezra story, resonating with Nehemiah, "holiness" bears multiple levels of applicability, including the racialized ethnocultural boundaries of Israel. As Israel wrestled with what it meant to be an Israelite or part of "the holy people," the construction of ethnic and cultural boundaries became necessary in order to navigate and negotiate the complex and contested processes in such a racialized culturally diverse context. The deeply theological meaning of Israel as "the holy people" received its concrete expression in the creation of ethnocentric, racialized cultural boundaries as markers to distinguish them from other groups.

The Ezra-Nehemiah passage has been a source of great debate in contemporary cultural, identity, and race theories. It would be a mistake to interpret Ezra's and Nehemiah's claims for "separateness" and insistence on endogamy as justification for segregation or to condemn interracial marriages or unions. It would also be a mistake to interpret these passages as outright xenophobic prejudices as understood today, particularly because contemporary racialized notions deploy flawed Eurocentric racialized ideas of purity-impurity and supremacy-inferiority that run counter the divine creative order. As I stated earlier, there are passages in the Bible where

---

70. Nasili Vaka'uta, *Reading Ezra 9–10 Tu'a-Wise: Thinking Biblical Interpretation in Oceania* (Atlanta: Society of Biblical Literature, 2011) 126.

71. Southwood, *Ethnicity and the Mixed Marriage Crisis in Ezra 9–10*, 126.

72. Ibid.

the Israelites welcomed those who voluntarily adopted their religious and cultural traditions (Ezra 6:21),[73] of which Ruth is one good example.

That said, it is possible that the Israelites in the story might have had sentiments toward racialized purity embedded in the cultural boundaries they established, which led to the rejection of other people. However, we cannot directly infer those from these passages. The intention here is neither to condemn nor condone the events described in the narrative. Rather, it is to elucidate the way the intimate interconnection between the religious, the racialized processes, and the cultural symbols play out, the way these are negotiated with contested notions of faith in YHWH, and the way people's devotion to God received expressions through them.

The Hebrew Bible is certainly the record of historical events over centuries and of the social, political, economic, religious, and human factors and conditions that contributed to those events. As I have been insisting, the Hebrew Bible also functions as the ethnocultural memory of the people of Israel. As such, it shows how over time the people's understandings of God became racialized and culturalized in the very fabric of Judaism and the identity of the Hebrew people. It also shows that questions of racialization, racism, and ethnic identity do not play a small role in the very social fabric. These factors often are mixed with religious overtones to give them legitimacy. This is where we have to be careful not to misread the text and make it say something that was not intended from the beginning.

By the time one arrives at the NT, it becomes evident that Israel's self-perception has undergone enormous developments. The record of the NT shows that first-century Palestine had become the crossroads of multiple ethnocultural groups and religious traditions and as a result was a culturally volatile context. In some instances age-old ethnic and racialized cultural conflicts persisted, but new clashes emerged based on different ethnoracial, cultural, religious, and social status. New kinds of social prejudices and discriminatory attitudes among the groups are recorded (e.g., from Jews toward Samaritans and Greeks, and from Romans toward Jews). We see that the system of differentiation of peoples based on ethnicity, culture, and geographical location is still operative: Greek (John 7:28; 12: 20), Syrophenician (Mark 7:26), Gadara (Matt 8:28), Jerusalem, Judea, and the ends of the world (Acts 1:8). As a result the complexity of the cultural milieu and differences among social groups trickle into the writings. Drawing on two examples from the NT (the conversation of Jesus with the Samaritan woman in John 4 and Peter's "conversion" experience and interaction with Cornelius and his family in Acts 10), I illustrate how racialized tensions and multilevel cultural, ethnic, social, and religious clashes play a central role in the stories. These passages illustrate very well the radical departure of Christianity

---

73. Coggins, *The Books of Ezra and Nehemiah*, 56.

from Judaism in terms of revising the previous ethnocentric understanding of the divine covenant.

The conversation between the Samaritan woman and Jesus brings to mind the crisis of mixed marriages in Ezra-Nehemiah discussed earlier, and the problem of mixed children that were born from those unions. Second Kings 17 records the historical circumstances that brought about the ethnic, cultural, and religious tensions between the Jews and the Samaritans.[74] The old tensions and differences between religious "factions" seem to remain unresolved in John 4, this time with added complexities. Jesus's "unplanned" visit through Samaria signals a cultural and religious shift and challenge to prevailing Jewish ideas about the Samaritans.

The passage can be understood as an encounter between members of two colonized peoples,[75] and a careful analysis shows that questions of culture-ethnicity, gender, and religious tradition haunt the interaction.[76] Teresa Okure claims, "the fulcrum . . . of the entire episode between Jesus and the Samaritan woman is her discovery of who Jesus is."[77] Their conversation revolves around redrawing the shifting lines of the existing ethnocultural boundaries in a way that Jesus's identity is presented as ambiguous, moving from being explicitly Jewish to being incorporated among the Samaritans.[78] Jesus represents the colonizer Jews, writes Sung Uk Lim, but the woman's act of anticolonial mimicry of mixing Jewish and Samaritan identities blurs the lines of distinction between them in a way that "the colonial authority of Jesus as the colonizer from the perspective of the Samaritans as the colonized is damaged."[79]

There is tension in the act of mimicry in the story (4:40–42). The woman represents the Samaritans "who are Jews but not completely." The Samaritans also claim to worship YHWH but are not part of mainstream Judaism. She too becomes the "missionary" to her own people, like Jesus, "but not completely." In the process Jesus's identity as the colonizer becomes more complex through the invitation to stay with

---

74. The mutual hatred of Jews and Samaritans intensified during the postexilic period as narrated by Ezra-Nehemiah, particularly when Zerubabel did not allow the Samaritans to help rebuild the Temple (Ezra 4). "So around 300 BCE the Samaritans built their own shrine on Mount Gerizim as a rival to the Temple in Jerusalem" (Teresa Okure, "Jesus and the Samaritan Woman [Jn 4:1–42] in Africa," *TS* 70 [2009] 401-418, 407).

75. Sung Uk Lim, "Speak My Name: Anti-Colonial Mimicry and the Samaritan Woman in John 4:1–42," *USQR* 62.3-4 (2010) 35–51.

76. See Okure, "Jesus and the Samaritan Woman," 406–07, 416. See also Musa W. Dube, "Reading for Decolonization (John 4.1–42)," in *Voices from the Margins*, R. S. Sugirtharajah (Maryknoll, NY: Orbis, 2006) 297–318, 309.

77. Okure, "Jesus and the Samaritan Woman," 409.

78. Lim, "Speak My Name," 46.

79. Ibid., 47.

them (4:42). At the urge of the villagers Jesus gets "Samaritanized"; his unwillingness to exercise his privileges gains him acceptance into the woman's ethnic group. As Lim puts it, in this move the colonizer is assimilated into the colonized; Jesus embodies the colonizer and the colonized at the same time.[80]

Curiously enough, Jesus's identity is later challenged in relation to the Samaritans in John 8, where he is accused of being a Samaritan, an accusation which he does not refute. In the other Gospels (particularly in Luke 10:30–36) Jesus takes the Samaritans, the very people who are looked down upon by the Jews, as an object lesson of piety, devotion, and love of neighbor.

This reading of Jesus's conversation with the Samaritan woman notwithstanding, the story also demonstrates the intersection of cultural and ethnic identity and how these change, shift, and move in the quotidian context. We also learn that issues of power relations cannot be removed from interethnic and cultural relations. There is, in fact, a privilege and power differential at play in the conversation between Jesus and the Samaritan woman. For John's mainly Jewish audience, the jarring effect of the story is that the ethnocultural "outsiders" are elevated in dignity. The Samaritans are not dismissed as unclean or impure (remember Ezra-Nehemiah) or required to relinquish or change their ethnocultural identity. Instead, the Jews are required to change their perceptions of the Samaritans. Most importantly, the passage concretely shows the dynamic, contested, and porous character of cultures and ethnic identities as they get configured and reconfigured in the day-to-day exchanges.

Similar dynamics of ethnocentrism and discriminatory attitudes toward other ethnocultural groups by the Jews appear in the interaction between Peter and Cornelius in Acts 10. The story is framed around issues of impurity and uncleanness, highlighting how the Israelites viewed themselves in relation to all other groups in the region (11:2–3). Chris Miller notes that food is a crucial point of debate in the passage.[81] The text revolves around "the sociocultural dynamics of food, meals, and table fellowship."[82] Much like the passage about the Syrophoenician woman, this text reveals the playful intersection between the racialized cultural and ethnic differences and the resulting tensions centered on eating. In this case Peter's (and the Christian Jews') inherited understanding of purity is put into question. His experience at the house of Cornelius causes his (and that of his Jewish companions') ethnic, cultural, and religious claims to exclusivity to collapse. He is forced to rethink fundamentally his sense of divine "chosenness:" "God has now granted the Gentiles not only repen-

---

80. Ibid., 50.

81. Chris A. Miller, "Did Peter's Vision in Acts 10 Pertain to Men or the Menu?" *BibSac* 159 (2002) 302–17.

82. Nguyen, "Dismantling Cultural Boundaries," 460.

tance unto life, but also the fullness of the Holy Spirit and full acceptance into his household as first-class citizens."[83] By having Peter enter the house of Cornelius, Luke no longer regards "Gentile homes as unclean and off limits for Jewish Christians."[84]

The encounter between Peter and Cornelius is also important because the Spirit is said to be poured on all those present in the house of Cornelius, despite the fact that there is no record that he or those present ever adopted Judaism. Peter himself in Acts 11:17 testifies that the incident at the house of Cornelius made him realize that he and the other followers of Jesus needed to rethink their inherited theological notions of distinction and separation. The book of Acts provides crucial insights as to how Jewish ethnocultural and religious perceptions of Gentiles were being fundamentally transformed even as Christianity was being born.

Conclusion

As I indicated at the beginning, the discipline of hermeneutics has changed enormously. Philosophers, Bible scholars, and theologians all have invested great efforts in devising new approaches to interpret the biblical text in a better way. Since the middle of the twentieth century, hermeneutics has changed at a faster pace in great part because the Eurocentric character of theology, biblical scholarship, and philosophy has been challenged. Those other cultural groups previously absent from prevalent versions of Christian scholarship and theology brought forth critical new approaches that reclaim the role of gender, social location, racial-ethnic background, and cultural tradition in the biblical text from its original production to its reading and interpretation in multiple settings today.

Indeed, while we affirm the foundational character of the both the Hebrew Bible and the NT for the Christian faith, a theological hermeneutics of absence cannot avoid talking about the experience of faith in God without engaging issues of racial, ethnic, and cultural backgrounds and dynamics. Those elements tend to shape the ways people relate to God, their immediate contexts, and to each other. Similarly, questions of racialized differences are not a recent development but have shaped all of human history, even since biblical times. In the midst of current issues of evident racialized violence directed to African Americans, racialized criminalization of Latin American immigrants and Latinas/os, and racialized cultural destruction of native Americans and First Nations, the single most important message from a hermeneutics of absence is the celebration and struggle for the sacredness of the life of the racialized, discriminated other. This is the mandate that the Spirit of God

---

83. Miller, "Peter's Vision in Acts 10," 316.
84. Nguyen, "Dismantling Cultural Boundaries," 458.

places on us, and it is with such people in their struggle for life that the Spirit of God is being made manifest and the kingdom of God is being built.

RESPONSE TO MEDINA

Bruce L. Fields

"And I have other sheep that are not of this fold. I must bring them also, and they will listen to my voice. So there will be one flock, one shepherd." (John 10:16 [ESV])

"I therefore, a prisoner for the Lord, urge you to walk in a manner worthy of the calling to which you have been called, with all humility and gentleness, with patience, bearing with one another in love, eager to maintain the unity of the Spirit in the bond of peace." (Eph 4:1–3)

The passages above affirm the biblical priority of unity in the church, not just in terms of common confession, but love for one another. Among the many contributions that Medina's work makes to a discussion on hermeneutics is the contribution of an awareness of the possible establishment and maintenance of positions of power in any seemingly harmless human encounter. Appeals to unity may indeed cloak such an establishment and maintenance. Calls to unity, though they can be abused, can never be ignored simply because of the danger of abuse. Movement towards unity can be applied to discussions, emergent methodologies, applications in the realm of hermeneutics, and with the focus on biblical texts. Medina, appropriately, has his own objectives in the production of his work, concisely summarized in a call for entering "the text's narrative" with the sensitivities aroused by the named stories and the unique "epistemological sources" of various interpretive communities. The uniqueness of various interpretive communities must be respected in the hermeneutical project, if for no other reason, than to facilitate blessings arising from the mutual sharing of understandings and applications from the biblical text.

Like Medina, my purpose in this response is not to construct "the" hermeneutical method. He has offered a multitude of determinative observations and analyses in this paper. I can comment, however, on only a few things. I will first identify some of Medina's reminders and challenges in the sphere of hermeneutics. I will then offer some cautions and questions in light of aspects of his thought. My overarching hope is that we learn and incorporate relevant elements of his thought to move us to greater authenticity and transformative power as we engage the biblical text. My cautions and questions arise from the burden for unity, whereby we respect the uniqueness of various hermeneutical communities, but we are also enabled to remember through the text, the instructions, the confessions, and the needed correctives to our communities that can empower us to be one.

It was extremely helpful to be exposed to the contributions of people who shaped hermeneutics in the previously dominant culture. I found the discussions of Hans-Georg Gadamer and Paul Ricoeur to be very informative. I especially resonated, however, with Medina's summary concerning these people who put so much confidence in their "rational capacities" for the hermeneutical project, while simultaneously demonstrating a lack of awareness of their own sociocultural location in formulating their thought. The three-fold impact of postmodernism and Michel Foucault's understanding of the "conditioning power" of knowledge, propagated in various social contexts and readings of Scripture, set the stage well for discussing the decentralizing impact on such dominant discussions by emergent interpreters from communities previously unrecognized or insufficiently engaged.

I was intrigued and encouraged by the knowledge that after two world wars there were countries in the global South, as well as in Africa and Asia, who were "engaged in systematic anticolonial movements with profound political, economic, and cultural implications." The rise of liberation, black, feminist, and womanist theological constructs, along with various anticolonialist movements, would have enormous impact not only on sociopolitical relationships in various settings, but also on the church, on theological reflection, and particularly on the reading and interpretation of Scripture. These interpretive communities alert readers to such realities as the fact that there are no "neutral" readings of Scripture, the presence of racial-ethnic dynamics in the text, power relationships, and the molding and shifting dimensions of identity.

I was both grateful for and challenged by many aspects of Medina's work, but I was particularly grateful for the "permission" to plumb the depths of my own black church heritage, seeking further transformative engagements with the Scriptures, which will lead to deeper communion with my Lord through these texts. I do have, however, some cautions and questions regarding his hermeneutic of absence project. The first is the probing for a heightened specificity on what is "missing" in hermeneutical discussions. Second, I want to comment briefly on the significance of an example of sociocultural blindness manifested in the Scriptures. Finally, the sensitivities arising from anticolonial readings of Scripture should still consider the contributions of intertextual readings within the Scriptures. I will revisit Jesus's encounter with the Samaritan woman in John 4 to address this potentiality.

Is there a more dominant understanding that should be associated with the meaning of "missing" in interpretive processes? Should we focus more on what may be missing in hermeneutical discussions, or should we focus on what may be "missing" in the text itself? For example, in a consideration of the narratives of the Lord's Supper, it is one thing to say that dominant hermeneutical discussions miss some points of meaning and application. It is another to suggest that something is missing in the text, calling for the insertion of some creative formulation. It may be beneficial to consider the perspective of food-preparers and servers, but do we have access to this perspective?

The absence of women's names in the totality of Scripture could indeed reveal underlying patriarchal tendencies in the sociocultural fabric of the biblical writers. Though this is a legitimate observation to bring to the biblical text, I would just raise another consideration. Where women's names are recorded, are they and the contextual surroundings significant? The number of times something appears or does not appear in Scripture can be an exegetical marker of significance. Sometimes, that which does not occur frequently may still have great importance. Many examples could be cited such as Sarah (Gen 17:15), Deborah, the judge (Judg 4:4), and Mary, the mother of Jesus (Luke 1:26–27). One can even bring to such reflections the meaning of Hagar (Gal 4:24–25), as in the case of the womanist theologian Delores Williams.[1]

Finally, a postcolonial reading of Jesus's meeting with the Samaritan woman in John can yield some interesting insights, as Medina demonstrates. Along with lessons learned from a consideration of Samaritans "who are Jews but not completely" and comparisons with the situations of mixed-blood people, there are still further gleanings arising from considerations of intertextuality that can enhance the understanding of this encounter. From 2 Kgs 17, for example, we learn that the northern tribes were repeatedly warned of judgment for covenant violations, and they did not listen. They were exiled to Assyria, and other groups were moved into the area by the Assyrians. These people worshipped God, but they also worshipped the gods of their previous lands, even burning their children in sacrifice (2 Kgs 17:31). Second Kings 17:41 reads: "So these nations feared the Lord and also served their carved images. Their children did likewise, and their children's children—as their fathers did, so they do to this day." The attitude of the Jewish people in Jesus's day toward the Samaritans had become sin-infested and deplorable. Still, lessons were to be learned from the OT background concerning the consequences of covenantal unfaithfulness that contributed to the reported hostility in John 4.

---

1. Delores S. Williams, *Sisters in the Wilderness: The Challenge of Womanist God-Talk* (Maryknoll, NY: Orbis, 1993) 4–5.

Medina's hermeneutical project succeeds in establishing "a stance of enquiry" for our purposes. I hope for future hermeneutical discussions that include respect for racial/ethnic, gender, and geographical uniqueness as a part of the study the Scriptures. There is so much that people can contribute to one another. May we listen to streams of diversity in biblical dialogue, while maintaining a movement toward agreement on the message of the text. May the church live with authenticity in the sphere of "one Lord, one faith, one baptism, one God and Father of all, who is over all and through all and in all" (Eph 4:5–6).

"LOST IN TRANSLATION: ETHNIC CONFLICT IN ENGLISH BIBLES"—THE GOSPELS, "RACE," AND THE COMMON ENGLISH BIBLE

An Introductory and Exploratory Conversation

Emerson B. Powery

Translation matters. Most readers of the Bible examine the ancient stories in translation. Few contemporary readers think about the process of translation itself. Translation can be an act of humility. It can, alternatively, be an act of violence.[1] In any case, as one theorist reflects, "translation is the most intimate act of reading."[2]

According to the recent extensive survey carried out by the Center for the Study of Religion and American Culture (at Indiana University-Purdue University Indianapolis), most North American readers read only one Bible. They do not divide up the time reviewing several English Bibles. Translation matters. Which translation a person reads has the potential to inform the Christian reader exclusively! Most do not participate in seminary activities comparing various English translations, even though Bible apps of most English translations are available. The majority of Bible users still tend to read only one English Bible, and according to the survey that majority prefers the King James Version.

One example from the KJV that dovetails with our area of inquiry is the classic example in the Song of Solomon,[3] as seventeenth-century British translators "interpreted" the ancient author's description of the lover in the story as "black but comely (or, lovely)" rather than "black and beautiful."[4] Even though the Hebrew conjunction

---

1. Randall C. Bailey and Tina Pippin, eds. *Race, Class, and the Politics of Bible Translation*. Semeia 76 (Atlanta: Scholars, 1996) 3.

2. Gayatri Chakravorty Spivak, "The Politics of Translation," in *Outside in the Teaching Machine* (New York: Routledge, 1993) 183.

3. One analogy in contemporary English translation is the rendering of *doulos* as "servant" rather than the more culturally visceral sounding "slave." For example, Jesus's saying "Well done, good and faithful slave" does not sound like an encouraging reminder for persistent discipleship. Cf. Clarice Martin, "The *Haustafeln* (Household Codes) in African American Interpretation: 'Free Slaves' and 'Subordinate Women,'" in *Stony the Road We Trod: African American Biblical Interpretation*, ed. Cain Hope Felder (Minneapolis: Fortress, 1991) 206–231.

4. The NRSV and CEB have the latter.

wāw can be translated as either "and" or "but," some English translations—the NIV and ESV—continue the tradition of the KJV. Nineteenth-century commentators followed the implications of the KJV's use of "but" with startling (to our ears) remarks, such as Adam Clarke's widely popular commentary: "I am black, but comely. This is literally true of many of the Asiatic women; *though* black or brown, they are exquisitely beautiful. Many of the Egyptian women are still fine; *but* their complexion is much inferior to that of the Palestine females" (my italics).[5] It is this kind of translation and interpretive tradition that leads to Crystal Valentine's lyric in her 2015 poem, "Black Privilege is being so unique that not even God will look like you."[6]

In this exploratory paper I am interested primarily in one question: did the Gospel writers have an ethnic bias? Or, as Cain Felder put it over twenty-five years ago, "The immediate significance of this New Testament tendency to focus on Rome instead of Jerusalem is that the darker races outside the Roman orbit are for the most part overlooked by New Testament authors."[7] This presentation is not, however, a study of the original texts and authors. Rather, I investigate four passages in the canonical Gospels available to contemporary English readers. So, an answer to the question may depend on which English translation one reads. That is really what I want to examine. I want to look at five "popular" English translations: KJV, NIV, NRSV, ESV, and CEB.[8] Does the 2011 Common English Bible, for example—with the most ethnically diverse and gender inclusive group of translators in the history of English versions—provide a more ethnically sensitive translation? Or, did

---

5. Adam Clarke, *The Holy Bible Containing the Old and New Testaments, With a Commentary and Critical Notes* (New York: Abraham Paul, 1825). When working on translation consistency for the CEB, one of the OT editors and I had conversations about a number of passages in which the simile "white as snow" was commonly used, a clear influence of the KJV that has lingered in several contemporary translations (cf. Num 12:10; 2 Kgs 5:27). Compare the NIV and NRSV. Despite its wide usage, Randall Bailey has argued, "It appears that the formula to be made white as snow is not a blessing in the Hebrew Bible. Rather it is a curse." ("They Shall Become 'White as Snow,'" in *Race, Class, and the Politics of Bible Translation*, 108). In the middle of the nineteenth century, one formerly enslaved individual, William Anderson, interpreted the use of this phrase—in the cursing of Elisha's servant, Gehazi (cf. 2 Kgs 5:1–20)—as the beginning of the origins of white skin color (*Life and Narrative of William J. Anderson, Twenty-four Years a Slave* (Chicago: Daily Tribune Book and Job Printing Office, 1857) 62.

6. https://www.youtube.com/watch?v=7rYL83kHQ8Y. I put the YouTube version of the poem because performance is crucial to the affective nature of this medium.

7. *Troubling Biblical Waters: Race, Class, and Family* (Maryknoll, NY: Orbis, 1989) 46.

8. Center for the Study of Religion and American Culture: KJV 55 percent, NIV 19 percent, NRSV 7 percent, other 8 percent. In a 2011 survey performed by the Bowker group (with 1700 respondents), the order of preference is similar, although the percentage of KJV users drops significantly in this study: KJV 30 percent; NIV 17 percent; ESV 7 percent; NRSV 4 percent; CEB 2 percent; other 8 percent.

the racialized impression of the KJV's tradition imprint itself also upon this recent translation effort?[9]

I need to offer a disclaimer. I was an Associate Greek Editor for the Apocrypha and the NT for the CEB, responsible for translating a couple of books, reviewing and revising many books, and discussing most books with other editors. The people contributing to the translation process included 120 biblical scholars from twenty-two faith traditions, and unlike previous translation work, one-third of the translators were from an underrepresented population with respect to gender and race. Also, seventy-seven reading groups from diverse ethnic and denominational congregations reviewed early drafts to ensure a natural reading experience.

"Greek, Syrophoenician by Birth"—Mark 7:24–30

Since this paper deals with the nature of translation, not issues on the relationships among the Synoptic Gospels (as interesting as these are), I will discuss parallel passages separately. Do any of the five translations investigated in this study create more or less racial ethnic tension between the characters in the story than its translation counterparts? Is Jesus more open or less open to the "other" in the renderings of these English translations? What might the readers who examine only one translation encounter with respect to ethnic tension in the ancient world?

Before we turn directly to the passage at hand, a glance at the CEB's sub-title to Mark 7:24–30 is worth noticing: "An Immigrant's Daughter is Delivered." The oddity, of course, is that Jesus is the "immigrant" in this story; he has transgressed borders to "rest" (apparently) from his mission. Jesus entered the region of Tyre; he went "into a house" to get away from the crowd. Josephus, the first-century historian, referred to Tyre as a foreign territory, even calling the Tyrians Israel's "enemies."[10] Mark 3:8 indicates that people "surrounding Tyre" (*peri Tyron*), probably Jews not Tyrians, were part of the large crowd attracted to Jesus in his early mission. More than likely, Jesus probably entered the "house" of a recent acquaintance for privacy. But Tyre was not Jewish territory.

This is the first time Mark introduces a character with her (or his) ethnic descriptors (cf. 15:21).[11] Of course, it is not the initial piece of information for the

---

9. Randall Bailey labels the KJV "the most racist of all English translations," in "The Danger of Ignoring One's Own Cultural Bias in Interpreting the Text," in *The Postcolonial Bible*, ed. R. S. Sugirtharajah (Sheffield: Sheffield Academic, 1998) 76. For understanding the more "conservative" or more "liberal" ideologies behind several of the English translations utilized in this study, see Peter Thuesen, *In Discordance with the Scriptures: American Protestant Battles over Translating the Bible* (New York: Oxford University Press, 1999).

10. *Against Apion* 1.70.

11. Although it is not the direct focus of the paper, *gender* particulars also flood this narrative. Cf.

audience. First, Mark introduces her as a mother with a young daughter who was ill. Second, Mark describes her as one well-connected to the community, since she heard about Jesus's visit "right away" (CEB). Third, Mark indicates she is a determined mother who seeks out Jesus.

Before Mark describes her ethnic background, the CEB and NIV provide language of "possession" to describe the child's condition. None of the other English translations surveyed utilizes this word. Does spirit-possession language matter for a study on ethnic difference? It might if this language is reserved only for non-Jewish characters associated with wrong spirits. The CEB, however, understands *echein* as referring to possession here and even for the charge against Jesus: "the legal experts were saying, 'He's possessed by an evil spirit'" (3:30).[12] At least, according to the CEB, the Jewish leaders thought it possible for a self-proclaimed Jewish prophet to be possessed by a spirit. The NIV does not follow suit. Their Jesus simply "has an impure spirit," disregarding the more forceful expression that Jesus was possessed. On the other hand, the NRSV never uses possession language for any of the cases with "unclean spirits," whether the association is with Jews or non-Jews. But the CEB utilizes the language democratically, that is, for both Jew and Gentile. In either case, no ethnic preference seems to occur.

The description of the woman's initial action when she visits Jesus may also be an indication of ethnic tension. Most English translations (e.g., CEB, ESV, KJV, and NIV) describe her act as "falling down" before Jesus, expressing an act of desperation, potential ethnic differences aside. The NRSV's depiction of this desperate woman, who is acting without a male proxy, as bowing at Jesus's feet sounds more like a thoughtful, controlled, subtle act of high respect, perhaps a way to endear herself to the Jewish healer. "Falling" appears frantic, irrespective of the setting; "bowing" seems reserved and may hide the character's intentions. "Falling" represents an act that illustrates the woman's condition; "bowing" demonstrates awareness of the other person's reaction. Was the woman's initial genuflecting movement an act of reservation and, thereby, cool contemplation of the ethnic other? The more reserved act of "bowing" may create a subtle form of ethnic distance that "falling" down would not capture. Only the NRSV pictures the more formal act.

Hisako Kinukawa, *Woman and Jesus in Mark: A Japanese Feminist Perspective* (Maryknoll, NY: Orbis, 1994) 51–65; Elsa Tamez, *Jesus and Courageous Women* (New York: United Methodist Church, 2001) 61–70. Further study into subtle differences in translation that affect an interpretation of gender issues would be worthwhile.

12. Even when the verb *echein* is absent, the CEB translates the non-Jewish Gerasene man's condition as a possession: "a man possessed by an evil spirit" (5:2); this is not the case in the NIV. The NIV, however, uses "possession" language for a Jewish person in 1:23, a use not found in the CEB.

Of course, the initial contact occurs before Mark actually describes her ethnic background. At 7:26 Mark indicates that she was a Syrophoenician, a descriptor every English translation includes.[13] But was she a Greek (CEB, KJV, and NIV) or a Gentile (ESV and NRSV), and does the different translation of *Hellēnis* matter? In either case, it states clearly that she is a non-Jew who lived in Tyre or the surrounding region. Yet, she too enters a Jewish home where Jesus was resting or planning out the strategy for his mission.[14] The story makes no qualms about her entrance into the house. Not only did she hear about Jesus's visit, she knew exactly where to go. Was the Jewish homeowner an acquaintance of this Greek/Gentile woman? Were they Tyrian neighbors?

The difference between the ethnic labels "Greek" and "Gentile" may be generally lost on readers of English translations, but the subtlety is important in the ancient world. All Greeks are Gentiles, but not all Gentiles are Greeks. One example of this distinction may be found in Acts 14:1–2. The effective preaching of Paul and Barnabas in a synagogue in Iconium led to the belief of Jews and Greeks. Several Jews who opposed their message convinced other Gentiles to stand in opposition against the believing Greeks and Jews.[15] By translating *hellēnis* as "Gentile" the NRSV and ESV associate the Syrophoenician woman with all other "Gentiles"; she is not to be distinguished from them. Mark, however, never uses the Greek word *ethnos* (i.e., "Gentile," "people," "nation") to describe any individual character who approaches Jesus; furthermore, he uses *hellēnis* only here (Mark 7:26). He has only six occurrences of *ethnos*, all in chapters 10–13. (Jesus's so-called "Gentile mission" will become a more pronounced theme in Matthew's Gospel, including its parallel to this account; see below.)[16] So, does the use of the term "Greek" establish less tension with the Jewish Jesus than the word "Gentile"? In Jesus's third prediction of his death he foretold that the "Gentiles" (*ethnoi*), among others, will be responsible for his death: "They will ridicule him, spit on him, torture him, and kill him" (Mark 10:33–34). The NRSV's "Gentile" woman from Syrophoenicia was not in good, liter-

---

13. Is there a difference between "by birth" (CEB, ESV) and "by origin" (NRSV)? The KJV's "by nation" could be interpreted in a different direction altogether. In my own personal history, I am a New Yorker by birth (i.e., a U. S. citizen) but I am a West Indian or Afro-Caribbean by origin. Both of my parents were born in the Caribbean.

14. Less likely is Eugene Boring's suggestion that the narrator probably sees the house as a Gentile home (*Mark: A Commentary* [Louisville: Westminster John Knox, 2006] 209). The narrative does not reveal Jesus's intentions for this geographical break from Judea.

15. Luke also provides evidence of "Jews" marrying "Greeks" (e.g., Timothy's parents; cf. Acts 16:1–2) in the early Jewish-Christian community.

16. Even then, the most significant use of the term "Gentile" with respect to Mark's portrayal of Jesus's mission may be found in his temple action, citing the inclusive words of Isaiah: "Hasn't it been written, My house will be called a house of prayer for all *nations* (*ethnesin*)?" (11:17; CEB). Of course, in the passage, "nations" apparently includes the people of Israel as well.

ary company. The CEB's "Greek" label may be an effort to portray the encounter between Mark's Jesus and the Syrophoenician woman as less ethnically tense.[17]

Except for the ethnic introduction, which is unique for characters in Mark's Gospel, translations fluctuate minimally. Most commentators rightfully focus attention on the image of the "dogs" in Jesus's response to the woman's request in order to understand Jesus's own cultural biases. That will not delay us here. More significant for our purposes, English translations vary over whether Jesus replied that it is not "right" (CEB, ESV, and NIV) or it is not "fair" (NRSV) to give away the children's bread to these animals. "Fairness" language may allude to the subjective nature of the act. "Rightness" seems to imply a religious duty of some kind, a kind of appropriateness before God.[18] A contemporary analogy may be the United States tax system. It is "right" that we all pay taxes; it is "fair" according to some that we all pay a flat tax rather than a percentage of what we earn, a progressive tax, which others favor. "Fairness" is more of an opinion. Does either translation establish more ethnic tension in Mark's portrayal of the encounter, if the distinctions between these two English terms stand? If Jesus says it is not "right," then he sounds as if he is adhering to a religious obligation. If he says it is not "fair," then he may be expressing a cultural bias borne out in the remainder of the encounter. Ethnic tension is present throughout the encounter and either occurrence seems to magnify the mistrust, but the NRSV's account of whether Jesus's assistance to the non-Jewish woman is "fair" places the onus on an individual's action rather than the community's cultural expectation.

Another significant difference in the English translations may have a bearing on our discussion. It is possible to understand the woman's address, "Lord" (CEB, ESV, KJV, and NIV), as a statement of cultural honor in the first-century world (similar to "Master"), while most English readers interpret it as a confessional word indicating a shift in this woman's religious orientation. She comes to recognize Jesus as her religious Lord, as a number of commentators suggest.[19] The NRSV, however, utilizes the translation "Sir," which maintains a cultural, respectful distance allowing this woman to preserve her own cultural, religious heritage while downplaying any implied ethnic tension. Confessional language like "Lord," on the other hand, does not necessarily relinquish the cultural tension. Readers could just as easily interpret

---

17. Is there another way to interpret this difference? Could the NRSV's translation team have an ideological desire to make clear that Jesus had a *Gentile* mission, which begins here if not in Gerasene (cf. Mark 5)?

18. Apparently there is a distinction in moral philosophy between "fairness" and "rightness."

19. E.g., Francis Moloney, *The Gospel of Mark: A Commentary* (Peabody, MA: Hendrickson, 2002) 147.

the confession as the elevation of one culture over another, dismissing one as completely inferior.[20]

Matthew's "Canaanite Woman"—Matthew 15:21–28

Matthew's parallel presents one immediate distinction. Matthew introduces the woman as a "Canaanite" woman. There are other crucial differences in Matthew's portrayal that may affect the assessment of this story. Several key differences are obvious in Matthew's account:

Matthew	Mark
She is a "Canaanite woman"	She is a "Greek, Syrophoenician woman"
Jesus is addressed as "Lord" three times	Jesus is addressed as "Lord" once
Jesus initially responded with silence	[omitted]
The disciples ask Jesus to dismiss her	[omitted]
Jesus acknowledges his ethnic mission	[omitted]
Jesus is sent only to lost sheep of Israel	[omitted]
Jesus acknowledges her faith	Jesus acknowledges her spoken word

Despite the significant differences in Matthew's account, these need not distract us unless the English translations diverge at these points. Do English translations provide additional features that create or lessen ethnic tension between Jesus and the "Canaanite woman"? Matthew immediately introduces the character with her ethnic label; unlike in Mark's account, nothing occurs in Matthew prior to this introduction. All translations mention her "Canaanite" status.

After the ethnic label there are other points of interest in the various translations. The Canaanite's opening confession, "Lord, son of David" (ESV, KJV, NIV, and NRSV) is less of a confession in the CEB, which omits any direct translation for the Greek *kurie* ("Lord"). If Matthew's objective was to present a non-Jewish woman's awareness of appropriate Jewish labels, including a potential high confession, then the CEB does not quite capture it. Instead, the CEB ignores the potential religious commitment of this non-Jew, offers a picture of a gradual shift in the story (i.e., she will say "Lord" in vv. 25 and 27 in the CEB), and maintains a more reserved initial acknowledgement from her lips, which creates more distance between her and the Jewish healer. The NRSV and CEB apparently switch places in Matthew, when compared to their depictions of the parallel story in Mark.

---

20. Cf. R. S. Sugirtharajah, "Textual Cleansing: A Move from the Colonial to the Postcolonial Version," in *Race, Class, and the Politics of Bible Translation*; also, Tat-siong Benny Liew, "Mark" in *A Postcolonial Commentary on the New Testament Writings*, eds. F. F. Segovia and R. S. Sugirtharajah (New York: T. & T. Clark, 2009) 126–28.

It is not clear in Matt 15:24 whether Jesus speaks only to the disciples or to the Canaanite woman. More evident is the Matthean Jesus's transparent sense of his exclusively ethnic mission, a theme repeated earlier in Matt 10:6. On the surface the distinction between the CEB's "people" and the NRSV's "house" (also ESV and KJV) seems minor. The NIV omits both qualifications with a terser "lost sheep of Israel." A "house," however, may imply a place in which "Gentiles" (i.e., as God-fearers) could participate, as they did in Jewish synagogues (cf. Acts 14:1–2; 17:4).[21] The CEB's choice of the word "people" does not allow for that possibility. If so, the NRSV and other translations that use "house" may be the more inclusive translation and may depict less ethnic tension than the NIV's omission altogether or the CEB's "people." The ethnic tension is more subtle, though present, in the latter two translations.

In 15:25 the CEB, NRSV, ESV, and NIV all say the woman "knelt before him." The KJV's "worship" language shifts the honor and respect afforded Jesus in another direction entirely. This language elevates Jesus and fits in more neatly with the translation of "Lord" for *kurios* (as a confession) rather than "Sir." Matthew has a preference for the Greek *proskunein* ("to prostrate" or "to worship"), a term that occurs four times as often as in Mark's Gospel.[22] Often the object of this verbal action is "Jesus," and such veneration frames Matthew's narrative (cf. 2:2; 28:17); so, this woman fits in line with several narrative characters that perform this activity. The Canaanite woman, however, is the only non-Jew to perform this act, a coincidence that the KJV translators may have recognized and wanted to exploit.[23]

Finally, in Jesus's words in 15:26 we encounter again the variation between "fairness" and "rightness." While the NRSV remains consistent with its use of "fairness" language, as do the ESV and NIV with respect to the use of "rightness," the CEB alters its Markan translation of "right" (for *kalos*) to "good" in its Matthean parallel. English readers may not understand the term "goodness" in the same way as "fairness" or "rightness." "Goodness" carries more cultural preference, determining whether an act or saying is fitting or not in a specific cultural setting. "Rightness" sounds like a religious obligation or perhaps a legal one. Whether something is "fair" seems more individualized and takes into consideration one's perspective on human nature rather than whether something is "right" (as I define it). Does one term offer more of an ethnic bias on Jesus's part? Whether it was "good" or "fair" suggests more of an ethnic bias on Jesus's part. If something is not "right" religiously speaking, then

---

21. This may be implied in the KJV's "worship" language in 15:25.
22. Matthew has thirteen occurrences and Mark only three.
23. This may also fit neatly with the end of Matthew's Gospel (cf. Matt 28). Cf. David Sims, "Christianity and Ethnicity in the Gospel of Matthew," in *Ethnicity and the Bible*, ed. Mark G. Brett (Boston: Brill, 2002) 185.

the blame may be placed upon the entire religious culture. So, the CEB's "goodness" is similar to the alternate translation "fairness" as one way to depict more ethnic conflict between individual characters and less between cultural groups.

Simon of Cyrene—Matthew 27:32; Mark 15:21; Luke 23:26

We turn our attention to another character in the Gospels, one whose appearance is brief but conspicuous: Simon of Cyrene carried Jesus's cross at the forceful entreaty of Roman soldiers. Is it possible with this singular verse to determine whether any English Bible generates more or less ethnic tension than its counterparts between the characters in the story? In this instance the tension may reside between Roman representatives—not Jesus—and Simon, probably a Jew from Cyrene in northern Africa.[24] One can safely imagine that the brutality that the Roman soldiers inflicted on Jesus transferred also to Simon.[25]

Before we turn to the translation variations, let us acknowledge a few differences among the Synoptic Gospels. First, Luke offers a slightly more violent scene, saying the soldiers "seized" Simon, although all three accounts mention that the soldiers "force" Simon to perform this act. Second, only Luke mentions that the soldiers "placed" the cross on his back, as if Simon was physically unable to lift the crossbeam to his shoulders without assistance. Finally, only Luke mentions that Simon carried the cross while walking behind Jesus (rather than beside or in front of him) on this short journey.

Reviewing the translations in light of potential ethnic tension, the CEB—along with the ESV, KJV, and NIV—attempts to maintain the word order of the Greek text of Mark 15:21. This places the emphasis on carrying the cross. On the other hand, the NRSV accentuates the one who carries it, that is, Simon of Cyrene. Does the NRSV's rendering highlight Simon because his family was well-known to the Markan community: "the father of Alexander and Rufus"? Or, is the translation committee's objective to draw attention to Simon's difference, as one from Cyrene? In J. B. Phillip's idiosyncratic translation, the distinction is too hard to ignore: "They compelled Simon, a native of Cyrene in Africa."[26] Were the Romans intent on locating only a Jew from Africa to carry Jesus's cross? Certainly, there were other Jews in the crowd who the Romans could have coerced into this act. The NRSV's translation

---

24. Also Moloney, *The Gospel of Mark*, 318.

25. Cf. Stephanie Buckhanon Crowder, "Luke" in *True to Our Native Land*, eds. Brian K. Blount, et al. (Minneapolis: Fortress, 2007) 182–83.

26. J. B. Phillips's translation, *The New Testament in Modern English* (New York: Macmillan, 1960) 104.

is more ambiguous but potentially depicts more ethnic tension than other standard English translations!

In Matt 27:32 the CEB, ESV, and KJV use the verb "found," which describes an intentional action of discovery. The impression here is that the Roman soldiers were seeking out an individual who would fit their conception of who should carry the cross. Perhaps Simon's Cyrenian garb provided what the Romans sought. On the other hand, the NRSV translates the Roman activity as "they came upon," as if they stumbled onto Simon by chance. Along with the NIV's use of "met," the NRSV's depiction seems to describe a less intentional and less tense encounter, minimizing any potential ethnic tension that may have existed between the Romans, Simon, and Jesus.

Finally, a note on Luke's account is also in order. Although there are no significant differences among the major translations used in this study, Luke 23:26 offers an opportunity to recognize how contemporary translations utilize their own images and biases when translating ancient passages. J. B. Phillips's 1958 translation, more popular within evangelical circles in the 1970s and 1980s, depicts the cross-bearer in the following manner: "Simon, a native of Cyrene in Africa, who was on his way home from the fields."[27] This African who apparently worked in the fields became Jesus's cross-bearer! In other translations Simon was unassumingly a man travelling home "from the countryside."

Samaritan Woman—John 4

Unlike other passages which have significant amounts of narrative description, John 4 is primarily a dialogue between two characters, which provides a lengthy theological engagement of a Samaritan woman with Jesus. She is not the first woman to speak in the fourth Gospel, since Jesus's mother encouraged him to respond to the wine shortage at the wedding in chapter two, but that was not a dialogue between Jesus and his mother. His mother assumed that he would implement her wishes, telling the servants: "Do whatever he tells you!" (NRSV).

Although issues of "gender" come to the forefront in this passage—notice the disciples' reaction that Jesus was speaking with a woman (4:27)—the concern of this paper is primarily with issues of ethnic difference.[28] A short summary of the

27. In the translations of Luke 23:27 confusion surrounds the ambiguous pronoun "him." If it refers to Simon, then the people were mourning the tragedy that had fallen on Simon to be included in this incident. When Jesus reacts, in 23:28, the potential confusion is cleared up. The CEB replaces "him" with "Jesus" in v. 27 to avoid the confusion altogether.

28. *gunē*: 22x in FG; John 2:4; 4:7, 9 (2x), 11, 15, 17, 19, 21, 25, 27, 28, 39, 42; 8:3, 4, 9, 10; 16:21; 19:26; 20:13, 15. The majority of occurrences fall within chapter 4. Only in John 4 is a woman a "major" character; the woman of John 8 does *not* speak although the debate centers on her action.

structure of the passage will show where we should concentrate our efforts. The opening section entails a lengthy conversation about water (4:4–15). When the unnamed Samaritan woman requests the water Jesus provides (4:15), the discussion turns to relationships (4:16–18). Jesus shifts the conversation into a gendered one, implying (in light of 4:15) that the woman cannot receive the "water" alone; she apparently needs male representation. She recognizes Jesus to be a "prophet." In the next sequence, the central issue focuses on proper worship, particularly as it relates to issues of space. Ethnic history, choice, and geography take center stage as the Samaritan woman initiates the theological tensions raised here (cf. 4:20, 25). Although the Fourth Gospel presumes Jesus's superior knowledge (vv. 21–24), this perspective also establishes an anti-Samaritan bias.[29] From earlier in the story ethnic tension is already emphasized: "Jews do not share things in common with Samaritans" (4:9). Eventually, the disciples arrive and question Jesus about his company (4:27–28, 31–38). Their shock highlights gender but not the woman's ethnic background, although they kept the matter to themselves (cf. 4:27). Sandwiched between the disciples' query of Jesus, the Samaritan departs to proclaim the possible arrival of the Messiah (4:29–30). Because of this woman's announcement, other Samaritans approach Jesus. Some believe the woman's testimony, so she must be a trustworthy figure within the community; others believe after meeting Jesus (cf. 4:39–41).

There are a number of noteworthy issues related to concerns of ethnic relationships in the ancient world that appear in the various English translations under review. In John 4:9 the CEB paints a mental picture of both ethnic and gender tension by juxtaposing a Jewish man with a Samaritan woman.[30] In other translations the emphasis falls on their ethnic difference only. Although there were significantly more female translators involved in the CEB project, a full study is needed to determine whether the CEB is actually more sensitive to gender inclusive concerns than its counterparts.[31] Perhaps in 4:9 the CEB may simply be more attentive to the flow of the story, as the disciples will eventually think to themselves (since it is not publicly acknowledged) about the gender of Jesus's dialogue partner (cf. 4:27).

Outside of John 4, although Jesus recognizes the experience of a woman's labor (16:21), he directly addresses females rarely: Jesus addresses his mother (cf. 2:4; 19:26); he speaks to Mary Magdalene (20:15; cf. 20:13).

29. On the other hand, in comparison to the Synoptic Gospel tradition, Jesus reveals himself as "Messiah" to a Samaritan woman (a non-disciple), not evident in the earlier Gospel tradition; of course, in the FG, (some) disciples follow him initially because they thought him to be the Messiah (1:41).

30. Earlier, at 4:7, the NIV *may* depict less ethnic tension with a more polite Jesus, *asking for*—not demanding—a drink of water!

31. One interesting passage to compare is 1 Tim 2:11–15, in which the CEB translates the Greek as a situation between a "wife" and a "husband" and not the more general "woman" and "man."

Furthermore, in a narrative aside the author informs his audience of the relationship between these two ethnic groups, revealing as much about the Fourth Gospel's audience base as it does the apparent tension itself. In 4:9 it is the NRSV that is unique, since its translation that Jews and Samaritans "do not share things in common" offers a slightly different meaning from the "association" language in the CEB and NIV. These two latter translations seem to follow the sentiment of the KJV's and ESV's "have no dealings" with each other. The NRSV's language implies that "association" may occur, even if there were recognizable differences between the two groups. They may have traded with one another in the marketplace or dipped into the same well for water, for example, even though they did not "share" common eating practices. So, the language of the CEB and similar translations creates more distance between the Samaritans and the Jews than the NRSV, implying that Jesus's contact with the Samaritan woman at the well was an isolated event.[32]

The language is quite compatible in the English translations throughout the remainder of the story until we arrive at John 4:20–22. In a phrase repeated by the Samaritan woman and Jesus, the CEB's "but you and your people" ("ye" in the KJV) strikes an odd tone compared to the NRSV which has "but you say that the place where people" (the ESV is quite similar).[33] The NIV, more in agreement with the CEB's direction, extends the tension with a more offensive tone in 4:20: "but you Jews say." In the CEB the Samaritan claims that Jesus and the Jewish people hold a different theological position from Samaritans; on the other hand, in the NRSV and ESV the Samaritan woman only *seems* to blame Jesus for this belief. As mentioned, Jesus will repeat the phrase in the CEB, "you and your people," in 4:21 and 22. If this is a fair description, then the CEB depicts more ethnic group tension instead of simply an immediate, individual conflict. Perhaps this communal dimension is significant for the end of the story when the entire Samaritan community, apparently, "believes" (4:39–41). On another note, the CEB, at least here, associates Jesus more clearly with his Jewish heritage than other English Bibles.[34]

---

32. More significant is the KJV's punctuation that implies that the Samaritan woman is the one saying, "For the Jews have no dealings with the Samaritans." It is not simply a narrator's aside.

33. The CEB is attempting to account for the *plural* verbs in each instance; if the NRSV had added "you *all*," that would have captured the same sentiment; as it stands, the NRSV's pronoun could be read as a reference to the individual.

34. One significant example of this is the CEB's translation of *Ioudaios*. cf. Tina Pippin, "'For Fear of the Jews': Lying and Truth-Telling in Translating the Gospel of John," in *Race, Class, and the Politics of Bible Translation*, 81–97.

SUMMARY

This is a limited study. Even within the Gospel narratives there are other passages that should be investigated: the centurion's slave (Luke 7), the Gerasene demoniac (Mark 5), the use of *Ioudaios* ("Jew, Judean,"), the use of *ethnos* ("Gentile, nation"), and other passages. But there are a few results in this initial exploration of Gospel passages.

In many passages, no consistent, significant differences exist that show ethnic tensions in English translations. In some cases, where variations occur, the individual translation itself might be inconsistent, which makes assessment difficult. For example, with the use of "possession" language in Mark's account of the Syrophoenician story, the NRSV avoids the language altogether, while the CEB uses this language to apply across ethnic groups.[35]

In other instances it is not uncommon for a translation to stand out in an individual story. For example, in Mark's account of Jesus's encounter with the Syrophoenician woman, the NRSV more than any other translation seems to depict a more tense ethnic encounter between Jesus and this unnamed woman. Yet, this is apparently not the case in Matthew's parallel story in the NRSV, a story in which the ethnic tension seems slightly more pronounced in the translations of the CEB and NIV (with their exclusion, for example, of the language of the "house").[36] However, in Jesus's encounter with the Samaritan woman the CEB, not the NRSV, stood out as a more tense depiction of the Jews and Samaritans.

In some cases, it is difficult to determine what is more or less tense for ancient ethnic groups. For example, is confessional language (e.g., a non-Jew's acknowledgement of Jesus as "Lord") less or more problematic for diverse ethnic cultures? Does the acceptance of the religious commitments of a person from a different ethnic background indicate a privileging of one culture to the detriment of the religious traditions of one's own ethnic group? One's theology and ideology matter.

What might all of this mean for the presence of "ethnic conflict" in English translations? Does the 2011 Common English Bible provide a more ethnically sensitive translation, or did the racialized impression of the KJV's tradition imprint itself also upon this recent translation effort?[37] Perhaps the answer is not "which

---

35. This emphasis may have more to do with the theological assumptions of translators rather than cultural ones.

36. This inconsistency, if we may label it as such, is also true for the NRSV's depiction of Simon of Cyrene in the accounts of Mark and Matthew.

37. Cf. Bailey, "The Danger of Ignoring One's Own Cultural Bias in Interpreting the Text," 76.

translation do you read" but what is a person's "theology of race" and how does that play into the translation process itself.[38]

Let me close by returning to Cain Felder's thesis: is Luke simply providing the "historical" record of the westward advancement of Christianity, or is he relaying the story with an ethnic bias toward the Latinized world? Others would have to relay the spread of the gospel eastward into India and China or southward into Africa. Furthermore, why is (only?) Cain Felder concerned about the relaying of this story as the whitening of the early Christian movement with its avoidance of "the darker races outside the Roman orbit"?

I began this investigation with hopes of discovering a more ethnically sensitive translation in the Common English Bible when compared to its peer translation efforts. What I discovered was that the CEB, generally speaking, offers a mixed impression of ethnic tensions among ancient groups when compared with other English translations, especially as it relates to the contact Jesus had with non-Jewish people in the stories of the Gospels. Of course, before a final assessment can be made, a fuller study of the entire Bible would have to be performed, but a look at ethnic stories surrounding the chief protagonist, Jesus, was an excellent foray into a complicated topic of identity politics, religious commitments, translation, and ethnicity.

What might it mean if the CEB, from the most diverse Bible translation team in the history of English Bibles, offers more intense conflict between ethnic groups in some passages and less tension in others when compared to other English Bibles? Perhaps a fuller investigation into which translators—and their ethnic origins—contributed to which stories in the Bible would allow us to assess more carefully the concern of this paper. Does the contemporary experience matter, and is it possible not to view ancient biblical stories through a contemporary bias? As language changes English translations represent modern attempts to update (even interpret?) ancient stories for contemporary communities. The CEB's use of "immigrant" for the Hebrew term, *ger*, is one excellent example: "Don't oppress an immigrant. You know what it's like to be an immigrant, because you were immigrants in the land of Egypt" (Exod 23:9).[39] In light of recent discussions on immigration in this country, is the CEB taking a political stance? Are translations responsible to present ancient tensions in new ways to help "address" our contemporary concerns and conversations, or should they translate what "they see," which is always interrelated in com-

---

38. Cf. Willie James Jennings, *The Christian Imagination: Theology and the Origins of Race* (New Haven, CT: Yale University Press, 2010); J. Kameron Carter, *Race: A Theological Account* (Oxford: Oxford University Press, 2008).

39. The Hebrew term is traditionally translated as "stranger" (KJV), but by "sojourner" (ESV), "foreigner" (NIV), and "resident alien" (NRSV) in KJV influenced translations.

plex ways with how translators view their own contemporary world. It is not only the language that changes, however; perspectives with regard to ethnic conflict also change. So, are translators responsible to present ancient tensions in new ways to indirectly "address" contemporary conflicts?[40]

If English translations are less intentional about their work with respect to ethnic difference in the ancient texts, perhaps they should become more aware in light of the recent growing tensions in the United States and the rest of the world. Can translations do anything to assist more peaceful relations among various ethnic groups? Should they? Let us think together about the implications of our translation tendencies on contemporary events that involve people from other ethnic groups. Let us think together about how our perspective on contemporary events—in particular, the multi-ethnic environment in which we find ourselves and the distribution of power and resources associated with these various ethnic groups—shape the way we translate and interpret our sacred texts.

---

40. Cf. Tina Pippin, "'For Fear of the Jews.'"

RESPONSE TO POWERY

Michael O. Emerson

I cannot help but begin by commenting on the overlap of our names. Emerson O. Emerson, there is Powery in that name. Pure poetry.

In the paraphrased words of Donald Trump, we have been building a wall, a big, beautiful wall between English Bible translations. Powery proposes in his paper to build a very nice door between these translations, and he is going to get Mexico to pay for it.

Powery begins his work by stating, "Translation matters." He repeats this phrase in the next paragraph, noting that for most readers, they read only one translation of the Bible. Thus the translation is everything; it is what people memorize, it is what they take as truth, and it provides the "feeling" readers get in reading the Bible.

In this paper Powery is interested in one main question: Did the Gospel writers have an ethnic bias? What he actually asks in the paper is even more focused: Does the answer to this question depend on which English translation one reads? It is an intriguing question to be sure.

He attempts to answer this question with a specific method. He examines the same four passages from the Gospels by comparing them across five English translations.

Starting from the supposition that the King James translation is racially biased (he argues in his paper why he takes this starting position), he explores whether subsequent translations vary in the extent of ethnic bias or whether subsequent versions merely repeat the problem.

I would have liked to have seen more argument in support of the supposition that the King James translation is ethnically biased. It is too central to the paper to not have more "proof" or force of argument, but let us move to consider the results of Powery's analysis.

Greek, Syropoenician by Birth (Mark 7:24–30)

Three translations say this woman was a Greek, and two say she was a Gentile. All Greeks were Gentiles, but not all Gentiles were Greeks. This is in the same way that all New Yorkers are Americans, but not all Americans are New Yorkers. Powery suggests that the Greek label may be an effort to portray the encounter between Jesus and the woman as *less* ethnically tense. This seems a leap of inference, at least with the evidence and context provided in the current version of the paper. Even more difficult to square, if this inference is correct, it means that not only is the supposedly most balanced of translations (the CEB) included in this group, but so too is the supposedly most racially biased translation (KJV).

The Other Three Passages: Matthew's Canaanite Woman (Matt 15:21–28), Simon of Cyrene, and the Samaritan Woman

Analyzing these passages across the five translations, Powery finds it is difficult to interpret in light of his main question. No clear pattern is evident. At times a version seems to depict more ethnic tension, but it is not always clear if this is so. The CEB does seem to depict greater ethnic tension in the story of the Samaritan woman. In the end, though, these passages do not much help us answer the question under consideration, at least in any way in which we can be confident.

So we see that in most passages, no significant differences in the expressed ethnic bias were found. When it does occur that a translation stands out from others on this question, Powery does not find any consistency across the passages within any given translation. This inconsistency means in effect that any differences found seem to wash away. What is more, it is clearly difficult to determine what is more or less tense for ancient ethnic groups. We would have to do extensive study of the respective cultures and know intimate details of the meaning of titles, greetings, and much more to interpret fully the implied level of ethnic tension.

After conducting his analysis, Powery returns to his original guiding question: Does the degree of ethnic bias in these passages differ by translation? He answers it this way: "Perhaps the answer is not which translation do you read, but what is a person's theology of race and how [does] that play into the translation process itself."

It seems the result of his analysis is to highlight the complexity not only of translations, but of the people reading the translations. In short, he seems to be saying that ultimately we would have to know how each person translates each translation. Now that is complicated. Indeed, it brings us full circle to this conclusion: interpretation matters.

Suggestions for Furthering the Study

The end result and conclusion of this study leads me to two suggestions for furthering this work. Both focus on developing the method by which the question is addressed.

The first suggestion is to consider what in my field (sociology) is called *intercoder reliability*. Given that the meaning of each of these translations for the question at hand is subject to possible interpretation biases, we can guard against this by having multiple scholars classify these same sets of verses. Do the multiple "coders" arrive at similar interpretations? If so, then we have much greater confidence in the results. Do they reach different interpretations? Then we have evidence for Powery's suggestion that what may truly matter is the interpretation by the reader of each translation.

Second, perhaps the most meaningful method to answer the question of this paper is not to have scholars do this classification at all. Rather, I would suggest a different approach, which has two components.

Have lay readers read the five translations and have them discuss with a scholar any differences they see between the translations and what the differences mean to them. Then, have a second set of readers, and assign them to read only the translation they most commonly read. Have them provide their interpretation of each of these four passages to a scholar. When comparing the interpretations of the people across the translations they read, do any differences in their interpretation emerge?

By having knowledge of how these two sets of readers—those reading multiple translations and those reading only one translation—interpret the passages, the scholar will have the evidence needed to both know if one translation or another suggests greater ethnic tension and if interpretation of the level of ethnic tension varies by the readers themselves.

It seems that only with such methods could we truly know if translation matters. I applaud Powery for asking such an important question and for beginning the work on answering it. He has made it possible to take the next steps in pursuit of knowing whether any of the English translations communicated greater ethnic tensions when compared to other translations.

The meaning of translations for knowing God and the Bible has rightly been a long-standing topic of discussion and debate. Bringing greater methodological rigor to such questions promises to help us better know the actual implications of translation decisions. Doing so will serve Christendom well and will show that focusing on the methods we use to answer such questions are well worth our time.

AN INDIGENOUS REINTERPRETATION OF REPENTANCE

Raymond Aldred

The idea for this paper flows out of the task to try and hold two identities together within one person, Christian and *Nehiyaw* (Cree, Indian) or *Nehiyawiwin* (Cree identity).[1] This task is difficult for a variety of reasons, but it is necessary. James Treat highlights some of the common reasons indigenous people pursue this project.[2] Indigenous people take seriously their indigenous and Christian heritage. Both identities are valued, and so there must be a way to work through the difficulties. Indigenous people value the spiritual legacy of their ancestors and their own indigenous experiences. This legacy includes sacred ceremonies and teachings, which have enabled indigenous life to prosper for many centuries. However, historically, particularly during the last 150 years, room was not always made for the indigenous experience and spirituality within North American "Christian" identity. Bringing indigenous and Christian together is important for the well-being of the individual and the community. Therefore, this paper is an attempt to work through some of these difficulties in hopes of promoting the possibility of a peace or "treaty" between the two. In order for this to happen some reinterpretation needs to happen. This paper will revolve around the ideas of repentance and conversion and their use with regard to indigenous people situated primarily in Canada.

    I propose that under the Canadian colonial enterprise salvation for indigenous people was defined as becoming Western and civilized. Conversion for indigenous people meant repenting of indigenous identity, putting it off, and becoming Western and enfranchised into Canadian society. Conversely, contextual Cree theology would reinterpret conversion and repentance as an embracing of the Creator's fulfillment of all that our traditional spirituality longed for. It is a repentance of turning to Christ by embracing a God-given indigenous identity of becoming a true human being. This reinterpretation of repentance is also sufficient for nonindigenous people as they embrace their own responsibility through repentance and move toward

---

    1. Arok Wolvengrey, compiler, *Nēhiýawēwin: Itwēwina* (*Cree: Words*), 2 vols. (Regina: Canadian Plains Research Center, University of Regina, 2001).

    2. James Treat, *Native and Christian: Indigenous Voices on Religious Identity in the United States and Canad*a (New York: Routledge, 1996) 2–8.

a reconciliation that can be described using principles of restorative justice. This involves telling the truth with complete disclosure, listening with the heart and not just the intellect, and engaging in a shared plan which is built upon returning to the ongoing historical and indigenous treaty process.

Colonized Conversion and Repentance

This paper is written primarily from an indigenous perspective. How did many indigenous people living under the assimilationist policies of the Canadian government understand the Christian gospel? These policies were implemented in partnership with churches. It is important to note that the problem in Canada was not just as a result of the enforcement of assimilationist policies by some denominations through the residential schools. These policies were energized or made possible because in Canada there was a general consensus among Euro-Canadians that indigenous people were a problem to be solved. For example, Mohawk lawyer Patricia Monture observes that as recently as 1991 Judge McEachern of the British Colombia court, ruling on an aboriginal land claim, describes aboriginal people as "disadvantaged" and part of a "national problem."[3] The judge's words could be construed as paternalistic at best, which describes the last 150 years and encapsulates our current state of affairs in indigenous Canadian relations.

Western Christian theology was complicit in this annihilation attempt. Therefore, it is necessary to appropriate the language of Christian theology in order to help heal the damage done by this same theology in the gospel proclaimed by North American missions. The problem with the Western church was not necessarily its definition of salvation but its interpretation and application of salvation, repentance, and sin that proved problematic. Perhaps some definitions of salvation focus primarily upon individuals and forget the broader strokes of creation. However, theologians such as Stanley Grenz point out "God's activity encompasses all creation, but humankind is his focus. The Spirit applies Christ's work to humans effecting our union with the Lord and with each other in Christ's community."[4] This definition of salvation is suitable for the purposes of this essay. The problems lie not with the definition but rather with the Euro-Canadian conception of indigenous people. Indigenous people were looked down upon and seen as wild people who were part of a wild land. John West, a Church of England missionary to the Indians, stated his

---

3. Patricia A. Monture, *Journeying Forward: Dreaming First Nations' Independence* (Halifax, NS: Fernwood, 1999) 50–53.

4. Stanley J. Grenz, *Theology for the Community of God* (Grand Rapids: Eerdmans, 2000) Kindle edition: chapter 15, "Dynamic of Conversion."

goal was "to cultivate the heath and convert the heathen."[5] His missionary work was cultivating spiritual practices among the indigenous people that would eventually lead to the cultivation of the wild land.

Of necessity indigenous people had to repent of their old way of life and turn to the Christian way of living. In my undergraduate theology class I remember memorizing a definition for repentance. Repentance was a contrite turning from sin, an essential part of conversion, and an ongoing aspect of the Christian life. This definition, although debated by some, is adequate to frame the way repentance was heard in aboriginal communities in the past. Repentance was a contrite turning from sin, but for Canada, developing as a modern nation-state, aboriginal sin and all sin was about morality. In colonial Canada, like much of the civilized world, it was necessary for all things wild to become settled. "Settlement, with its attendant emphasis on property and possession, is the bridge that links socioeconomics of colonial civilization with the Christian ideology of moral cultivation."[6] Key to this "settlement" process was moral development. Moral failure or loose morals were the result of sin. Aboriginal people had a problem fitting into Canadian society because they were immoral. The wild land needed to be cultivated and wild indigenous people needed to be converted and civilized.

This was a popular view of all colonized indigenous people, as postcolonial scholar Laura Donaldson points out. Thomas Jefferson, like most Euro-Americans of his time, considered aboriginal men and women as not following proper decorum.[7] In other words, he thought they were immoral and hypersexual. A generation later on the Canadian side of the border John A. MacDonald continued this colonial way of thinking, believing the problem with Indians was a moral problem.[8] The solution then was to have proper moral training, which could be achieved through the residential schools.[9] This view of indigenous people was largely shared by the Canadian people. A Royal Commission describes the thinking this way: "Cardinal among these virtues was moral training for, as a memorandum from the Catholic principals explained, 'all true civilization must be based on moral law.' Christianity

---

5. Alvyn Austin and Jamie S. Scott, *Canadian Missionaries, Indigenous Peoples: Representing Religion at Home and Abroad* (Toronto: University of Toronto Press, 2005) 22.

6. Ibid., 29.

7. Laura Donaldson, "The Sign of Orpah: Reading Ruth Through Native Eyes," *The Postcolonial Biblical Reader*, ed. R. S. Sugirtharajah (Oxford: Blackwell, 2006) 159–70, 162

8. J. R. Miller, "The State, the Church, and Residential Schools in Canada," in *Religion and Public Life: Historical and Comparative Themes* (Queen's University: 1999).

9. The Davin report entrenched residential schools, modeled after American industrial schools, as the way to resocialize indigenous children. See Flood Davin, "Report on Industrial Schools for Indians and Half-Breeds, 1879," in *Reconciling Canada: Critical Perspectives on the Culture of Redress* (Toronto: University of Toronto, 1879).

had to supplant the children's Aboriginal spirituality, which was nothing more than 'pagan superstition' that 'could not suffice' to make them 'practice the virtues of our civilianization and avoid its attendant vices.'"[10]

Moral training would cure or purify aboriginal people and enable them to avoid vices and develop virtue. Thus, the Western conception of Christianity was aimed at making "Indians" better behaved by giving them a civilized European identity. The goal of this kind of civil religion maintains the status quo, and the Canadian federal government was intent on assimilating aboriginal people and all the land into a European conception of the status quo. At this point Christianity in Canada had already begun to be reduced to a call to be more pious and better behaved.[11] Conversion to Christianity became synonymous with becoming "white" civilized "natives" while at the same time conquering and taming the wilderness to something that could be bought and sold.[12]

Residential Schools

The goal of the residential schools system was to resocialize indigenous children.

> The residential school system was an attempt by successive governments to determine the fate of Aboriginal people in Canada by appropriating and reshaping their future in the form of thousands of children who were removed from their homes and communities and placed in the care of strangers. Those strangers, the teachers and staff were, according to Hayter Reed, a senior member of the department in the 1890s, to employ "every effort . . . against anything calculated to keep fresh in the memories of the children habits and associations which it is one of the main objects of industrial education to obliterate." Marching out from the schools, the children, effectively re-socialized, imbued with the values of European culture, would be the vanguard of a magnificent metamorphosis: the "savage" was to be made "civilized," made fit to take up the privileges and responsibilities of citizenship.[13]

The residential schools and assimilation policies were to "obliterate" every relationship indigenous children had with their traditional way of life. The primary relationships of communal indigenous identity needed to be destroyed systematically so that they could become civilized Christians.

---

10. *Report of the Royal Commission on Aboriginal People: Looking Forward, Looking Back 1996.* 1.315. Online at http://caid.ca/RepRoyCommAborigPple.html.

11. Lesslie Newbigin, *Foolishness to the Greeks: The Gospel and Western Culture* (Grand Rapids: Eerdmans, 1986) 7.

12. Austin and Scott, *Canadian Missionaries*, 22–23.

13. *Report of the Royal Commission on Aboriginal People*, 1.312.

Children were removed from their homes so that the relationship with the land would be severed. Terry LeBlanc, a *Mikmaq* scholar, notes the residential school system failed to understand the deep connectedness indigenous people had with the land.[14] The schools needed to make indigenous children view land, not as part of the family, but as a resource. The land would no longer be the mother of indigenous children; the residential school would be their "mother" and "would fit them for a life in a modernizing Canada."[15]

Not only were the residential schools to break the relationship between land and indigenous children, they were also to destroy the children's relationship with their family. The justification for this process included co-opting aboriginal leaders' permission to remove children from homes and place them in schools.[16] Even if parents resisted sending their children to residential school, the policy was enforced because government and church officials believed that if the children were to be "saved" they needed to be taken from the negative influence of their parents who were stuck in their "wigwam ways."[17] Children were taken from their homes and many were not allowed to return as long as they attended the residential school.

Another key relationship that was targeted for "obliteration" was the relationship between indigenous children and their traditional culture or spirituality. Indigenous culture was their spirituality.[18] Therefore traditional spirituality was to be replaced with European and Christian values and morals. Above all the children were to be taught that the world is a European place in which only European values and beliefs had meaning. "A wedge had to be driven not only physically between parent and child but also culturally and spiritually."[19]

Indigenous children were subjected to institutional pressure, which destroyed, or severely damaged all of the primary relationships of their human existence: their relationship with the land, their relationship with their parents and community, and their relationship with the creator through their spirituality. If the effects of the cursing of creation and humanity, as seen in Gen 3, are a warping or severing of the relationships between humanity and creation; between man and woman or family; and between God as creator and human beings, then the residential schools entrenched the curse or followed the same pattern of cursing in its impact on indigenous people's

---

14. "Residential School: Policy, Power and Mission," in *Edinburgh 2010: Mission Today and Tomorrow*, ed. Kirsteen Kim and Andrew Anderson (Regnum, 2011) 393.

15. *Report of the Royal Commission on Aboriginal People*, 1.309.

16. Austin and Scott, *Canadian Missionaries*, 24.

17. *Report of the Royal Commission on Aboriginal People*, 1.309.

18. James William McClendon, Jr., *Systematic Theology*, rev. ed. 3 vols. (Waco, TX: Baylor University Press, 2012) 3.66–74.

19. *Report of the Royal Commission on Aboriginal People*, 1.316.

lives. Salvation or conversion then was seen as a need to repent or turn from the sinful indigenous life and put on the "white robes"[20] of Western Christianity.

Relocation of Sayisi Dene

Residential schools were not the only assimilationist policy of the last 150 years that "obliterated" aboriginal relationships. The relocations and forced settlement policies of the 1950s also took their toll on aboriginal identity. The forced relocation of Sayisi Dene to Churchill, Manitoba, serves as an exemplar of these policies and shows the impact of relocation on the same primary relationships of indigenous people as seen effected by the residential schools.

The Sayisi Dene were nomadic hunters long before the coming of the Europeans. Europeans came to Canada and wanted land. The missionaries helped pave the way by learning the language of the people and converting people to Christianity. It was a former Methodist missionary who was the treaty commissioner in 1910 and who signed the reluctant Sayisi Dene to Treaty 5. Even though they would not be forcibly moved until 1956, this was the beginning of the move. Eventually the people were seen as a problem for they were thought to be causing the extinction of the caribou. After World War II, Western people become convinced that every fur bearing animal was endangered, and to keep the caribou safe the Dene were moved to Churchill. Over a third of the people died from various causes. The people were taken from the land.[21] They were given little time to pack their things. Taken to Churchill without proper shelter, the ability to hunt, or a means to earn a living, they were reduced to living on "welfare vouchers and macaroni rations."[22]

Again Western society did not take into account the relationship that indigenous people had with land. A survivor of the move, Charlie Kithithee, said, "The land and the people were one. That was the secret of our life. . . . this is how the creator looked after us. He puts animals onto our land so that we could provide for our people."[23]

As a result of the separation from the land there was a cascading effect on the other primary relationships. After they were relocated to Churchill, many of the people developed drinking problems. The relationships between family members

---

20. William Apess, *On Our Own Ground: The Complete Writings of William Apess, a Pequot*, ed. Barry O'Connell, Native Americans of the Northeast. (Amherst: University of Massachusetts Press, 1992) lxvi–lxvii.

21. Ila Bussidor and Üstün Bilgen-Reinart, *Night Spirits: The Story of the Relocation of the Sayisi Dene*, Manitoba Studies in Native History (Winnipeg: University of Manitoba Press, 1997) 50–55.

22. Ibid., 4.

23. Ibid., 37.

eroded. "In 1968, community development worker Phil Dickman wrote: 'There is practically nothing today that binds the children to their parents and prepares them to carry adult responsibilities...'"[24]

The relationship with the land was broken, which led to a breakdown in the relationship with family, which resulted in such spiritual and social destruction that Ila Bussidor tells of the shame she felt over her own identity: "We lived in a slum in total darkness. As a child, I learned what it felt like to be inferior to another race, to be less than the next person because I was Dene. Because of the racism we faced every day, I was ashamed to be Dene. I wished I belonged to another race of people."[25] It is small wonder then that historically and recently, on the level of popular theology in "Indian country," Indian identity is seen as a negative thing. Many have seen all of their relationships damaged through generational trauma. Therefore, repentance for Indian people has been cast as a negative thing. Just like conversion, repentance meant to give up one's identity, to repent from being First Nations and embrace the new Christian identity, an identity that just happened to look like Western European identity.[26] To be converted to Christ meant you gave up being Native. You developed hatred and a regret for being made this way, and you longed to be "whiter than snow."

This is the narrative of many aboriginal people in Canada. As a result of the degradation that has come about as a result of the assimilation policies such as relocation, residential schools, and underlying racism, many indigenous people are left feeling conflicted about their own identity. A friend of mine once said to me, "I grew up hating I was an Indian and that is why I liked the gospel; it hated Indian too." The gospel was used to try to annihilate aboriginal identity. Catholic and Protestant alike did this. It was systematic and pervasive. Conversion and repentance became synonymous with giving up aboriginal identity.[27] In order to be Christian one had to repent of being an "Indian" and embrace a Western conception of identity and Christianity.

Repentance is seen as embracing one's own depravity and turning to God, but this translated into self-hatred by aboriginal people. I am the third generation of my family growing up not wanting to be Indian. My grandfather told everyone he was Chinese and learned some Cantonese because he experienced less racism when he did this. My mother told everyone we were mostly French and Scottish. At my

24. Ibid., 90.
25. Ibid., 37.
26. Marie Therese Archambault, "Native Americans and Evangelization," in *Native and Christian: Indigenous Voices on Religious Identity in the United States and Canada*, ed. James Treat (New York: Routledge, 1996) 132–54, 139.
27. James L. West, "Indian Spirituality: Another Vision," in *Native and Christian*, 29–37, 33.

grandmother's funeral my brother, in true Cree fashion, made a joke to ease the pain. As all the indigenous people were entering the place of the funeral, he leaned over and said, "I wonder when all the French and Scottish relatives are going to get here." I also grew up hating that I was aboriginal, wanting so much to just fit in, because in fitting in, I would escape the pain, or so I thought.

This self-hatred of indigenous identity was kept alive by well-meaning pastors and church elders when I would go forward during an alter call. I wanted help to deal with the pain in my soul. They would routinely say that they had noticed that I was Native. Their next question was whether I had ever taken back the ground my ancestors had given to Satan. This ended up being a proliferation of the idea that my people's ways are the devil's ways, that somehow there was something in my Native identity that needed to be repented of. John West, missionary enshrined in the stained glass at Wycliffe College's Founders chapel, justified doing violence to convert aboriginal people by noting that aboriginal people themselves thought violence should be done to their own to advance the gospel.[28] Thus the church justified its actions of seizing children before the indigenous way of life could influence them.

Indigenous people themselves denigrate their own identity. I often hear converted aboriginal people saying, "I am a Christian first and Indian second." Somehow our indigenous identity and ways are seen as not being appropriate for living at the same level as Christianity. Some even suggest our communal identity as nations of indigenous people is not redeemable by God. *Boundary Line*, a book published by the Christian and Missionary Alliance in the United States, expressed this message by saying that people were redeemable but not their culture.[29] This could be construed as saying in order to be Christian we must give up our indigenous culture or spirituality,[30] which amounts to our humanity. This kind of statement is a continuation of the teaching of the residential schools that reduced aboriginal identity to something less than human.

This idea is compounded by folks who think that First Nation identity is only on the level of identity in a nation state like Canada. To be *Nehiyaw* (Cree) or *Haudenosaunee* (Iroquois), or *Siksika* (Blackfoot) is to be human with all of the attendant relationships. Western Christian nations have convinced many of our own people that we were less than human and to be human beings we must convert to their

---

28. Austin and Scott, *Canadian Missionaries*, 24.

29. *Boundary Lines: The Issue of Christ, Indigenous Worship and Native American Culture* (USA: Native American Association of the Christian and Missionary Alliance, 2001).

30. Jacqueline Ottmann notes that spirituality and culture are used interchangably by First Nations in Saskatchewan. See Jacqueline Ottmann, "First Nations Leadership and Spirituality within the Royal Commission on Aboriginal Peoples: A Saskatchewan Perspective" (MA Thesis, University of Saskatchewan, 2002).

religion and give up our "Nation State" citizenship and assimilate into the Canadian politic. To stop being Nehiyaw would mean to stop being human. There is a need to teach what it means to be indigenous in Canada.

As Ila Bussidor expressed shame over her own identity, many indigenous people become self-conscious about their "otherness" and feel shame. In a sense they feel estranged from themselves. They feel shame for their own identity. They want to be something else, and to solve this pain in their soul they resolve to stop being "Indian." Sadly, many have taken it further and thought that the only solution to pain is to stop feeling. They then go to any length to accomplish that, even if it means taking their own life. Self-contempt or "other-contempt," all flowing out of illegitimate shame, is the legacy of the assimilation policy of the Canadian government and the churches.

Thankfully we have turned a page or changed our minds, in keeping with the idea of repentance. The woundedness, or narrative of woundedness, continues. Aboriginal people continue to struggle against institutionalized, assimilationist pressures. However, a shift in the understanding of indigenous people about their identity is occurring. An embracing of indigenous identity by aboriginal people could be described as a repenting from self-hatred to embracing a God-given indigenous identity, an identity that gives hope despite continued attempts by Western hegemony to suppress or assimilate indigenous identity. This hope could flow out of Christianity, not with any thought of replacing indigenous identity, but with a desire to heal or fulfill indigenous identity.

Repentance as a Decision to Live

There are two aspects of repentance that could fit within an indigenous world that would allow repentance to be reconfigured as a decision to turn and embrace the life our Creator has provided. *Michiyuwasewin* in Cree captures the idea of feeling sorry or repenting. This is an older word used in some of the teaching material of the early Methodist missions.[31] In a modern Cree dictionary the word for repentance, *kweskatisiw*, has the idea of changing your way of life.[32] Both of these definitions would fit within a theological definition of repentance, but they must be reinterpreted within a changing context.

---

31. John Semmens, William Isbister, and John McDougall, *The Hand-Book to Scripture Truths, or, the Way of Salvation: Words of Admonition, Counsel and Comfort* (Toronto: Methodist Mission Rooms, 1893) 3. See E. A. Watkins, compiler, *A Dictionary of the Cree Language* (London: SPCK, 1865) s.v. "Repentance."

32. *Nēhiýawēwin: Itwēwina (Cree: words)*, s.v. "Repent."

Repentance remains, as from the outset of this paper, a contrite turning from sin. Sin in a First Nations context refers to a "falling out of balance" into self-consciousness, which causes shame.[33] Indigenous people, whose relationships have been under attack and severely damaged, have been pushed "out of balance" resulting in illegitimate shame which can be construed as sin. Calling this illegitimate shame sin is not another attempt to heap guilt upon abused people by telling them they are to blame for their problems. Rather, it is conceiving of sin as something that traps people and leaves them unable to effect change without grace from the Creator. This is a grace that is available if one embraces his or her own situation and identity provided by the Creator. Repentance then involves sorrow for a lost identity. It is understanding and rejecting the shame that was put upon indigenous people, turning to embrace a Creator-given identity, and taking responsibility to work toward healing all relationships.

This version of repentance could be understood as taking responsibility. Responsibility is not primarily about guilt but about an opportunity to live in another way. As such, repentance could become an act of dreaming about what it would be like to put relationships back together, healed and made whole. The idea of taking responsibility could fit within modern indigenous thought. Mohawk author, Patricia Monture, believes taking responsibility is what is at the heart of indigenous freedom or self-determination, as she says: "I have realized that self-determination is both a personal issue and a collective yearning. As I have come to understand it, self-determination begins with looking at yourself and your family and deciding if and when you are living responsibly. Self-determination is principally, that is first and foremost, about our relationships."[34]

Thus, the gospel of Jesus Christ could bring hope to aboriginal people. This hope can be described as a hope for a better day in the future. The vision of Black Elk, of the prairies being rolled up as a scroll and then being unrolled to be restored as they were before the coming of the white-man is an apocalyptic vision that perhaps some continue to cherish.[35] I am struck by the hope the wounded Christ brings to aboriginal people, the hope that we will not die, that somehow, even in the midst of great pain and the intensity of rage, there is one who understands. This is not the cosmic Christ who sanctions residential schools or establishes theocracies;[36] it is

---

33. Joseph E. Couture, Virginia Margaret McGowan, and Ruth Couture, *A Metaphoric Mind: Selected Writings of Dr. Joseph Couture* (Edmonton: AU Press, 2013) 15–16.

34. Monture, *Journeying Forward*, 8.

35. See John G. Neihardt, *Black Elk Speaks: Being the Life Story of a Holy Man of the Ogala Sioux* (Lincoln: University of Nebraska Press, 1979).

36. This idea in part was developed after hearing Richard Kearney comment that behind many violent acts is an imagined deity that supports the idea. See Richard Kearney, "The God Who May

the abused Christ who identifies with our own abuse. It is from this place that one can then turn to this Christ and embrace life. Repentance has then ceased to be a decision to hate one's own earthly identity and has become a decision to embrace our broken identity and to live. It is recast as a decision to live, to stop self-hatred and embrace my own communal identity as an aboriginal person and the resiliency that comes from my mother and all my relatives. This means changing my mind and viewing my own despised identity as something having value.

When my mother was six years old, her mother left her and her three younger sisters because my grandfather was a very abusive drunk. My mother would stand on a wooden box to change her youngest sister's diapers. When she was eight, her father left for the war and was gone overseas for ten years. I asked her, "How did you survive raising children when you were still a child?" She said, "Every day I would pray. My grandmother would make me go to mass every morning, and I would pray." Her solution to life is to embrace where you are, pray, and work.

This turning to live and find hope in the gospel is not a kind of triumphalism. It is embracing one's own limitations. It is not hope in surpassing our finiteness; rather it is embracing our existence as human beings. Hope that is based primarily upon surpassing our finite existence continues to nurse some kind of escapism that puts people and countries always pursuing some mythical idea of progress that justifies itself by the ideology it pursues. The hope that lies in indigenous identity begins with the community. It is in seeking to maintain relationships that one finds hope.

Hope is found in taking responsibility and turning to heal the relationships that have been damaged. For the Sayisi Dene it meant returning to their former territory. They are attempting to restore relationship with the land. Returning has enabled some to begin to work on healing their wounds. The Dene understood that if we do not heal our wounds they will be passed on to the children.[37] The land is the place where this healing can occur. Again, responsibility for relationship with the land must be understood as a primary human relationship.[38] This is fundamental for healing because health is connected with the land. For example, Naomi Andelson writes, "A sense of health is ultimately rooted in what it means to 'be Cree,' and being Cree has everything to do with connections to the land and to a rich and complex past."[39] Turning to embrace indigenous identity then could mean to reject the teach-

---

Be," in *Best of Ideas*, ed. Paul Kennedy (Canada: Canadian Broadcast Corporation Podcast, 2006). See also Richard Kearney, "Thinking after Terror: An Interreligious Challenge," *Journal of Interdisciplinary Crossroads* 2.1 (2005).

37. Bussidor and Bilgen-Reinart, *Night Spirits*, 142.

38. Sophie McCall, *First Person Plural: Aboriginal Storytelling and the Ethics of Collaborative Authorship* (University of British Columbia Press, 2012) 120.

39. Naomi Adelson, *"Being Alive Well": Health and the Politics of Cree Well-Being* (Toronto:

ing of the residential schools that land is a commodity[40] and to remember it as part of family, as our mother.[41]

Christian theology is not without images of the earth as family. Francis of Assisi in his Canticle of the Sun uses familial terms to speak of human relationships with creation and the Creator.[42] Colin Gunton reminds Christians that we share a continuity with all that is nonhuman by virtue of our being created.[43] Therefore, one of our primarily relationships is with creation and land. Indigenous elder and Anglican priest Andrew Wesley teaches that at the heart of indigenous spirituality is understanding your creation story, a story that tells you of your connection to the land.[44] When this connection is made you can stand on the land and feel it welcome you home.[45]

Repentance as turning to embracing indigenous identity also includes taking responsibility for healing the wounds of abuse that have separated family members and communities. It is a healing from colonialism, but the trauma from the residential schools is more complicated than just removing colonial or neocolonial policy. Monture makes this point:

> If colonialism brought our nations to this point, then undoing colonialism must be the answer. . . . It is not just colonial relations that must be undone but all of the consequences (addictions, loss of language, loss of parenting skills, loss of self-respect, abuse and violence and so on). Colonialism is no longer linear, vertical relationships—colonizer does to colonized—it is horizontal and entangled relationships (like a spider web).[46]

Repentance can involve trying to work through the wounding by revisiting the "dark stories,"[47] which can serve as a tool for healing. It is reimagining the individual story by embracing the good things from our past history but also remembering the difficulties. The act of embracing one's story and continuing to share it recasts pain and difficulty as a source of hope by showing that indigenous identity remains de-

---

University of Toronto Press, 2000) 15.

40. LeBlanc, "Residential School," 93.

41. Couture et al., *A Metaphoric Mind*, 4; Monture, *Journeying Forward*, 60.

42. Paschal Robinson, "The Writings of St. Francis of Assisi," (1905). http://www.sacred-texts.com/chr/wosf/wosf22.htm.

43. Colin E. Gunton, *The One, the Three, and the Many: God, Creation, and the Culture of Modernity* (Cambridge: Cambridge University Press, 1993) 3, 13.

44. Personal notes from a lecture of Andrew Wesley, "Traditional Aboriginal Spirituality," Consultation on First Nations Theological Education (Thornloe University, Sudbury, Ontario: 2009).

45. Neal McLeod, *Cree Narrative Memory: From Treaties to Contemporary Times* (Saskatoon: Purich, 2007) 61–70.

46. Monture, *Journeying Forward*, 11.

47. Bussidor and Bilgen-Reinart, *Night Spirits*, xix.

spite facing traumatic events. Telling and listening to our stories ensures we do not forget our relatives who have passed on. It also ensures that we are not romanticizing some lost ideal, trying to engage in a kind of "primitivism" as a form of escape to some premodern period.[48] Rather, it is trying to embrace identity, as it exists, by trying to build upon roots of strength within indigenous culture. This is accomplished by retelling difficult stories in a way that advances healing.[49] The importance of story for healing will also figure into repentance for newcomers.

It is not only relationships between individuals in one's own family or group that need to be healed, but there is also a responsibility to attempt to return to and heal the treaty relationships between indigenous people and the newcomers. This idea is part of what it means to be indigenous and connected with the land. Right relationship requires a location; it must be grounded upon the earth.[50] As covenant, treaty has a spiritual and locative dimension. The relationship with the other is captured in the shared narrative of the treaty, particularly as the practice of treaty making in Canada developed. J. L. Miller points out that treaties evolved in Canada from "friendship compacts" eventually to covenants between newcomers, indigenous people, and the Creator.[51] By the time the numbered treaties were signed in Saskatchewan, the sweet-grass prayer ceremony included all the people and the land represented in the treaty. The braid of sweet-grass illustrates this idea. One strand represents the newcomers, another strand the First Nations, and the third represents the Creator. For the Lakota the smoke from the sweet grass fills the whole universe, and in doing the ceremony we make peace as we become like relatives.[52] The newcomers, including church officials, engaged in the indigenous ceremonies that made us like relatives or family.[53] Thus, in the healing of relationships treaty relationships must be healed. The treaty also serves as a source of healing. As a shared narrative it legitimates or creates shared space. The treaty will hold the individuals and groups

---

48. Robert J. Schreiter, *The New Catholicity: Theology between the Global and the Local*, Faith and Cultures Series (Maryknoll, NY: Orbis, 1997) 25.

49. McCall, *First Person Plural*, 120.

50. Monture, *Journeying Forward*, 36, 60.

51. J. R. Miller, "Compact, Contract, Covenant: The Evolution of Indian Treaty-Making," in *New Histories for Old: Changing Perspectives on Canada's Native Pasts*, ed. Theodore Binnema and Susan Neylan (Vancouver: UBC Press, 2007) 66–91, 84.

52. Black Elk, Joseph Epes Brown, and Michael F. Steltenkamp, *The Sacred Pipe: Black Elk's Account of the Seven Rites of the Oglala Sioux* (New York: MJF, 1996) 103. Leo J. Omani, "Perspectives of Saskatchewan Dakota/Lakota Elders on the Treaty Process within Canada" (PhD diss., University of Saskatchewan, 2010) 2, 159.

53. Jennifer S. H. Brown, "Rupert's Land, *Nituskeenan*, Our Land: Cree and English Naming and Claiming Around the Dirty Sea," in *New Histories for Old: Changing Perspectives on Canada's Native Pasts*, ed. Theodore Binnema and Susan Neylan (Vancouver: UBC Press, 2007) 18–40, 34–35.

they represent together because, as covenant, the relationship is more important than the exact particulars.[54]

The healing of all relationships is premised on returning to an indigenous identity that affirms the goodness of the created world. The starting point for indigenous spirituality is the appreciation of a beautiful world. Doug Cuthand writes: "Our people believe that the earth and all the creatures that live on it are a gift from the Creator. This beautiful land of lakes, forests, rivers, plains, and mountains is a gift from the Almighty and it must be respected and treated properly."[55]

Indigenous spirituality shows that appreciation for a beautiful world is thanksgiving. The circle of harmony is lived as seen in the indigenous teaching that says, "If you receive something, you give something back; in this way we live in harmony with all things."[56] Repentance is seeking to live in right relationships and in balance with Creator and creation. This is the vision and ideal that indigenous spirituality is seeking. However, it will take time to heal. Ila reminds us "healing doesn't happen just once. We have to be healed again and again."[57] In seeking the healing of significant relationships with creation, family, clan, community and all others, indigenous people return or reinvigorate their relationship with *kise-manitow* (the Creator).

A reinterpreted understanding of repentance as a turning to embrace an identity given by the Creator is therefore in keeping with traditional understandings of what it means to be indigenous in Canada. Interestingly, the basic meaning of repentance as a contrite sorrow for sin and a turning to a new way of living has not needed to be altered. The context has meant repentance has to be reconfigured as hope through taking responsibility. If Christian repentance and salvation are large enough concepts to conceive of turning to Christ as being a return or embracing of a Creator-given indigenous identity, it is possible to conceive of conversion or salvation in Christ as fulfillment instead of being a replacement for indigenous spirituality.[58]

---

54. Miller, "Compact, Contract, Covenant," 83.

55. Doug Cuthand, *Askiwina: A Cree World* (Regina: Coteau, 2007) 1.

56. Clara Sue Kidwell, Homer Noley, and George E. Tinker, *A Native American Theology* (Maryknoll, NY: Orbis, 2001) 33.

57. Bussidor and Bilgen-Reinart, *Night Spirits*, 132.

58. In proposing fulfillment I am not precluding that the relationship between indigenous spirituality and Christianity could be complementary. Fulfillment might be viewed by some as placing indigenous spirituality in a lower or lesser role. It is beyond the scope of this paper to address this question, but it is worth noting. George Lindbeck offers a brief taxonomy of possible interfaith relationships in his *The Nature of Doctrine: Religion and Theology in a Post-Liberal Age* (Philadelphia: Westminster, 1984) 52–53.

Repentance for Canada

Turning to nonindigenous or newcomers to Canada, the task becomes thinking through what repentance looks like for all Canadians. Could there be another way of living together in the land that embraces indigenous identity as being true human beings? What does repentance look like for a Canada that has violated the treaty relationship and is complicit in the abuse of indigenous people? Would repentance as turning to embrace a God-given identity as a human being be sufficient to work through the difficulties from a nonindigenous side of the relationship? The answer is positive particularly if treaty relationship is seen as shared narrative. It is a large enough concept to include a narrative of troubled relationships but also have a coming back together for healing. Some of the principles from restorative justice will be put to use in this description.[59] Restorative justice is an attempt to heal the damage. In this process the effected parties must tell the truth, they must listen, and they must come up with a shared plan to repair the damage. All of these steps come together as an attempt at reconciliation between indigenous peoples and the newcomers. These steps presuppose that indigenous and newcomers will both, through repentance, embrace their indigenous identity as created human beings.

National repentance is not something that should be entered into lightly. C. S. Lewis warned that national repentance is an office of the church but should be done with humility,[60] remembering that national repentance does not absolve an individual from responsibility for personal repentance. Oliver O'Donovan points out that a national repentance that is rooted in Scripture must embrace a community or a nation's collective history and return to its social covenant.[61] O'Donovan was thinking about the atrocities committed in India by Britain. He states that repentance for the British people involves owning those things on a personal, individual level. In this way history functions as a moral mirror. He writes:

> Until we learn to root that sense of "us" in the history of a living community, it is an empty, powerless thing to speak of what "we" shall do now, what "our" good intentions are. There is an immense pathos in a community's good intentions—a point to recall at a moment when a modern democracy is heady with excitement of making new beginnings, setting its hand to do things which it is conscious of having failed to do.[62]

---

59. Pierre Allard, "Restorative Justice: Lost Treasure," conference lecture (Regina, Saskatchewan: Canadian Theological Seminary, March, 11, 1999).

60. C. S. Lewis, "Dangers of National Repentance (1940)," *Transformation: An International Journal of Holistic Mission Studies* 14.4 (1997) 10–11.

61. Oliver O'Donovan, "Community Repentance?" *Transformation: An International Journal of Holistic Mission Studies* 14.4 (1997) 12–13.

62. Ibid., 13.

By remembering past actions and owning them on an individual level, a nation may keep from making the same mistakes again. If the focus is on right relationships, this rules out the idea of a new national strategy or policy that is going to fix all of the problems inherited from the past.

New national "blanket" policies that are applied to indigenous people would just be a continuation of colonialism. Healing will come when we base our relationships upon "caring, sharing truth and strength."[63]

Canada could heed O'Donovan's observations of remembering and returning to work through its own repentance. Remembering could follow the principles of restorative justice of telling the truth and listening. Returning could embrace the historical treaties as a way forward to heal and affirm relationships in Canada. Canada needs to remember the past and confess its shortcomings—not in an apology as a one-way speech act but as a dialogue.[64] In so doing they could embrace the stories of past abuse as gifts to be a mirror for repentance.

The Canadian government has engaged in at least two national attempts to effect reconciliation with aboriginal people; the Royal Commission on Aboriginal People and the Apology to the Survivors of Residential Schools. However, up to this point, their effectiveness has been limited because they limited their telling of the truth.[65] They did not make full disclosure. Sophie McCall offers the opinion that the Royal Commission on Aboriginal Peoples, commissioned in 1991, missed an opportunity for reconciliation because it reduced the stories of people's trauma at the hands of the Canadian government and churches to recommendations.[66] As a government report with recommendations it does not allow the reader to enter the Royal Commission as the second person—"you." Recommendations sterilize the past and render it incapable of providing the emotive energy to dream what repentance looks like. The Royal Commission was limited in its ability to help individuals enter into the shared Canadian narrative to reconfigure our history. Instead it tended to see reconciliation as a way to forget the past.

In McCall's words: "In order for reconciliation to be more than a case of amnesia, it must prioritize a politics of difference and a testimony. However, the tendency of RCAP's report is to subsume the testimony within a dominant narrative of progress—from assimilation to self-government, from loss to recovery, from mutual

---

63. Monture, *Journeying Forward*, 12.

64. Eva Mackey, "The Apologizers' Apology," in *Reconciling Canada: Critical Perspectives on the Culture of Redress*, ed. Jennifer Henderson and Pauline Wakeham (Toronto: University of Toronto Press, 2013) 47–62, 48.

65. See n. 10 and *Honouring the Truth, Reconciling for the Future*, available at http://www.trc.ca/websites/trcinstitution/File /2015/Findings/Exec_Summary_2015_05_31_web_0.pdf.

66. McCall, *First Person Plural*, 110.

mistrust to reconciliation."[67] McCall explains that the Canadian state's conception of reconciliation saw indigenous people needing to reconcile themselves to being under the Canadian state.[68] This was not a return to the treaty relationship and a reconciliation of equals. Thus, the Royal Commission was ineffective in allowing Canada as the offender to enter into the shared narrative of the treaty. It was limited in its ability to help individual Canadians think through what repentance looks like.

Another opportunity for reconciliation occurred with the 2008 apology by the Government of Canada for the residential schools. Making the apology was better than not making the apology. The apology by the prime minister has been used by indigenous people to embrace their wounded identity. Again, the continual denial of wrong doing over generations meant that aboriginal people not only had to labor under the continual attacks upon their identity but they were also blamed for their problems. Many aboriginal people received the apology as an admission by their abuser that "they," not aboriginal people, are guilty. Indigenous people have used the apology as an opportunity to turn a page and begin to work toward healing themselves and their world, a healing that continues to mean making room for the other.

However, Eva Mackey points out that the apology also seems to have been used by the Canadian government not to enter into a dialogue but, as in the Royal Commission, to forget about the past and impose new national strategies for fixing aboriginal people.[69] Mackey suggests that an apology that is not a dialogue is only a one-sided speech act, which fails to bring about a change or, in the words of this paper, fails as an act of repentance because it does not lead to a new way of living for the abuser. A real sign of repentance would be a return to the treaty relationship.

Even after being abused by the Canadian people, indigenous people continue to pursue right relationships as a testimony to the resiliency of indigenous identity. This is in contrast to an institution that was so enamored with its own progress it sought to eradicate another people's identity. It is fascinating that after the apology by the Canadian government in 2008, several aboriginal people sought to offer forgiveness to the government.[70] They started a movement, or tried to start a movement, from community to community holding forgiveness summits. Their basic message was that since the government had offered an apology we should forgive them. As I have argued earlier, it is always indigenous people who seem be proactive to try

---

67. Ibid. 113.

68. Ibid., 111–12.

69. Mackey, "The Apologizers' Apology," 50–51.

70. News CBC, "Native Residential School Forgiveness Granted," CBC News. Available online at http://www.cbc.ca/news/canada/native-residential-school-forgiveness-granted-1.956939.

and heal relationships.[71] I find it disconcerting that the Canadian government did not issue another statement of the need to work through what repentance looks like for themselves. This would have shown that the Canadian government would want to take time and seek to inquire how deep this institutional racism was. They should also take time to think through what repentance from this institutionalized abuse looks like, but they did not say anything. (However, Justice Sinclair, since the completion of the public Truth and Reconciliation Commission, has said that the apology and the public testimony do not amount to reconciliation. There is a need to stop racism toward aboriginal people and others and to work towards healing the relationship.[72]) The Canadian people must face the past of their own failures. In a turn of repentance to their identity as human beings in a treaty relationship Canadians would build on the historic treaty process and move toward reconciliation with indigenous people. An ideal apology must lead to dialogue, which involves listening. The Truth and Reconciliation Commission was set up as a response to the apology so that people damaged by the residential schools could share their stories and perhaps find healing.[73] The public testimonies given at the Truth and Reconciliation Commission meetings were a gift. They are received as a gift if one enters into a reciprocal relationship with the speaker. If we enter into the story and embrace the pain that we have caused and use the emotional energy to begin to change, then we are embracing our own identity as a true human being. This is the kind of listening necessary to continue to move toward reconciliation. Sophie McCall would call it entering the story as the second person.[74] This is not easy, and the stories of trauma cause some to disassociate. This can be mitigated if the speaker and the listeners understand the goal is healing and restored relationship.[75] Healing and restored relationship are legitimate goals for all who call the land of Canada home.

Finally, repentance as turning to a new way of life for newcomers could mean a return for all to the treaty relationship where they are also treaty people. As treaty people Canadians themselves are healed from being strangers in the land. The idea of treaty is the idea of making relations. Through the treaty newcomers and indigenous people were to live like family. This secures a place for the First Nations, and it secures a place for newcomers. The following quotation from the office of the treaty commissioner in Saskatchewan emphasizes this point.

71. Ray Aldred, Adrian Jacobs, and Terry LeBlanc, "Thoughts on Forgiveness," *Indian Life*, 2010.

72. See http://www.cbc.ca/news/aboriginal/reconciliation-not-opportunity-to-get-over-it-justice-murray-sinclair-1.2614352.

73. Truth and Reconciliation Commission of Canada, "Our Mandate," Truth and Reconciliation Commission of Canada http://www.trc.ca/websites/trcinstitution/index.php?p=7.

74. McCall, *First Person Plural*, 111.

75. Ibid., 120–21.

> Treaties are beneficial to all people in Saskatchewan. They are considered mutually beneficial arrangements that guarantee a co-existence between the treaty parties. Newcomers and their descendants benefit from the wealth generated from the land and the foundational rights provided in the treaties. They built their society in this new land where some were looking for political and religious freedoms. Today, there are misconceptions that only First Nations peoples are part of the treaties, but in reality, both parties are part of treaty. All people in Saskatchewan are treaty people.[76]

Repentance for Canada could mean to turn and own the mistakes of the past and embrace identity as a human being under covenant, and for those in Canada this includes the treaty.

By way of anecdotal evidence, I have a friend who was born Saskatchewan, and in a recent conversation he captured this idea when he referred to himself as a Treaty 4 person. He has embraced his identity as a kind of indigenous person, one related to the land. This relationship is premised on his people making treaty with the First Nations through treaty.

Repentance then, as defined in the first section of the paper as a contrite turning from sin and as a turning to embrace an indigenous identity, is large enough to include newcomers. By entering into the shared narrative of the treaties as equals, the possibility exists for a shared identity that does not necessitate the eradication of identity. Instead, it is an opportunity to embrace the past and be open to a future of walking together in the Creator's land in a good way. Treaty functioning as a shared narrative allows for a re-envisioning of history and becomes a tool for healing.

Conclusion

Repenting of self-hatred means indigenous people embrace their own broken identity so that they can begin to live again. The decision to repent and live is a decision to begin to put back together the relationships that have suffered so much over the years. Though these relationships have been damaged, they remain in the stories and memories of my people. This repentance is not primarily about guilt but is about taking responsibility and seeking to rebuild what was broken. It is a decision to embrace the hope that there is another way of life possible, one which exceeds just surviving.

Aboriginal identity begins with the idea that we are related to everything. This is in contrast to identity as alienated individuals, or as the West saw our "lives, brutish and short, bereft of hope."[77] This is a better description of life in the era of

---

76. "We Are All Treaty People," Office of the Treaty Commissioner. http://www.otc.ca/education/we-are-all-treaty-people.

77. This description of primitive life is attributed to Thomas Hobbs. It was used to characterize

residential schools. Indigenous identity reminded me that I was related to the land. It was part of who I was. I belong here. The knowledge that each person and each people who share this space are also in relationship is why aboriginal people continue to advocate for a return to nation-to-nation relationships. This gives hope and resources as we continue to develop as a multicultural society. Aboriginal identity has long sought to live in right relationships—not only individual to individual but also people group to people group, right relationship with land, and right relationship with the Creator.

This reinterpretation or reconfiguration of repentance is large enough to include nonindigenous people who make up the nation of Canada. They can repent by entering the shared narrative of the treaty. Embracing the stories of trauma from residential schools and relocation is an effort to own the pain and move toward healing. By becoming the second person in the story, the listener is able to work through the pain of the past without merely wishing it away. This repentance is a turning to embrace the shared narrative of the treaty process in Canada and goes further than a one-way approach that cuts off dialogue. It is possible to see this returning to the treaty relationship as fitting within the rubric of restorative justice as telling the truth, listening with the heart, and creating a shared plan. This is an attempt at reconciliation by healing the treaty relationship or returning to the treaty relationship for healing. The treaty can be a narrative and an instrument for healing.

Repentance, as a contrite sorrow for sin and a turning to a new way of life, is understandable in a Canadian context by both indigenous and Christian. It is then possible to see Christian repentance and salvation as a fulfillment of what was hoped for in indigenous spirituality, right relations, and harmony.

---

indigenous life before the coming of Europeans to Canada. See Dale Turner, "Oral Tradition and the Politics of (Mis)Recognition, in *American Indian Thought: Philosophical Essays*, ed. Anne Waters (Malden, MA: Blackwell, 2004) 229–38, 236.

RESPONSE TO ALDRED

Mark Tao

Let me first express my appreciation to Professor Aldred for his valuable work on the subject of repentance. While Aldred's title suggests that his task has been "reinterpretation," it just as well could be titled "An Indigenous Recovery of Repentance," since his project actually rescues repentance from its corruption by nineteenth and twentieth-century colonial treatments and places it in accord with a proper biblical view, though in general I think the treatment as a whole could have benefited from a greater consideration of the biblical texts.

In his paper Aldred rightfully asserts that repentance is not only a contrite turning from sin but a decision to live truly as one was created to be. Repentance therefore is in part an existential matter. The embrace of one's true created self is especially compulsory for Canadian aboriginals who have long lived with an internalized self-hatred derived from colonial subjectivity. Aldred suggests repentance means a wholesale denial of cultural self-loathing and rejection of whiteness but with that the embrace of one's ancestral roots and customs as invaluable to the Creator God.

Aldred points out that the task of repentance is not merely restricted to the personal rectification of self-hatred. It also seeks the "healing of all relationships" and particularly a desire to be restored to others, the earth, and the Creator for the sake of harmony. This restorative outlook of indigenous thought is codified in the "treaty" ritual in which committed parties covenant together to become family and pursue restorative relationship. Newcomers may also participate in "treaty" relationships, and in taking "treaty relationships" as shared narrative they may become "treaty people" and no longer "strangers in the land." Newcomers also do not enter into treaty lightly. For newcomers to become treaty people, it requires naming mistreatment of indigenous populations and acting to repair harm done. Lastly, Aldred claims that the "treaty" relationships thus become the cornerstone for national repentance in Canada and reconciliation between newcomers and indigenous peoples.

In response let me first say that I recognize his observation that indigenous natives and newcomers all need to be engaged in the work of repentance, i.e., seeking the healing of all relationships and to be in right relationship with one another.

I further appreciate that he names this conviction, not as a result of a master/slave dialectic and a recapitulation of imperialist logic, but rather as a sentiment arising indigenously within native communities.

Second, I am grateful that he has affirmed that repentance looks different depending on one's own social location, power, and privilege. A native's act of pursuing restorative justice will look different from a newcomer's pursuit of that same end. A native pursuing restorative justice means liberation from colonial subjectivity and self-hatred. For newcomers pursuing restorative justice means acknowledging one's complicity in whiteness and the colonial enterprise by virtue of one's very own embodiment irrespective of individual actions. It means learning to hear well the voices of the oppressed in order to become allies and advocates against the organizing logics of white establishment thinking. In both cases—natives and whites—a certain kind of "death" is required in order for a restoration to right relationship to occur.

Arguably this death leading to true reconciliation must be more costly for newcomers. If newcomers are sincere about pursuing right relationship and becoming a "treaty people," it will come at a high cost, for they must be willing, as Aldred suggests, to tell the truth, listen with heart, and create a shared plan. Even further, I would suggest they must put to death their own quest for traditionalism so that "foreign" and subaltern traditions may flourish in a pluralistic society. Elevating a subaltern tradition in the political sphere is not only risky but unpopular, but when conflict inevitably arises and "liberal" justice is violated, the perennial question is whether a liberal democratic society can muster enough political resolve to take proportionate reparative actions such that the defined "good(s)" of subaltern populations are given due process and even elevated over against white traditions, access, and privilege in the national consciousness.

Death, especially death of white, colonial traditionalism is hard to achieve. Quebec is a good example[1]. In 1982 after adopting the Canadian Charter of Rights, in the face of a rising multiculturalism, they quickly enacted language legislation to protect Francophone interests. Unsurprisingly, this also placed restrictions on other minority groups, including aboriginals with whom they had a "treaty," whose own national interests were displaced. The question is why? Why take these measures to elevate the French language considered "good" by the Quebecois at the expense of the aboriginals shortly after affirming the broader goal of promoting multiculturalism?

Again the answer I think is traditionalism. Language legislation was enacted not as a willful desire to continue to subjugate subaltern interests. Rather, they were enacted to protect the traditions which constituted Quebec's provincial identity (at

---

1. See Charles Taylor, "The Politics of Recognition" in *Multiculturalism: Examining the Politics of Recognition*, ed. Amy Gutmann (Princeton: Princeton University Press, 1994) 52.

least in the minds of the dominant culture). Their will for their own culture to survive superseded their desire to risk the death of their way of being in order that a new way of being centered in indigenous history could flourish. In surveying United States relations with native Americans and blacks we see similar patterns, even in more allegedly "reconstructive eras" from more "progressive whites." Abolition is good until we realize it disrupts the entire economy of the South and puts us into poverty. Black lives matter until they require us to suffer estrangement with our own biological families. So how far are newcomers willing to go in the name of upholding "treaty," i.e., social contract, especially when facing imminent death in their own identities and social existence?

The only way for newcomers to participate in a true national repentance is to see "treaty" as much more than binding social contract which generates fraternity. "Treaty" is never inviolable as social contract; it may always be annulled. But if "treaty" is taken as sacrament, visible means of invisible grace, it may never be broken. To partake of "treaty" as sacrament is really the only way newcomers can stay committed to the task of the death of traditionalism and the resurrection of a new way. This new way is a hybrid way that fundamentally sustains the experiences of the subaltern and interrogates whiteness and the colonial enterprise.[2] Entering into a "treaty" relationship sacramentally is to say to your neighbor, "I am committed to dying and rising again with you in Christ" no matter the cost and whatever the odds. Further, it is to avow sharing in all other aspects of sacramental life, especially Baptism and the Holy Eucharist. Affirming "treaty" relationships as sacramental is the only way restorative justice may be achieved and indigenous and newcomers reconciled.

I conclude by posing a few final questions. If achieving restorative justice is contingent upon accepting "treaty" as sacrament, is it even possible for true national repentance to emerge as driven by political secularism? I would argue it cannot. The state as church can produce civil religion, but civil religion is alone insufficient to produce true repentance. This said, what is the church's role and responsibility in promoting an alternate vision of "treaty" as sacrament? How is this achieved in praxis, and how does it interface with the work of the nation state? Where can the church be involved in the work of national repentance and reconciliation between people groups in Canada, taking into account decisions of the state? These are important questions, still left to be worked out in the imminent future.

May our Creator God continue to bless all of God's people, the church universal, in forging "treaty" relationships so that through this sacramental act we may

---

2. For more elaboration on this idea see Brian Bantum, *Redeeming Mulatto: A Theology of Race and Christian Hybridity* (Waco, TX: Baylor University Press, 2010).

demonstrate what it means to live into a more faithful communion and find a new way to live in true peace together.

TWO SONGS BY PANDITA RAMABAI[1]

Trans. by M. Bobbie Pothen and Boaz Johnson

Geet 118

Where may I go for help
Where may I go for restfulness
I am weary
I am beaten down
I carry the load of sin
Systemic sin
I searched hard in the temples
Hindu temples
But all I found
Was sin and evil
There was no happiness
No respite
in this world
Then I encountered
I intrinsically heard
Deep down in my inner being
The WORD of the Pritam,[2]
The Beloved, the Messiah
I will give you rest
I was irreversibly changed
With that encounter
Yeshu the Messiah

---

1. These two songs are still sung by hundreds of girls every day at Ramabai Mukti Mission, Kedgaon, Maharashtra, India. These are girls who have been rescued form human trafficking, child widowhood, and orphans.

2. *Pritam* means "the Beloved." Ramabai came up with very unique words in her poems and Bible translation. She sought to avoid high caste Brahmanic hegemonic terms. She also sought to avoid terms which were intrinsically sexist and expressed high caste male dominance.

Trans. by M. Bobbie Pothen and Boaz Johnson   Two Songs by Pandita Ramabai

He alone is my Deva[3]

He is dearer to me than life

In him

I know fullness of life

He saw me

Beaten down to death

With that encounter

I knew life

Life, Life, Real Immense LIFE

He is dearer to me than life

I will give you rest

My daughter

Come to me

Evil has beaten you down

In him I saw real humility

I tasted real sweetness

Yeshu, in you I saw real love

In turn, to you, I give my love

And so will I serve you all the days of my life

My life

May it be a praise to my Muktidata[4]

My Savior

From now on

There will I go

Him alone

The Pritam

will I serve

Him will I love

So will my low caste family, my tribe

---

3. *Deva* is the simple word for God. Ramabai refused to use high caste names of God like *Parameshvara* or *Mahadeva* often used in Indian translations of the Bible, for these names of God expressed the subjugation of low caste people and especially women.

4. *Mukti* and *Muktidata* mean "salvation" and "Savior" respectively. Ramabai refused to use the high caste word *Moksha*, since it expressed the idea of an escape from the cycle of *Karma* and *Samsara*, the cycle of birth, life, death and rebirth (also called reincarnation). For Ramabai salvation was from systems of sin seen in Hindu society. She also rejected the related theme of salvation in high caste Hinduism. This is the idea of *svarga*, or heaven. She reasoned that *svarga* is the place where only high caste men go, where each are given many virgins. Ramabai reasoned that *Mukti* is starkly different from this idea of salvation and heaven.

All my days on this earth
Will I spend in loving and serving you
And your creation.

Geet 257

They told me
I had no hope
Condemned was I
to the hell of enslavement
That was destiny
Then I encountered Yeshu
To me He drew near
Me He redeemed
From systemic sin and injustice
That haunting fear He removed
The fear of evil
Done to my soul
Forever
Yeshu spoke
Ever so lovingly
You have I saved
You have I redeemed
And so I gaze
Always gaze upon his wonderful face
The wonderful miraculous face
Sweet Word I hear
Yeshu Word
Never will I leave you
Never will I forsake you
And so I hear
So I believe
That Word is mine
Forevermore
Gone was my pain
Gone was my sorrow
He took it all away

Trans. by M. Bobbie Pothen and Boaz Johnson   *Two Songs by Pandita Ramabai*

The fear of death
The fear of punishment
He wiped my heart
From all that deep sadness
He saved me from systems of sin
Sin that caused me to sin
Out of fear
That fear is gone
His blood flowed down
Me it led to the way
The way of release to Mukti
On this amazing path
His hand I hold
His Spirit guides
And gives me strength
His love gives power
He becomes my desire
In my deepest heart, my deepest soul

TRUTH BE TOLD: A NECESSARY FUNERAL DIRGE IN THE MIDDLE OF OUR CONVERSATION

Soong-Chan Rah

This semester I am on sabbatical, and one my goals for my sabbatical is to get more fit. I did some research to find out what is the most popular program for fitness. I found out that now the most popular program is called CrossFit. CrossFit is based upon the concept of muscle confusion. I was really excited by this discovery, because the concept of muscle confusion has been my approach to exercise for many years now. Here is how I have applied the concept of muscle confusion. I do not work out for months, and when I finally go to the gym, my muscles are really confused. Sometimes a little bit of holy confusion and holy disruption is a good thing, a necessary thing.

I recently completed a commentary on the book of Lamentations called *Prophetic Lament*.[1] I worked about five years on this project, and I am expecting to sell about four books. There is not a huge demand for a book on lament or on the biblical book Lamentations. Lamenting is not a common practice in the American church. Lament, however, may be the holy confusion and disruption we desperately need. Particularly when we are engaging the topic of race and racism, we cannot do without the practice and discipline of lament.

The genre of lament offers an alternative narrative of holy disruption. Lament is found quite often in the Bible but is often neglected in the church. The loss of lament may be attributed to the excessive triumphalism of American culture. We live in a culture where we think we can quickly and easily solve all problems. Lamentations challenges those assumptions.

The first two chapters of Lamentations employ a specific subgenre of lament. Both chapters 1 and 2 begin with the Hebrew word *'êkâ*, which is simply translated as "Alas" or "How?" or more fully translated as "How can it be?" It is often the opening cry of a subgenre of lament, the funeral dirge. The first two chapters also employ an uneven metering system, which along with several other notable characteristics

---

1. Soong-Chan Rah, *Prophetic Lament: A Call for Justice in Troubled Times* (Downers Grove, IL: InterVarsity, 2015).

demonstrate that the first two chapters of Lamentations are a funeral dirge. The city of Jerusalem is a corpse, and the funeral dirge is conducted over the dead body.

There is a significant difference between a funeral dirge and a typical individual lament. A typical individual lament is like a pastoral visit when someone is in the hospital. We cry out in lament to intercede for the sick person. We have hope that the sick person will get better, so we offer up an individual lament as an intercession and as a plea. A funeral dirge operates differently. The body is no longer in the hospital. The body in the room is a dead body. It would be inappropriate to pray for healing for a dead body during a funeral. A funeral dirge means that the body is already dead, and we have to deal with the reality of that dead body.

"The funeral dirge does not allow for the denial of death, nor does it allow for the denial of culpability in that death. The funeral dirge is a reality check for those who witness suffering and allows mourning that is essential for dealing with death. Rather than denying reality, Lamentations portrays suffering and death in gritty detail."[2] Lament is honesty before God. Something has died and we must deal with this reality.

Dead bodies litter American history, and we must deal with the reality of these dead bodies. The dead bodies in our history are found in a broken racial history. Truth must be told about these dead bodies. Most of these bodies are the bodies of black men and women. We struggle with truth-telling and truth-hearing when it comes to dead black bodies. We do not want to acknowledge the dead bodies in the room. There are times when there is a visceral response when confronted with a challenge to the status quo.

Recently I gave a sermon on this topic in a nearby suburban church. I raised the issue that Lamentations challenges us with the need to deal with history and that we need to learn the truth from the breadth of history. We needed to deal with the dead bodies in the room. In the sermon I mentioned that #blacklivesmatter provides a challenge for us to learn more about our broken history and why dead black bodies are found throughout our nation's history. In response to this sermon I received the following gem: "You endorsed the 'Black Lives Matter' movement which openly and proudly endorses killing police officers. Michael Brown was a felon . . . who was possessed by a demon. Brown and all of the other unrepentant, sinister criminals in this country, who President Obama is so quick to praise, deserve admonishment. That movement is funded by people that profit from chaos and disunity in our society."

The above e-mail was copied to his brother, who sent me the following e-mail: "Having been contacted by my family regarding the utterly perverse and despicable, and certainly inspired not by God but by the evil one, message which you delivered

---

2. Rah, *Prophetic Lament*, 46.

last Sunday." (So he actually was not there when I delivered the sermon but heard about it from his brother, but he still felt qualified to comment on a sermon he had not heard.) He continued, "The dog turns back to its own vomit / The sow is washed only to wallow in the mud. You are going to hell, and will have one of the worst possible places reserved for you. For you simply chose not only to disbelieve the Word of God, but to pervert it, being of the world, in order that you may drag many souls to hell with you."

I responded: "Thank you for your concern. I do not agree with your assessment but respect your right to hold your opinion." To which, he responded with the following e-mail: "Your reply is indicative of exactly what I expected you to be, a pseudo-intellectual, morally deviated coward. I will pray for you, and mostly so that you will be truly saved. For you are as lost as the man who has never heard the name of Jesus Christ."

The challenge of telling the truth, or even calling people to pursue the truth, is that folks will respond with an extremely defensive posture. We do not want to deal with the dead body in the room—even to the point of condemning those who would point toward the dead body in the room.

The history of the United States is littered with dead bodies, bodies that we have to deal with—bodies of black men and women, black women used for objects of sexual abuse, black men used for free labor and portrayed as animals, demons, and violent criminals. We need to know the history of dead bodies that led to the shooting of Michael Brown in Ferguson, MO. Missouri was allowed into the union as part of the Missouri Compromise. Missouri was a slave state that allowed for the furtherance of the institution of slavery and the enslavement of black bodies. St. Louis is the home of the arch that symbolizes the gateway to the Western half of the United States. The arch and gateway would further the application of "manifest destiny" which would wipe out Native American communities. The Dred Scott decision, which denied personhood to a former slave, was issued on the Federal Court House steps in St. Louis. The consistent message from our nation and from this region of the country has been black lives *do not* matter. Ferguson now is the place where #blacklivesmatter is being elevated. We must know how those dead bodies ended up there in the first place. Have we had a proper funeral dirge for the dead bodies?

In Lamentations the funeral dirges of chapters one and two look toward the moment when all the voices of suffering are heard. There are questions about the traditional attribution of the authorship of Lamentations to the prophet Jeremiah. Lamentations features the voice of a prophetic narrative that weaves together various voices of the remnant in the city of Jerusalem, but the prophet's voice is not the only voice in Lamentations. There is a strong feminine voice as well. Lamentations may prove to be the most feminine book of the Bible because most of the able-bodied men, the leaders, the priests, and the elders have been taken away into exile.

The survivors—the women, the children, the lame, the blind, the old and the infirmed—gather at the city gate after the destruction of Jerusalem. Various voices gather there and share stories from a cross-section of society. It is not the privileged voices of the ruling culture that speak after the tragedy. It is the voice of the suffering. Lament requires the elevation of the voices of those who have suffered. Lament is not a time to hear the prominent voices of the privileged. In the midst of a national dialogue that necessitates the disenfranchised voices to speak, it is not appropriate for a prominent evangelical leader to tell blacks and Latinos to "listen up" or to denigrate minority voices who speak up. Lamentations calls for the voice of the suffering to be heard.

Hearing from all the voices challenges the notion that only the privileged have the right to speak. A dysfunctional narrative elevates the privileged over and against the suffering. Theologian Willie Jennings points towards an existing Christian imagination that asserts the supremacy of whiteness over blackness. In American Christianity and American society there is an assumption of the superiority of white bodies over black bodies. Ideas of beauty in American society focus on white bodies as the ideal expression of beauty.

The assumption of the supremacy of whiteness extends to the assumption of the superiority of white minds over black minds. The cultural product of white minds would be considered superior to the product of nonwhite minds.[3] Even white emotions can be assumed to be superior to nonwhite emotions. When my family and I first moved to Chicago and the Midwest, I was introduced to the something called "Minnesota nice," which I think is a behavior that can be extended to the whole region as "Midwest nice." The way "Minnesota nice" was explained to me was the picture of a large dog licking your face while simultaneously urinating on your shoes. I was told that "Minnesota nice" was the appropriate way to express emotions in the Midwest. As a Korean I express my emotions in a different way. Koreans are a passionate people. We have prayer mountains in Korea where we tear up grass and knock over trees as we pray. As a passionate Korean my passion is oftentimes mistaken for anger. I have been told in so many words and looks that Korean passion is a lesser way of expressing emotions than "Minnesota nice." My emotions were deemed as inferior.

---

3. See Soong-Chan Rah, "Racialization of the Image of God" in *The Image of God in an Image Driven Age: Explorations in Theological Anthropology*, ed. Beth Felker Jones and Jeffrey W. Barbeau (Downers Grove, IL: InterVarsity, 2016) forthcoming.

Willie Jennings points out that salvific viability is based upon approximation to whiteness. The more the nonwhite person could mimic or reflect whiteness, the more there would be legitimation within the Christian community. Lamentations shows us a counter example of hearing all the voices to form that community. As we engage on the topic of race and racism as an academic community, can we hear from all of the voices? Did God intend for there to be a community where a myriad of voices could be heard? A symposium like this allows us to hear from the myriad of voices that now make up our society and also make up our church. May our efforts here this week lead to the deepening of the work of the church.

Benediction (adapted from Lamentations 5, when the people pray for themselves)[4]

[1] Remember, Lord, what happened to Michael Brown and Eric Garner;
look, and see the disgraceful way they treated their bodies.

[2] Our inheritance of the image of God in every human being
has been co-opted and denied by others.

[3] The children of Eric Garner have become fatherless,
widowed mothers grieve their dead children.

[4] We must scrap for our basic human rights;
our freedom and our liberty has a great price.

[5] Corrupt officers and officials pursue us and are at our heels;
we are weary and find no rest.

[6] We submitted to uncaring government agencies
and to big business to get enough bread.

[7] Our ancestors sinned the great sin of instituting slavery;
they are no more—but we bear their shame.

[8] The system of slavery and institutionalized racism ruled over us,
and there is no one to free us from their hands.

[9] We get our bread at the risk of our lives
because of the guns on the streets.

[10] Michael Brown's skin is hot as an oven
as his body lay out in the blazing sun.

[11] Women have been violated throughout our nation's history;
black women raped by white slave owners on the plantations.

[12] Noble black men have been hung, lynched and gunned down;

---

4. Rah, *Prophetic Lament*, 210–12.

elders and spokesmen are shown no respect.

¹³ Young men can't find work because of unjustly applied laws;

boys stagger under the expectation that their lives are destined for jail.

¹⁴ The elder statesmen and civil rights leaders are gone from the city gate;

young people who speak out their protest through music are silenced.

¹⁵ Trust in our ultimate triumph has diminished;

our triumphant dance has turned to a funeral dirge.

¹⁶ Our sense of exceptionalism has been exposed.

Woe to us, for we have sinned!

¹⁷ Because of this our hearts are faint,

because of these things our eyes grow dim

¹⁸ for our cities lie desolate

with predatory lenders and real estate speculators prowling over them.

¹⁹ You, Lord, reign forever;

your throne endures from generation to generation.

²⁰ Why do you always forget us?

Why do you forsake us so long?

²¹ Restore us to yourself, Lord, that we may return;

renew our days as of old

²² unless you have utterly rejected us

and are angry with us beyond measure.

ANNOTATED BIBLIOGRAPHY

Race and Racism

Adams, Jason, and Arum Saldanha, eds. *Deleuze and Race*. Edinburgh: Edinburgh University Press, 2013. This collection of essays from scholars of various disciplines offers insight into the application of Gilles Deleuze's thought to race and racism. This is the first volume addressing these issues in his work and is an important introduction for those interested in exploring a major philosophical contributor to race theory.

Anderson, George M. "White Supremacy and Theology: An Interview with James Cone." In *America: The National Catholic Review*, November 20, 2006. http://americamagazine.org/issue/592/article/theologians-and-white-supremacy. The interview is brief but clear on the absence of white theologians writing on the topic of racism. Cone is not offering an invitation as a much as a critique to white theologians that the silence or superficial nature of their writing is part of the ongoing curse of white supremacy in American theology.

Bailey, Randall C., Tat-siong Benny Liew, and Fernando Segovia, eds. *They Were All Together in One Place? Toward Minority Biblical Criticism*. Atlanta: Society of Biblical Literature, 2009. This collection of essays by minority biblical scholars takes seriously both the social location of the reader and the received history of the Bible. The essays treat historical, theoretical, and rhetorical issues in biblical interpretation.

Bailey, Randall C., and Tina Pippin, eds. *Race, Class, and the Politics of Bible Translation*. Atlanta: Scholars, 1996. This is a collection of essays from scholars in various disciplines, which challenges the assumption of the neutrality of translation and investigates alternative ways to approach the task of translation.

Bantum, Brian. *Redeeming Mulatto: A Theology of Race and Christian Hybridity*. Waco, TX: Baylor University Press, 2010. *Redeeming Mulatto* explores the intersection of race, discipleship and identity. Bantum considers race as a form of either true discipleship or distorted discipleship and explores how race shapes the lives of those who are rendered "interracial," "in-between," or "neither/nor," and how they must navigate this space. A consideration of the incarnated Word as occupying a neither/nor existence ultimately draws all who confess Christ into a disruptive and liberating mode of discipleship.

Barth, Fredrik. *Ethnic Groups and Boundaries: The Social Organization of Cultural Difference*. Long Grove, IL: Waveland, 1998. Widely regarded as pivotal in the discipline of anthropology, this book of essays begins by outlining issues encountered in the process of defining ethnicity and practical concerns which arise in the study of ethnicity. The majority of the book focuses on examples using the framework developed by Barth in the initial chapter and includes discussion of dynamics and relationships between ethnic groups worldwide.

Bieberstein, Sabine. "Disrupting the Normal Reality of Slavery: A Feminist Reading of the Letter to Philemon." *Journal of the Study of the New Testament* 79 (2000) 109–111. This interpretation of Philemon focuses on the context of the civil codes of the Roman

Empire. Bieberstein sees Paul's letter as an illustration of the contrasting messages of the world and the kingdom of God and an important resource for contemporary Christian engagement with the marginalized and oppressed.

Bradley, Anthony B., ed. *Aliens in the Promised Land: Why Minority Leadership Is Overlooked in White Christian Churches and Institutions*. Phillipsburg, NJ: Presbyterian and Reformed, 2013. This collection of essays from an ethnically diverse group of pastors and theologians addresses the history and contemporary manifestations of racism in theological education and ministry in North America, especially in the evangelical tradition. The essays address issues often overlooked in evangelical formulations of missiology, ecclesiology, and spiritual formation.

———, ed. *Black Scholars in White Space: New Vistas in African American Studies from the Christian Academy*. Eugene, OR: Pickwick, 2015. This interdisciplinary collection of essays addresses intersections of race and a variety of topics. The authors are African American scholars and include an unprecedented number of essays by African American female scholars teaching in Christian colleges. Especially helpful is the essay entitled "Erasing Race: Racial Identity and Theological Anthropology" by Vincent Bacote.

———. *Liberating Black Theology: The Bible and the Black Experience in America*. Wheaton, IL: Crossway, 2010. This is a very critical consideration of black liberation theology, specifically that advanced by James Cone. Over five chapters Bradley argues that Cone's reaction to his sociopolitical context was coupled with a misappropriation of Marxism and led to the development of a "victimologist" theological framework. In the final chapters Bradley asserts that black theology must reassess its relationship with Scripture in order to be truly liberating.

Braxton, Brad R. *No Longer Slaves: Galatians and African American Experience*. Collegeville, MN: Liturgical, 2002. Braxton places Galatians in dialogue with the African American experience and explains that Paul's letter was deeply concerned with issues of race and ethnicity. He views union of different ethnicities and cultures in Christ as an essential aspect of the gospel. He gives a helpful historical overview of the emergence of various interpretive lenses and their consequences.

Brett, Mark G. *Decolonizing God: The Bible in the Tides of Empire*. Bible in the Modern World. Sheffield: Sheffield Phoenix, 2008. Brett wrestles with questions of whether biblical texts are overwhelmingly pro- or anti-empire and examines the ways in which an increasing number of biblical scholars are paying attention to the colonial/imperial content of the Bible. Written with exceptional clarity, this book demonstrates the relevance of postcolonial and decolonial approaches to biblical scholarship.

———, ed. *Ethnicity and the Bible*. Boston: Brill, 2002. This is an international collection of essays investigating the conceptual development of ethnicity in the ancient world and the implications of biblical texts from the perspective of various contemporary ethnic groups.

Brogdon, Lewis. *No Longer a Slave but a Brother: An African American Reading of Paul's Letter to Philemon*. Atlanta: Scholars, 2013. Brogdon acknowledges the use of Philemon by American Christians to defend the institution of slavery, which led to later dismissal of this epistle by African Americans. He proposes that the text be placed in dialogue with current trends in African American biblical interpretation. This yields an understanding of Philemon which finds desire for and practical movement towards deeper relationships across ethnic and racial boundaries.

Buell, Denise K. *Why This New Race: Ethnic Reasoning in Early Christianity.* New York: Columbia University Press, 2005. Buell draws on history, biblical studies, and feminist theology to offer a distinctive take on the development of early Christian understandings of community and the church. While many seem to take for granted that Christianity goes beyond ethnicity, she argues that Christianity—at least in its earliest expressions—actually sought to establish its own ethnic boundaries, and then invite others into this new community.

Byron, Gay. "Race, Ethnicity, and the Bible: Pedagogical Challenges and Curricular Opportunities." *Teaching Theology and Religion* 15.2 (2012) 105–24. Byron criticizes current practices in theological education for failing to deal with race issues in Bible classes that comprise an important aspect of almost all theological curricula. Drawing on her years of experience teaching NT in a variety of different academic contexts, she outlines a methodological framework for introducing students to issues of race and ethnicity in Scripture and their ministerial applications.

———. *Symbolic Blackness and Ethnic Difference in Early Christian Literature.* New York: Routledge, 2002. Byron argues that both positive and negative assumptions about color or ethnicity were ubiquitous in Greco-Roman and early Christian writings. Through her examination of several apocryphal texts, Byron shows that ancient understandings of Egyptians and Ethiopians contributed to associations with black or blackness as marking that which was other, and the color black was eventually viewed with negative theological and sexual connotations.

Caliendo, Stephen, and Charlton McIlwain, eds. *The Routledge Companion to Race and Ethnicity.* New York: Routledge, 2011. This important volume is an incredibly wide-ranging and accessible introduction to race and ethnicity and contains essays from the perspectives of history, sociology, philosophy, and economics.

Callahan, Allen D. *The Talking Book: African Americans and the Bible.* New Haven, CT: Yale University Press, 2006. Callahan exegetes art produced by African Americans through history and examines the interplay between Scripture and the African American experience of suffering and oppression, especially with the themes of exile, exodus, Ethiopia, and Emmanuel. Callahan argues that Scripture is a decisive point of contact in the development of African American identity and past resistance to dominant cultural narratives of oppression.

Cannon, Mae Elise, Lisa Sharon Harper, Troy Jackson, and Soong-Chan Rah. *Forgive Us: Confessions of a Compromised Faith.* Grand Rapids: Zondervan, 2014. The writers argue for a biblically informed repentance which is illustrated in Nehemiah, the Psalms of lament, and NT accounts of Jesus and the pastoral letters of Paul. In addition to looking at sins committed against people on the basis of their sexual orientation and religious beliefs, *Forgive Us* includes chapters which specifically address racism against indigenous people and people of different ethnicities.

Carroll R., M. Daniel. *Christians at the Border: Immigration, the Church, and the Bible.* Grand Rapids: Baker Academic, 2008. Carroll is an OT scholar who looks at the biblical basis for welcoming migrants. His treatments of *imago dei*, sojourner, and hospitality in both Testaments allow his focus on the historic Hispanic religious experience in America to function as an example of how theological engagement with these topics should influence how the church encounters immigrants.

Carter, J. Kameron. *Race: A Theological Account.* New York: Oxford University Press, 2008. This is a far reaching, well structured, and meticulously researched book arguing that Christianity made itself "white" as it identified itself with the West in its attempt to separate itself practically, ideologically, and theologically from the apparently eastern religion of Judaism. According to Carter, bridging this divide requires dialogue between traditions and across disciplines. After addressing Michel Foucault, Cornel West, and Immanuel Kant, Carter asserts the necessity of the content and nature of theological imaginations like those of Briton Hammon, Frederick Douglass, and Jarena Lee.

Cleveland, Christena. *Disunity in Christ: Uncovering the Hidden Forces that Keep Us Apart.* Downers Grove, IL: InterVarsity, 2013. Drawing from her experience and research as a social psychologist, Cleveland explains why bias happens and how the resulting division harms individuals and communities. Each chapter ends with questions for reflection and practical application. Running throughout the book is the invitation for churches to shift from "them" to "we" in terms of community composition and worship expression. Especially insightful are chapters on group construction and identity in the latter half of the book.

Coffey, John. *Exodus and Liberation: Deliverance Politics from John Calvin to Martin Luther King Jr.* New York: Oxford University Press, 2014. This is an excellent examination of how the themes of exodus and deliverance are invoked throughout Christian history. The author demonstrates how cultural context has a vital impact on the interpretation of biblical texts and offers a fascinating account of Christian responses to the exodus narratives.

Cone, James H. *The Cross and the Lynching Tree.* Maryknoll, NY: Orbis, 2011. Cone relates the practice of lynching, especially the lynching of Emitt Till, to the crucifixion of Jesus at Golgotha. Cone's theological narrative challenges twenty-first-century American Christians, especially white Christians, to understand how their ignorance of racism, segregation, and lynching does not allow them to fully understand the story of God and the story of African Americans.

Dawson, John. *Healing America's Wounds.* Ventura, CA: Regal, 1994. Dawson proposes that cultural, community, and personal reconciliation begins with the intentional choice of individuals to associate themselves with the guilty party. This act initiates what he terms *identificational repentance*, which he argues is the key to the healing of rifts between people and cultures in America, particularly those caused by racism.

DiAngelo, Robin. "White Fragility." *International Journal of Critical Pedagogy* 3 (2011) 54–70. DiAngelo explains how the privilege that white Americans enjoy often results in an inability to process and lack of skills to engage with racism, which results in automatic deployment of instinctive defensive behaviors that perpetuate racism. This seminal article explores the obstacles in the cultivation of an antiracist identity development among whites and provides definition and explanation of "white fragility," an important term in contemporary discussion of racism.

DuBois, W.E.B., *The Souls of Black Folk.* New York: Barnes and Noble, 2003. This collection of essays, originally published in 1903, is regarded as seminal in several fields of study. Chapter one, which contains development of his concepts of *double-consciousness* and *the veil*, and chapter ten, which is a historical analysis of the black church, are especially relevant. The final chapters are important illustrations of the integration of Scripture and tradition in individual narratives. This is a pivotal book in Africa American history and an important resource for discussions of racial reconciliation.

Elizondo, Virgilio. *The Galilean Journey: The Mexican-American Promise.* Maryknoll, NY: Orbis, 2000. In this important contribution to Hispanic theology Elizondo outlines the various points of contact between the experience of Jesus Christ and the experience of Mexican Americans. Just as Mexican American identity is marked by the tension between difference and similarity, Jesus also experienced life as *mestizo*—someone who simultaneously is and is not. Elizondo's work is similarly characterized by critical engagement with Hispanic history and hope for the future of Mexican Americans.

Ellis, Carl F., Jr. *Free at Last? The Gospel in African-American Experience.* Downers Grove, IL: InterVarsity, 1983. This book is a primer of the history of African Americans, written by an African American pastor and scholar with an African American audience in mind. He outlines the distinctive development of African American Christianity, what he calls the "theological soul dynamic." The book has a glossary of African American culture which is very interesting, although understandably a bit out of date.

Emerson, Michael O., Jennifer Bratter, and Sergio Chavez. *The (Un)Making of Race and Ethnicity: A Reader.* New York: Oxford University Press, forthcoming, fall 2016.

Emerson, Michael O., and Christian Smith. *Divided by Faith: Evangelical Religion and the Problem of Race in America.* New York: Oxford University Press, 2000. Drawing from over two hundred interviews and from historic and contemporary statistics, Emerson and Smith assess contributing factors to current segregation within the evangelical church and offer a gracious and constructive critique of white evangelical engagement with ethnic minorities, particularly African Americans.

Emerson, Michael O., and Jason E. Shelton. *Blacks and Whites in Christian America.* New York: New York University Press, 2012. In this award winning book the authors argue that the religious practices of black American Protestants are primarily constructed from five "building blocks" (experiential, survival, mystery, miraculous, and justice) which are uniquely and profoundly shaped by the historic experience of racism. Drawing primarily from sociological analysis, the book offers an extensive examination of how and why the thoughts, beliefs, and practices of black American Christians contrast with their white counterparts.

Felder, Cain Hope, ed. *Stony the Road We Trod: African American Biblical Interpretation.* Minneapolis: Augsburg Fortress, 1991. A landmark book of essays written by black biblical scholars which engage issues at the intersection of race and Scripture. Especially helpful are chapters written by Thomas Hoyt Jr. and Cain Hope Felder, which respectively provide helpful historic and thematic analysis of biblical interpretation as it relates to African Americans.

Fernandez, Eleazar S., ed. *Teaching for a Culturally Diverse and Racially Just World.* Eugene, OR: Cascade, 2014. This volume of essays, written from different ethnic and interdisciplinary perspectives, seeks to assist teachers, students, and others in theological education in their assessment of the roots and fruit of racialized and racist practices embedded in curricula, pedagogy, and educational structures.

Fields, Bruce. *Introducing Black Theology: Three Crucial Questions for the Evangelical Church.* Grand Rapids: Baker Academic, 2001. Fields outlines major biblical, theological, and philosophical roots of black theology and places it in its historical context as an important expression of liberation theology. In his examination of the black theologian, he seeks to move the reader from theory to practice and encourages members of both traditions to engage with and learn from each other. The goal is racial reconciliation and the general health of the body of Christ.

———. "The One and the Many: What Can Be Learned from a Black Hermeneutic." *The Covenant Quarterly* 73 (2015) 41–52. Fields argues that treating black churches as important parts of the church will lead to a more complete expression of Christianity in America. He outlines four ways the church might gain from a black hermeneutic: a more complete view of the world, resistance to prevailing cultural themes, exposure of breakdown between belief and act, and a fuller understanding of the *imago dei*. He argues for a black hermeneutic that operates with the tension between theory and practice and participates in the multifaceted life and work of the church.

Franklin, John Hope, and Evelyn Brooks Higginbotham. *From Slavery to Freedom: A History of African Americans*. 9th ed. New York: Knopf, 2010. This book was originally published in 1947. It is an engaging and widely used textbook which provides a historical overview of African American history. Subsequent editions have been updated in terms of historical content as well as with pictures, tables, maps, and excerpts of first person narratives.

Gilbreath, Edward. *Reconciliation Blues: A Black Evangelical's Inside View of White Christianity*. Downers Grove, IL: InterVarsity, 2006. With compassion and a touch of humor Gilbreath merges his own personal experience with statistics and interviews to produce an engaging and practical look at the complex nature of racism in American evangelicalism. Although American evangelical theology may be "tainted by individualism," Gilbreath still holds out hope for racial reconciliation in the church.

Grant, Jacquelyn. "Sin of Servanthood and Deliverance of Discipleship." In *A Troubling in My Soul: Womanist Perspectives on Evil and Suffering*, edited by Emilie Maureen Townes, 199–219. Maryknoll, NY: Orbis, 1993. Grant's essay shows how white supremacy diminishes the power of language in Scripture. She critiques the use of "servant" language and its history of interpretation. She questions dominant interpretive histories and white feminist approaches through a womanist hermeneutic.

Goff, Phillip, and Brian Steensland, eds. *The New Evangelical Social Engagement*. New York: Oxford University Press, 2014. This collection of essays examines the role of the evangelical church in America. It treats the history of the evangelical movement and its interactions with the political and civic spheres and acknowledges the presence of both conservative and progressive roots in this movement. This is an important treatment of evangelical history, and it provides valuable insight into factors which promise to influence the future of evangelicalism.

Goodman, Diane J. *Promoting Diversity and Social Justice: Educating People from Privileged Groups*. New York: Routledge, 2011. This book is widely recognized as an important educational resource for those in education, management, and social work. It provides perhaps the most extensive examination of the psychological costs of racism to white people currently available. Following consideration of specific benefits of a shift in privileged populations away from oppression and towards inclusion, it contains helpful explanation of practical tools and structures for stimulating reconciliation.

Harvey, Jennifer. *Dear White Christians: For Those Still Longing for Racial Reconciliation*. Prophetic Christianity. Grand Rapids: Eerdmans, 2014. Harvey's extensive historical investigation fuels her critique of the concept of racial reconciliation often discussed within Christian circles. She argues that reparations, rather than reconciliation, provide a paradigm that has proven both to be more effective throughout history and more closely aligned with the concrete realities of oppression.

Hays, J. Daniel. *From Every People and Nation: A Biblical Theology of Race*. New Studies in Biblical Theology 14. Downers Grove, IL: IVP Academic, 2003. This monograph surveys ethnic tensions in both Testaments from a theological perspective. Hays couples examination of passages which explicitly address race with analysis of the relationship between the people of God and other nations to provide a biblical basis for practical engagement with issues in race and ethnicity by the contemporary church.

Higuera Smith, Kay, Lalitha Jayachitra, and L. Daniel Hawk, eds. *Evangelical Postcolonial Conversations: Global Awakenings in Theology and Praxis*. Downers Grove, IL: InterVarsity, 2014. This collection captures the multiple intersecting changes that evangelicals are undergoing. Although uneven in addressing the challenges elicited by postcolonial critical frameworks, this set of essays does a great job in creating the conditions for evangelicals to engage their own colonial history and legacy. Of particular interest are the evangelicals' colonizing and racialized attitudes towards the "brown" peoples, among which Native Americans and African Americans figure prominently in this collection.

Hill, Johnny Bernard. *Prophetic Rage: A Postcolonial Theology of Liberation*. Grand Rapids: Eerdmans, 2013. This book enters the complex multidisciplinary debates of liberation theologies, including recent criticisms and attempts to reclaim the liberation ethos and long-standing legacy of struggles for justice by African Americans. Hill insists the greatest threat liberation struggles face today is nihilism: the lack of hope and lack of desire and courage to organize and struggle against social, political, and economic forces of subjugation in this world. The best response, he claims, is prophetic rage, the prophetic praxis of resisting evil and speaking truth to empire.

Isaac, Benjamin. *The Invention of Racism in Classical Antiquity*. Princeton: Princeton University Press, 2004. In this award-winning historical analysis Isaac examines Greek art and literature and argues that modern conceptions of racism are rooted in the social imagination of the classical period.

Isichei, Elizabeth. *A History of Christianity in Africa: From Antiquity to Present*. Grand Rapids: Eerdmans, 1995. Africa has recently been the site of tremendous growth for Christianity. Isichei examines the spread of Christianity across the continent over the past thousand years and addresses political, sociological, and theological issues in its development. This book is a valuable resource for understanding cultural and religious influences that have informed the religious experience of many around the world. It is an insightful study of the complexity of Christian identity within African culture.

Jennings, Willie James. *The Christian Imagination: Theology and the Origins of Race*. New Haven, CT: Yale University Press, 2010. Jennings peels back the layers of Western theological architecture to show its inherently white supremacist logic. He analyzes the Reformed tradition and its emphases, including sovereignty and the vernacular translation of Scripture. The result is a theology centered in desire, intimacy, and belonging, which expects a descent into history and the logic of white existence. This volume is a celebrated treatment of the role of the imagination in producing segregation and racism in Western society and theology and in the necessity of a renewed Christian imagination in racial reconciliation.

Johnson, Matthew V., James A. Noel, and Demetrius K. Williams, eds. *Onesimus Our Brother: Reading Religion, Race, and Culture in Philemon*. Minneapolis: Fortress, 2012. This book is a collaborative effort of African American biblical scholarship. The collection of essays places Philemon in dialogue with Paul's other letters, with philosophy, and with African American experience of marginalization. It deals with Philemon's contemporary significance and the treatment of the epistle historically within the African American community, especially from the standpoint of those engaged in oppression.

Annotated Bibliography

Kabri, Nazli. *Becoming Asian American*. Baltimore: Johns Hopkins University Press, 2002. Kabri's personal interviews with children of Asian immigrants in the urban centers of Boston and Los Angeles inform her assessment of the racial and ethnic identity development of Asian Americans. Although Asian Americans may not always share the same negative experiences as other ethnic minorities, Kabri's research shows that the work necessary to sustain their image as the "model minority" takes its toll, and she proposes possibilities for future improvement of the situation.

Keener, Craig S., and Glenn Usry. *Black Man's Religion: Can Christianity be Afrocentric?* Downers Grove, IL: InterVarsity, 1996. Through an overview of the development of origins of Christianity in ancient Israel and its development in Africa, Keener and Usry assert that suffering is central to the African American experience and has provided vital shape to African American Christianity. They stress that it is this intimate relationship with suffering that goes beyond color, race, and ethnicity to form a "deeper basis" for African American identity. This opens the possibility that even white people may become allies insofar as they sincerely identify with the suffering of African Americans.

Kidwell, Clara Sue, Homer Noley, and George E. Tinker. *A Native American Theology*. Maryknoll, NY: Orbis, 2001. Informed by their differing tribal backgrounds, the authors offer helpful insight into the development of a Native American hermeneutic and subsequent systematic theology, particularly the complex relationship between the Jesus narrative and the narratives of Native people, which they propose should in some way also function as "sacred texts." They deal with the tension between Native American familial and spatial emphases and traditionally Christian emphases on doctrine and time. The explanation of a Native American understanding of the unpredictable nature of the supernatural is perhaps the most intriguing element of this work.

Kim, Grace Ji-Sun. *Embracing the Other: The Transformative Spirit of Love*. Prophetic Christianity. Grand Rapids: Eerdmans, 2015. Kim draws on themes in feminism and Asian culture as she addresses racism and gender inequality. While the first three chapters of the book establish the separation and subordination of women, the remainder of the book argues that this harmful separation may be overcome when we participate in the divine work of love. Love, which is the work of the Spirit, reflects the Trinitarian nature as it breaks down walls to restore peace and unity to the world.

Lewis, C. S. "Dangers of National Repentance." *Transformation: An International Journal of Holistic Mission Studies* 14 (1997) 2. In this article, originally published in 1940, C. S. Lewis critiques the concept of national repentance and points out that the call for "us" to repent may actually mask condemnation of the sins of others while functioning as a distraction from personal, contemporary sin. Rather than dismissing the need for corporate apology, Lewis points out the importance of owning one's own sin before condemning others. Although Lewis is addressing a British audience more than seventy-five years ago, his critique still applies to contemporary discussions of racism in America.

Lincoln, C. Eric, and Lawrence H. Mamiya. *The Black Church in the African American Experience* Durham, NC: Duke University Press, 1990. This is a detailed analysis of one of the most in-depth surveys ever conducted on the subject of black churches in America. By contextualizing thousands of ministerial interviews and statistics within the historical progression of several black denominations, the writers provide a valuable understanding of the nature of the black church in America and its relationship to a wide variety of important issues. It has an extensive bibliography.

Marsh, Charles. *God's Long Summer: Stories of Faith and Civil Rights*. Princeton: Princeton University Press, 1997. Marsh offers multiple narratives from a broad range of perspectives—including a civil rights activist and a white supremacist—of the pivotal summer in 1964 to remind Americans of the civil rights struggle and its painful story. These divergent stories capture the reader's attention and invite them to continue the fight for injustice through Christian convictions and a deeper understanding of history.

Maxwell, David. *Race in a Post-Obama America: The Church Responds*. Louisville: Westminster John Knox, 2016. Maxwell seeks to educate and equip American Christians who are eager to engage in racial reconciliation. This is a concise and accessible introduction to the historic roots and contemporary dynamics of racism in America, and it provides helpful explanation of terms and issues often encountered in activism.

McCall, Sophie. *First Person Plural: Aboriginal Storytelling and the Ethics of Collaborative Authorship*. Vancouver: UBC, 2011. McCall considers complex issues associated with the compilation and interpretation of stories—"told-to narratives"—emerging from concerted efforts of aboriginal storytellers and those who record them. She surveys the profound political impact of these texts throughout aboriginal history in Canada.

McCoskey, Denise. *Race: Antiquity and its Legacy.* London: I.B. Tauris, 2012. McCoskey provides an overview of racial and ethnic dynamics in ancient classical culture and argues that this legacy continues to be perpetuated in contemporary society. This book is particularly helpful in its examination of the impact of race and ethnicity on other economic, political, and sociological issues such as class and gender, and vice versa.

McKenzie, Steven L. *All God's Children: A Biblical Critique of Racism*. Louisville, KY: Westminster John Knox, 1997. McKenzie offers interpretation of passages which appear to favor nationalism and ethnocentrism in light of the overall biblical narrative of sacrificial love and unity which he asserts honors and embraces difference.

Medina, Néstor. "U.S. Latina/o Theology: Challenges, Possibilities, and Future Prospects." In *Theology and the Crisis of Engagement,* edited by Jeff Nowers and Néstor Medina, 141–60. Eugene, OR: Pickwick, 2013. This article serves as an introduction to the wide range of issues, themes, and theological concerns of the Latina/o communities. The author focuses on the centrality of culture in theology and biblical scholarship and outlines some of the key contributions to theology and biblical criticism by Latina/o scholars.

———. "Transgressing Theological Shibboleths: Culture as Locus of Divine (Pneumatological) Activity." *PNEUMA* 36.3 (2014) 432–46. This paper proposes a reinterpretation of the cultural dimension as *locus* of divine activity. This methodological shift requires that the historically-culturally specific event of Jesus be interpreted as opening the door for the celebration of other ethnocultural traditions. When coupled with the event of Pentecost, this move provides grounds for discerning the Spirit at work at the level of culture. The two events of Jesus and Pentecost challenge us to reconceive the culturally bound ways in which the Spirit is involved in the process of divine disclosure, leading us toward the recognition of the contextual, plurivocal, and multicultural nature of theological reflection.

Obama, Barack. "A More Perfect Union." Public Speech. Philadelphia, PA. November 17, 2008, Constitution Center. http://www.huffingtonpost.com/2008/03/18/obama-race-speech-read-th_n_92077.html. In this speech Obama responded to the controversial remarks of Rev. Jeremiah Wright which were dominating the news and media discussions of his presidential campaign. Obama situated his former pastor's statements within the historical context of racism in America and provided a balanced and constructive critique of factors from multiple perspectives of the racial divide.

Oden, Thomas. *How Africa Shaped the Christian Mind: Rediscovering the African Seedbed of Western Christianity*. Downers Grove, IL: InterVarsity, 2007. Admittedly limited in its scope, this book outlines the basis for reconsideration of the role of Africa in the development of Christianity. Oden introduces evidence that theological issues surfaced in Africa prior to being dealt with in Europe, invites Western Christians to appreciate the theological contributions of the historic African Church, and challenges scholars to support future research of ancient Africa, especially by Africans. Especially interesting is his chronological account of Christianity in Africa.

Painter, Nell Irvin. *The History of White People*. New York: Norton, 2010. Painter develops a detailed narrative as a black woman disclosing white experience. She complicates the story of race by starting with the identities that diminished others. The volume is thorough and uncovers often taken for granted language and practices that are carriers of white supremacy.

Park, Sydney, Soong-Chan Rah, and Al Tizon. *Honoring the Generations: Learning with Asian North American Congregations*. Valley Forge, PA: Judson, 2012. The three writers draw on their experience and training in ministry, theology, and biblical studies to weave together insights from Scripture with themes from Asian culture. They pay special attention to the ways these factors are manifested differently in first, second, and third generations of Asian North American immigrants. This book is full of real life examples and ideas for practical application and is a valuable resource for those leading multigenerational ministries.

Perkinson. James W. *White Theology: Outing Supremacy in Modernity*. New York: Palgrave MacMillan, 2004. Perkinson takes up Cone's call for white theologians to develop an antiracist theology from a theological interrogation of the experience of white supremacy. Perkinson is prophetic and provocative in his antiracist hermeneutic and exposes how white Americans are largely unable to analyze their own privilege and power.

Rah, Soong-Chan. *The Next Evangelicalism: Freeing the Church from Western Cultural Captivity*. Downers Grove, IL: InterVarsity, 2009. Rah develops an ecclesiology from the growing ethnic immigrant and multiethnic communities in the United States. He investigates what is happening to monocultural and dominant white churches. The center of his argument is a critical analysis of three major ecclesial movements: church growth, emergent church, and globalization. He responds to the problems of Western captivity with ecclesial practices of Native American, African American, immigrant, and second generation multiethnic churches.

Rattansi, Ali. *Racism: A Very Short Introduction*. New York: Oxford University Press, 2007. This concise and accessible overview of racism defines important terms and identifies social, theological, and scientific factors that have contributed to the perpetuation of racism throughout Western history. It also examines contemporary manifestations of racism.

Robinson, Elaine A. *Race and Theology*. Nashville: Abingdon, 2012. Robinson assesses the treatment of racism in theology and the consequences of the lack of quality theological studies throughout American history, including current manifestations of racism in America. Although she sharply criticizes the church's relative absence from discussions of race, her gesture toward constructive engagement is hopeful.

Robiteau, Albert. *Slave Religion: The "Invisible Institution" in the Antebellum South.* New York: Oxford University Press, 2004. This work was originally published in 1978, and Robiteau's afterword to the 2004 edition provides helpful application in light of the contemporary context. Drawing from both primary and secondary sources, Robiteau looks at the historical and social development of Christianity among slaves in America prior to the Civil War. He shows how their religious practices shaped their identity, their relationship with their present physical reality, and their views of the afterlife.

Romeny, Bas ter Haar. *Religious Origins of Nations? The Christian Communities of the Middle East.* Boston: Brill, 2010. This interdisciplinary collection of essays focuses on the emergence and definition of Christian groups in the Middle East such as the Syriac Orthodox, Armenians, and Byzantine Orthodox. Close attention is given to the interplay between religion and ethnicity in the development of the self-awareness of these communities.

Rothenberg, Paula S, ed. *White Privilege: Essential Readings on the Other Side of Racism.* 5th Edition. New York: Worth, 2015. This is a seminal collection of essays focusing on how those who are part of the dominant white culture in America benefit from racism. Rothenberg has updated each edition with essays addressing contemporary expressions of racism in various contexts, including politics, economics, education, and immigration.

Ruiz, Jean-Pierre. *Reading from the Edges: The Bible and People on the Move.* Maryknoll, NY: Orbis, 2011. This book questions the traditional division between biblical studies and theology and issues a refreshing challenge to read the Bible using contemporary lenses of immigration. Biblical texts are coupled with personal anecdotes from his childhood, seminary, and clerical experiences. Ruiz asserts that the Bible has much to say to immigration issues and the plight of immigrant peoples and demonstrates the practical benefits of making room for multiple levels of interpretive meaning.

Said, Edward W. *Orientalism.* New York: Random, 1994. Originally published in 1978, this is a pivotal book in cultural studies. The book condemns much study of the Eastern world as an exercise in intellectual imperialism. The author asserts that the portrayals of the East emerged from methodology tainted by Western bias and that these depictions then served to fuel further colonialism. Said's post-structuralist work informed later critical study of literature, culture, and other geographical regions. The latest edition is updated with a prologue and epilogue in which Said answers several criticisms of the book.

Sechrest, Love L. *A Former Jew: Paul and the Dialectics of Race.* New York: T. & T. Clark, 2009. In this published version of her doctoral thesis Sechrest examines the relationship between race, ethnicity, and religious identity in the ancient world, specifically in the NT writings of Paul. She begins with a comparison of ancient and contemporary understandings of race and ethnicity and then shows that for Paul conversion to Christianity includes conversion to a new understanding of one's own race. She concludes with an assessment of how this finding might positively shape racial reconciliation within the church.

———. "Identity and the Embodiment of Privilege in Corinth." In *1 and 2 Corinthians: Texts@Contexts*, edited by Yung Suk Kim, 9–30. Minneapolis: Fortress, 2013. This article describes the concept of privilege in relation to ethnic pride and stereotyping in ancient Greco-Roman culture and analyzes these dynamics as they appear in Paul's defense of his apostleship in Second Corinthians.

Annotated Bibliography

———. "Race, Ethnicity, and Biblical Criticism." In *The Oxford Encyclopedia for Biblical Interpretation*, edited by Steven L. McKenzie, 189–97. 2 vols. New York: Oxford University Press, 2013. This dictionary article gives a concise yet substantive overview of ethnicity and race in biblical societies and biblical scholarship. A bibliography is included.

———. *Race Relations and the New Testament*. Grand Rapids: Eerdmans, forthcoming.

Segovia, Fernando F. *Decolonizing Biblical Studies: A View from the Margins*. Maryknoll, NY: Orbis, 2000. This volume introduces important elements involved in decolonizing postcolonial biblical studies. Drawing from cultural studies, Segovia reformulates the role of culture and experience in the task of biblical criticism. Writing from the Latina/o vantage point, he emphasizes the important role of social location in hermeneutics and helps trace some of the developments biblical scholarship has been undergoing for the last couple of decades.

Skinner, Tom. *Black and Free*. Grand Rapids: Zondervan, 1968. Skinner contextualizes the Christian message within the black experience of individual and institutional racism with the patience and compassion that marked his ministry as a bridge builder. Although dated, this is an accessible introduction to issues in race and ethnicity which incorporates Scripture and includes Skinner's own personal narrative.

———. *How Black is the Gospel?* Philadelphia: J. B. Lippincott, 1970. Skinner was an evangelist, pastor, and founder of Skinner Associates (now Skinner Leadership Institute, which seeks to equip young people to lead racial reconciliation efforts). This book defines the gospel and relates this "true Christianity" to the black experience. Written almost fifty years ago, this historic portrayal of practical involvement by an evangelical pastor and chaplain with race and ethnicity provides valuable insight for contemporary engagement with these issues in the ministerial context.

Smith, Anthony D. *The Ethnic Origins of Nations*. Malden, MA: Blackwell, 1986. Smith disagrees with the popular understanding of the nation as a modern invention and seeks to establish that the concept of the nation actually has its roots in historic conceptions of the ethnic community, which he refers to as *ethnie*. The book is divided into two parts. The first half contains Smith's definition of *ethnie* and examination of the nature of these communities in the premodern era, and in the second half he outlines the shift toward the nation.

Smith, Efrem, and Phil Jackson. *The Hip-Hop Church: Connecting With the Movement Shaping Our Culture*. Downers Grove, IL: InterVarsity, 2005. This is a practical look at the incorporation of hip-hop culture into liturgy and ministry in the local church. The authors point out theological themes in hip-hop and draw on Scripture to argue for appreciation and integration of hip-hop culture by the church in America. The second section seeks to introduce newcomers to hip-hop's major themes, cultural manifestations, and historical context.

Takaki, Ronald. *A Different Mirror: A History of Multicultural America*. Boston: Little, Brown, 1993. By concentrating on the historical experience of Japanese and Chinese immigrants, groups often relegated to the margins of American history books, Takaki shows the necessity and possible contemporary benefits of engagement with the histories of the numerous immigrant populations that comprise American culture.

———, ed. *From Different Shores: Perspectives on Race and Ethnicity in America*. New York: Oxford University Press, 1987. This volume features essays on race and ethnicity written by scholars coming from very different political perspectives. By placing them in dialogue with one another, *From Different Shores* illumines the processes and end products of differing methodologies within racial and ethnic studies.

Tatum, Beverly Daniel. *"Why Are All the Black Kids Sitting Together in the Cafeteria?" And Other Conversations About Race*. 5th ed. New York: Basic, 2003. This often cited book contains a good introduction to issues in ethnic and racial studies and pays particular attention to the psychological and sociological aspects of the development of racial identity by groups and individuals. She argues intentional and transparent discussion of racism, despite discomfort, is indispensable in the movement toward integration and reconciliation. She gives helpful tips on how to initiate and foster such conversations.

Thurman, Howard. *Jesus and the Disinherited*. Boston: Beacon, 1996. Originally published in 1978, Thurman, a black scholar, activist, and pastor, addresses the relationship between Jesus and the oppressed black person in America. Although he explicitly addresses African Americans, his challenge to exchange fear, hypocrisy, and hatred for a life driven by love for one another and God offers profound insight to anyone who can identify with the disinherited Jesus.

Toyama, Nicki A., and Gee Tracy, eds. *More Than Serving Tea: Asian American Women on Expectations, Relationships, Leadership, and Faith*. Downers Grove, IL: InterVarsity, 2006. This book contains essays from Asian American women who serve in American college ministries. These writers explore a wide variety of issues including gender, sexuality, community, media portrayals, and biblical role models within the tension of being Asian, American, and women. The book includes a study guide and recommendations for further reading.

Treat, James, ed. *Native and Christian: Indigenous Voices on Religious Identity in the United States and Canada*. New York: Routledge, 1996. This collection of essays from a diverse group of North American writers from various tribal backgrounds and different Christian traditions addresses subjects such as narrative, sacred texts, and liturgy. The book includes a bibliography of other articles and books by Native American writers on issues of spirituality and Christian community.

Twiss, Richard. *One Church, Many Tribes: Following Jesus the Way God Made You*. Ventura, CA: Regal, 2000. Drawing from First Nations' history and personal experience interwoven with biblical commentary, Twiss critiques American evangelicals' failure to include First Nations people in mutually beneficial relationships. He argues that moving beyond mission to full participation and inclusion in worship and ministry is essential for the health of the body of Christ. Twiss focuses on practical application and the importance of narrative and addresses missiological issues like religious and cultural syncretism. His book includes contact information of potential ministry partners.

Villafañe, Eldin. *The Liberating Spirit: Toward an Hispanic American Pentecostal Social Ethic*. Grand Rapids: Eerdmans, 2003. Hailed as a significant and much needed contribution to scholarship on Pentecostalism, this book looks at the history of Hispanic Americans, paying particular attention to how their experience of poverty and oppression shaped their religious practice and how their theological understanding influenced their relationship with suffering. He seeks to develop a Christian social ethic which is distinctively Hispanic and Pentecostal.

Volf, Miroslav. *Exclusion and Embrace: A Theological Exploration of Identity, Otherness, and Reconciliation*. Nashville: Abingdon, 1996. Using the image of embrace, Volf outlines the potential costs, benefits, and practice of reconciliation between conflicted parties. For the excluded and excluder, the oppressed and the oppressor, the vulnerability required

Annotated Bibliography

in the process of embrace may be worth the risk. As he explores both sides of the process, Volf contends that experiences of reconciliation with both God and others are essential aspects of the Christian understanding of salvation.

Warner, Stephen, and Judith Wittner, eds. *Gatherings in Diaspora: Religious Communities and the New Immigration*. Philadelphia: Temple University Press, 1998. This interdisciplinary collection of essays examines how religious beliefs in the second half of the twentieth century influenced the formation of immigrant communities, rituals, education, and social structures. Its examination of the influence of religions other than Christianity in the immigrant experience is especially helpful.

West, Cornel. *Race Matters*. Boston: Beacon, 1993. Expertly addressing specific concerns related to issues like sexuality, riots, and affirmative action, West offers critical analysis of wide-ranging structural and behavioral issues in the perpetuation of racism, examines the successful contributions of people and systems engaged in the fight against racism through history, and calls for revitalization of activism and the development of young activists.

Wills, Richard. *Martin Luther King Jr. and the Image of God*. New York: Oxford University Press, 2009. Wills places King within his historical and philosophical context as he charts the historical development of the Christian understanding of the *imago dei*. He provides a helpful overview of King's biblical and theological influences and addresses the extent to which these specifically shaped his understanding of the image of God and subsequently informed his pastoral practice and civil rights activism.

Wu, Frank. *Yellow: Race in America Beyond Black and White*. New York: Basic, 2002. Drawing on his experience as a law professor and journalist, Wu gives a historical analysis of Asian American immigrant culture and his own personal narrative. This is an engaging examination of contemporary issues in race and ethnicity, particularly as they relate to the lives of Asian Americans.

NORTH PARK THEOLOGICAL SEMINARY SYMPOSIUM ON THE THEOLOGICAL INTERPRETATION OF SCRIPTURE

SEPTEMBER 25–SEPTEMBER 27, 2015

Race and Racism

PRESENTERS

Raymond Aldred
Assistant Professor of Theology, Ambrose Seminary/Ambrose University

Lewis Brogdon
Assistant Professor of Religion, Claflin University

Bo Lim
Associate Professor of Old Testament, Seattle Pacific University

Néstor Medina
Independent Scholar

Emerson Powery
Professor of Biblical Studies, Messiah College

Love Sechrest
Associate Professor of New Testament, Fuller Theological Seminary

Elizabeth Sung
Assistant Professor of Biblical and Systematic Theology, Trinity Evangelical Divinity School

Soong-Chan Rah
Professor of Church Growth and Evangelism, North Park Theological Seminary

Kyle Small
Associate Dean and Associate Professor of Church Leadership, Western Theological Seminary

Presenters and Respondents

RESPONDENTS

Michael Emerson
    Provost, North Park University

Bruce Fields
    Associate Professor of Biblical and Systematic Theology, Trinity Evangelical Divinity School

Alexander Gee
    Pastor, Fountain of Life Covenant Church, Madison, WI

Rebecca Gonzalez
    Executive Director of Operations, Evangelical Covenant Church

Evelmyn Ivens
    Staff, Christian Community Development Association, Chicago, IL

Valerie Landfair
    Adjunct Professor, North Park University

Mark Tao
    Pastor, Immanuel Covenant Church, Chicago, IL

Al Tizon
    Executive Minister of Serve Globally, Evangelical Covenant Church

www.ingramcontent.com/pod-product-compliance
Lightning Source LLC
Chambersburg PA
CBHW081350230426
43667CB00017B/2783